Cadence of Hooves:
A Celebration of Horses

Contemporary Poetry
Edited by Suzan Jantz

Yarroway Mountain Press

Cadence of Hooves

Printed in Canada

10 9 8 7 6 5 4 3 2 1

For permissions and information, please contact

Yarroway Mountain Press

P. O. Box 98

Igo, CA 96047

yarrowaymountainpress@hotmail.com

www.yarrowaymountainpress.com

www.yarrowaymountainpress.blogspot.com

Permission credits begin on page 477

Book and cover design by Suzan Jantz

Cover design by Tony Camarota

www.camarotadesign.com

Cover art by Valerie Mejer

ISBN-10: 0-9801141-01

ISBN-13: 978-0-9801141-0-2

Library of Congress Control Number: 2007941139

With grateful acknowledgment to California State University Research and Creativity Foundation for their grant in support of this project.

Special thank you to Jeanne E. Clark, Casey Huff, Carole Simmons Oles, & Beth Spencer for generous and continued insight, feedback, support, friendship, & love.

for Bernita

Contents

Cadence of Hooves: an introduction

Suzan Jantz

Growing up in the late 1950s and '60s, a girl in middle-class suburbia, I galloped through our neighborhood, absorbed in my inner-life as a horse. The cadence of black patent leather shoes striking the concrete sidewalk was the sound of iron horseshoes; my animated nickering: a consciousness not yet realized, the innocent voice of innate happiness—ignorant, yet seeking, as all humans do, the matters of desire, complexity, a source of beliefs, convictions, expectations.

By my thirteenth birthday, I had appropriately evolved into walking erect, slowly having compromised my horse-like ways but finding comfort still in a pair of western-style suede cowboy boots. Meanwhile, my parents—perhaps missing the gradual disappearance of that once-galloping little girl—presented me with the gift of a twelve-year-old quarter horse mare.

While I had been busy growing up in a quiet residential subdivision with no living horses in sight, this beautiful sorrel mare had lived her past nine years with a herd of over 100 horses, running free-range on at least 10,000 acres of private land covered in oaks, sage, and wild mustard. No human contact to speak of—no saddle, no bridle, no bit, no cinch, no iron horseshoes.

We had a lot to learn about each other.

I was by that time, socially and exponentially removed from my equus roots. The mare, for her part, showed a curiosity for these man-made trappings but was naturally resentful about the sudden expectation that she assimilate to her new life as a trail horse under saddle.

The development of our relationship was chiefly dependent on effective communication—something that we slowly and sometimes agonizingly developed through a series of trials and error. The definitive evidence as to whether our communication was truly reciprocal was whether I got to ride home on her back, or as happened more times than I like to admit, I had to walk the long trails home on my own accord, returning to find her standing nonchalantly in her stall, swishing her tail at flies.

With a horse you know exactly where you stand.

A horse's entire being centers on communication—giving and receiving. A horse feels each subtle shift of human weight on its back. And with each signal, however subtle, the horse attempts to decipher the meaning and then responds accordingly.

In this way, horses demand attentiveness.

Many equestrians and first-time riders alike agree that horses have proven inherently attuned to forms of extrasensory communication. They attest to horses responding not only to humans' intentional forms of communication but to their inadvertent thoughts and emotions as well.

Show me your horse, and I'll tell you who you are.

Among horse handlers, there is an ancient belief that proficient equestrian skills require a kind of spiritual cross training in order to become as one spirit with the horse. This invisible thread between horse and rider demands that the rider communicate physically as well as mentally and spiritually—that they ride with the body, mind, and soul.

Throughout history, horses of legend and real life have served as mediums between the spirit and material worlds. And, unlike cats or dogs, to which similar extrasensory attributes are often given, horses reputedly carry their riders between the seen and unseen realms and hold the power to lead humans to forms of lost knowledge.

Preliterate petroglyphs, pictographs, and other artifacts remain as testament that the horse has inhabited cultural human experience throughout millennia. Horses have been with us in war, in work, in leisure, in sport, in symbol, and in all manner of art.

Here, in this anthology, I am delighted and honored to bring together the extraordinary voices of leading contemporary poets—who

with great attentiveness to body, mind, and soul—share diverse perspectives and immense wisdom through their eloquent and creative communication. There is palpable nourishment in this celebration of our unique and enduring relationship with equus caballus—the horse.

The Impossible Still-Life

A horse, as it stands along a ridge,
Looked-at against the sun
Rising, above you, the light
Making a pure, thick, coloring book line
Between sky and mountain,

That horse
Loped-back and with peaked ears,
A fine side rise and lift of neck,
The hillock of a nostril:

A horse looked-at against the sun,
In this way, becomes larger.
You see more of it. The whole thing

May be a trick of perspective,
Seeing in this place

The sudden angle of beginning.

Blessing, North of Perigoux

Morning comes, silver, fog hanging low,
gossamer along a river valley in southwest France.
You sit on your pack and watch young horses scatter
  across the field below.
Stopping just short of the limestone wall, they are all
  light and angle,
and it seems they should rise up, curl like autumn leaves
  on the next lip of air.
In a few hours you will enter a cave four miles north of
  this place,
and then you will know why cedar lined fields and the
  faces of your sisters are here
whispering a blessing against the back of your skull.
Your eyes will follow the glow of a red pen light across
  millennia,
and your mind, slowly, will reconcile each image—bear,
  water, piece of night sky.
But when your guide leads you into the deepest room,
the face of rock once reserved for only the most sacred
  shapes,
recognition will float up your spine, neck hair rising,
a prayer for horses and people, in which you will
  remember this moment,
morning and mares grazing along the hillside,
  a cathedral, glazed in an arm of early sun.

Prehistoric Horses

This is not a dream,
but it is like a dream,

like somebody else's,
in common:
                    into the mountain,

along moist corridors
flowing slowly with minerals,

walls that drip polyps
and twist, singly

follow the needle of light
in—
            till the tunnel tightens,

breaks open: onto
secret precincts, vault, rock sky.

*

First nothing. Half-dark, silence
and its repetitions. Then

like-angels are here, wheeling above
around us: scooping the paleolithic air,

rivers of muscle, outline-fur on the spine-sine-curve
and mane to the withers:

lunged against a ground of milk-stone, arc-flickering
and exact, to the flare of the whiskers!

Rearing light, they levade on their haunches.

Noiselessly among nothing

they whinny and flehmen and nicker,
flicking their delicate ears.

*

Because they cast no shadow, it is as if in this secreted
world they are their own light.
Because they leave no hoofprints, it is as if the field they
graze is hard and curved behind them, as the cave is,
arc tilting into plane, where their carved bodies
hover.
Each floats alone, and their singleness
feels like an original true thing, each beast in its outline.

Sometimes as they trot on their separate base-lines their
bodies intersect, and they pass
easily through one another,
and they do not notice, their apartness is that complete.

Even the little one stands contained in the contour of
another's belly, or pausing through her.
Maybe in their fullness they have nothing to do
with one another, coinciding in
stone. Or maybe the larger one is the mother,
or the little one is not yet born,
and the clear body of the first holds the next
one whole:
so that this transparency of their bodies must be how
time looks, each life contained, in part, in
another's, and another, as if solitude were refracted, each
itself the source of whatever other it can know, the
field where it is nourished and relinquished.

The little horse is here. As the other is, standing between
us and the next, or around
her compact body:
so that it is space, not time, that clarifies their bodies,
how high space looks when it
is curved, and shared, clean of creatureliness
and its errors of desire.

She would be no less horse, the mother, orange and
sturdy-thighed and singular,

for all that her body is a window onto that cold field.

*

Presences, if this were a dream I would know how to
  address you.
I would come toward you across the sepulchral air with
  something like a clot of
        sugar on my palm, pronouncing the dialect or
  the necessary gesture with my
        secret hand, and you would whuff and
  shimmer, urging yourselves calmly
        closer as I spoke and approached you.

And I wonder whether that is part of the pattern, that I
  should fail to know how to speak to you, or how you
        are called to yourselves and to your people, so
  that you go on and on, in the buried life,
and it should be enough to know that you are here:

as it is said to be enough in the upper life to know there
  are monks in high fortresses
        who pray for mercy for us endlessly, that we can
  continue, with the courage
        each summons, to conjugate virtue the best we
  can—in the cold bed, at the

        kitchen table, on the bus—,
whether or not constant prayer would be enough, or
  constant forgiveness.

With you I feel far from that world. In that city we kill
  our fathers and then become them.
We entreat our children, crying *O when will the killing
  end?*

Although in my city I am mostly solitary, here I find I
  contain my time even more than
        I personify its differences.
And it makes me oddly happy to think so, speaking my
  time into your time, a representative

deviate of my century, and speak to you, so,
from the end of a century of deviations.

*

I am a grown man from the late afternoon of a century
given over to power and to doubt,

and to what scaffolds we weave in the meshes of those
  helixes
to lift ourselves above the shaking ground,

high here in the banked air,
which is mostly brown here, with blue fringes.

Choosing from among what can be said, we imagine
  ourselves in their matrices
as small birds murmuring in a tree.

Our measure of the body is vertical: we call each layer of
  our homes *a story,* as if a language
        passes through and shapes us to a space.
Our horizon, time, is linear, the taste of the self invested
  with memory and small connectives
        like precocious green-veined leaves, as if we pass
  through a language and conform it
        to our bodies, which we have come to know as
  private

—so that, fixed in these intersections as if in safety, we
  are surprised to learn what we had
        forgotten: that we are, each of us, contained
in one another, and the tree, and the fire beneath us, at
  the level of the street, equal with the
        first—the common—story.

*

When I try to imagine the men and women of the clan
  that made and hid you,
I see the differences that separate them from me and
  from my people,

for whom the horse, after generations, is a figure of pure
  desire,
a grace without a means of production, and the body of
  a mercy stronger than ours,
        somehow erotic but displaced into a form of

power;

or an ideal archaic figure, suitable for girls, after the
  Modern lust for novelty and machines
      at the opening of our century;
or a dream of utopia mingled with the memory of a
  classless society

and therefore tainted too, these days,
like a tourist-postcard from Chincoteague.

And I wonder if this too is part of a pattern,
this knowledge of coming too late and failing to know;

or a dream even older than you,
or a glimpse of the female god.

*

Who painted her?
Someone who needed to see her.

What does she promise?
Somewhere to come from.

What is that community?
What we hunted
together. A property
of signs, recognized and chosen.

And history then?
The life of our design.
What we know because it is
embodied: having not yet
mastered them we represented
what we had not yet lost.

*

If you *are* a verb, how should I constitute a subject?
that I do not now and I sense that is part of a pattern;

that you do not speak, visible in a space opened by
  blindness and wavering in torchlight;
that you are mares and mothers hidden till the morning

of a century needing both; that
our breath corrodes you;

that you do not speak, but you are a made thing; that
you may have been useful and so
you were hidden, commodified magic;
that we hide our dead, and treasure, and desire; that we
the living return to the buried, though
our words incarnate them chiefly as images of
our desire;

that you do not speak, because to speak is to carve
dualities of flesh our words intend to heal;
that talking with you, nevertheless, I address the men
and women of my oblique century;

that because you do not speak you seem a form of
freedom, not a representation but the fact of the form;
that the gods are awful, in proportion to our capacity
for awe:

I make myself a subject
from these dry irreducibles of my century, whoever it is
we decide after all we will choose to
become in the upper world, in the fallen light.

*

In the world above we think of ourselves as contained in
a world below.
Therefore we feel tenderness for beginning things, colts
and introductions, human loves,
prepositions, pretty lurchings of the wind…

Early snows, also, move us, because we like to imagine
them as small compassionate angels
pulled to join us in distinguished, silent,
separate fallings. Nothing like you:
unless that difference, too, is part of a pattern, and so
what seems in you impassive and
singular embodies, instead, a larger compassion.

We have these thoughts and feelings and do not know
what to do with them.

Therefore we put them from us, and they move away, or
seem to,

and so they come to seem very beautiful.
Withdrawing, residual, they pause

and look back, hardly a part of us at all.
Outlined in black, their hooves and mane a fire,

they seem like something
to which we might aspire.

*

Mustangs

You camp along the deep Cheyenne,
the Lakota's sacred river flowing in all
four cardinal directions so summer-slow
you swear it's made of tar or crude oil dreams
you can't wade through. You're thirsty
as Crooks Mountain, waiting for mustangs
from the northern plains to cross here,
split into two herds, one moving to the thick interior
of western pines, the other to the east,
through high canyons where they'll graze
in landscapes grand and lavender. You want to stand
in that split, stretch your arms in both
directions, so you wait, skin cracking
like the Badlands under the golden sun.
Your rations gone, the hunger rings in you,
a pain so hollow you could play it like a flute
except your mouth is filled with sand,
not song, so you keep waiting,
drag yourself to the river's shallow bed
but see no reflection in the silt. You kneel
there. You have finally forgotten your name.
The ground shudders, but before you see them,
you hear the slow code of their pounding hooves
build in you like a cresting wave, your eyes
fixed on the ridge they'll shadow,
and you know you'd wait forever here
for their wind to cool your neck, for one clean look
into the wet mirror of a dark eye,
one chance to ride
bareback, thighs trembling at the strain,
a specter flashing through the raw Black Hills,
your hands knit like music and air,
inextricably, in a white mare's mane.

Horsewomen

Praise the semitendinocus muscle, the wide, rounded
  hindquarters of horses
and the strong thighs and round, muscular buttocks of
  women who ride horses;
praise incipient strength gaining in the thighs and spines of
  girls who ride horses
(gait of girlhood, its rising trot that leads to the canter of
  knowing about horses).
Women who have re-centered their lives owing, in part, to
  horses,
  are shy of nothing, strong as horses,
ample with muscle, like horses;
  their posture conveys respect from horses, and more than
  horses.
There are women who grew up with horses
or made their way through years to console themselves
  at last with horses—
horses, that do not question the authority of women,
  horses, that never criticize the shapes or stature of women,
horses whose backs accommodate women.
  Horses will listen to women,
even the awkward girl bulky with adolescence and not yet a
  woman.
She will develop from her thighs and spine into a woman:
woman broad and powerful on the powerful broad backs of
  horses.

Manipura, Out of Tiphereth

This fierce horse stumbles from my stable-plexus—
sixteen hands, star both fetlocks, sorrel coat,
no vices, tends to pace when nervous:
            caveat rider.

Earthcurve's grave and gravity, her cure
for yellow cantering. Fever-fled,
she's paddocked in the middle orchard
            facing east and ocean.

Chew that. She craters January pasture,
green shoots creeping under: succulents
and paralytics. A bridle ruse
            can check her.

Her dam's a famous champion, named
for beauty—she's got her eyelights, heat,
and tremor. Smooth her to the sea-fed sky,
            the vital nova.

You'll find she's tried, goes nicely driving double,
foot-clod, clad and roan, her bloodclash spurred
or coaxed with sugar. Keeps her head. Carries
            whom she will.

Control

Hard to judge the flesh,
you may think, but I *learned.*

I studied the integument, the bones—memorized
each one—the muscles, what they moved

and supported, the ligaments, tendons,
the filaments of connection. But the nerves,

the impulses, the shaking skin, the quiver
quaking the body—and the eye,

the sharp gleam, sudden, knowing,
seeing to you, as if to your own intelligence—

the package: conformation, disposition.
It was hard to decide until I mounted

and felt the animal, muscle
against muscle, the give, the take,

the heart. That's when you know
the soul. It's as if

you suddenly feel your own—because
the animal has freed you to believe

you are totally in control.

Turn and Look

The horse looks up wildly from grazing
toward the woods where some deep rock rang
or leaves shattered like glass in a freak of breeze
that leaves the rest of the woods undisturbed.
Quite simple, the rush of red mane from ground to
height,
then the head still, locked,
the mane like fire framing the stillness of the head,
the head turned slightly away from the woods,
the eye dead-set on the woods,
the thin rim of white around the eye,
the spray of green held fast in the teeth.

Oklahoma Family Portrait, 1928

Here is the family, lined up
like fence posts in the cotton field
for some itinerant photographer
with a black box and a silver tongue.
They're all studying the camera,
faces void as the bank account,
except for the small boy who
has turned his back to the lens.
He's looking behind at something
we can't see just as the shutter snaps,
his face lost forever to history.
What is it that makes him turn
just now? Does he hear the wild stallion
of his dreams stampeding by, fear
the gunshot his father, this man
in the sombrero to his left,
is said to have fired at one,
bringing it to its knees?
Has he heard the horse's cry
or the silence that follows?
When he finally turns back
to face the lens, already too late,
will we see what knowledge
he's acquired? The woman
stands to the right, her hand
on an older girl's shoulder,
driving her into the earth.
Unlike the boy, the girl
has her eyes nailed
to the man with the tripod,
fists clenched at her side,
having already learned the cost
of distraction, the price for imagining
the moonlight yipping of the coyote
to be anything but noise.

A Little Respect

From the farm next door, long after midnight, there came
one day last year the bray of a jackass, an unholy sound
I had not heard for years; by now it is nearly as much
a part of the air around me as the sound of my breathing,
but that first note set me off, down the hill and across
the meadow and up the road, then one farm north,
where old Foster was still working when I was a boy.
He assembled for haying a crew young and old, Black and white,
in an era when some men might have sent separate
and possibly equal water-cans to the field, but Foster
had one can, one dipper, with which each man took his turn,
swirling the last swallow, not taken, into a jeweled
arc as he passed the dipper on and let out a breath
through his cooled throat like a velvet shout, and turned to work.

Down toward the edge of the bottom, then back into the hill,
two thirds of the load on already, and the mules balked.
It is a term rarely used in connection with horses,
for instance, whose methods of subverting human wishes
might be called stopping, quitting, refusing, or pulling back.
They shift about, under duress, to avoid moving on.
Mules balk. They put all four hoofs in touch with a force
below the earth's surface, and enter into a state
of patient remoteness not unlike prayer, or trance;
their apparent indifference to shouts, jerks, and blows
can lead their oppressors to an unexamined belief
that what they are doing is no more cruel than beating a

rug.

So with Foster and his men. As usual, they tired first,
stepped back to take breath and wipe brow, and the air
settled, in nearly-noon sunlight, toward perfect stillness,
a transparency dense enough to suspend a fleck of chaff
or the odd wisp of hay, drooping weightlessly from the load
like a fern in a glass paperweight. Decreasingly labored
the sound of their breathing, and abrupt the halted buzz
of a fly landing somewhere. On the off side, the slight creak
of a strap under strain.
A boy spoke. Just a kid, a ward
of the county, sent out to this farm to be learning to work.
"Let me try," he said, and these grown men looked down
on this half-grown Black boy, then back at the team,
whose roots in the field were perceptibly deepening.
"What the hell," one of the men said, "he can't do no worse
than we done." So Foster stepped toward him, held out the lines.
The boy took them, made them right in his hands, stood
just to the near side of the rear of the team, and spoke
to the blindered heads. "Come up there, Mr. Mule."

First stillness, then a calm, slow lean into the collars,
a hoof lifted, and another, and they walked off
up the windrow as if bound for their hearts' desire.
The boy glanced back as he walked with them, and
grinned.
"Call em 'Mister.' It help sometime to talk to mules that way."

Tongue of a Horse

Five rubbery pounds between the fortress of teeth
would take an apple, touch-read, then lick
the hand. Tongue of a horse, *hyoglossus,* connected
to both the sternum and shoulder muscles, massive
as such. Tongue of a horse, never at rest, pulling up
the grass by its roots or clanging the empty pail.
Tongue of a horse, connected thus to muscles
of the front legs, where humerus, radius, and ulna
taper to each hoof, carrying both whinny and neigh
into the sweaty fields, the galloping stones of earth.

MARK IRWIN

A Painting at the Met

They are all four astride a horse.
The woman almost looking back
over the small child she clasps.

The man, in front, holds a boy
in one arm, the reins in the other.

They are fleeing something vast,
the map on which their bodies figure.
It is the 19th century. They are black.

I see: the ashen color of their clothes,
the dread that composes the woman's face,
the grip of distress in the man's holding
the horse steady. They are bold. I don't
know that, for them, there exists a choice.

Flight writes itself on their backs.

Under the White Scar of a Face

Not everything's about naming. We've heard
the stories, so bucolic
the hay dust in our throats is enough
to cut off hope of getting out
without loss leaving its prints on our neck.

Horses, we've been told, know their names & come
when called. Loyalty, the namers of horses
claim, has four sturdy legs & can be ridden
bareback, our hands holding its mane,
legs tucked in to its abdomen for good measure.

But it's the clowns of itinerant circuses,
standing on the backs of horses decked out
so gaudy we hardly recognize them
& doing back flips & playing, for laughs,
funny instruments, who know their true names.

Only a clown can measure a horse's heart.
Under the grotesque white scar of a face,
a clown knows the horse in ways no woman
could ever know it, no matter how much
light her skin-tight, blinding outfit reflects.

Beauty may ride the beast, but only a heart
whipped & broken & ridden by beauty
can know the heart of the beast. No matter
what name we give it, it's not
loyalty we put the bit in the mouth of.

Trick Rider

His handsprings and gesticulations are a semaphore of well-phrased questions. The hinge of his bent knees absorbs the shock. The daring Trick Rider has an abiding faith in three-four time. Teetering on the rump of the world, he trusts what his feet know. Clinging to the belly of the world, Trick Rider feels the enormity of the heart beating against his own, he senses the menace and the excitation of hooves stroking that thin amnion of air along his back. Trick Rider hears the audience roar as the fetus hears the father's voice. Now he's streaming off the side of the world like a flag. Vision is a ribbon of fluid color, thought an arc in the back. Sweat-streaked, unrepentant, he stands on top of the world, wreathed in a vapor of dust.

[Acrobats vanished behind a veil]

Acrobats vanished behind a veil of thick, blue smoke. Jugglers tossed hatchets and knives, but it was hot, my son was restless, and we wandered out to the deserted midway. My son ran between the empty amusements while a loudspeaker blared, come see the world's smallest horse. I could hear the animal whinny from its stall while the disembodied voice called, come on over, come on in, this is something that you'll never see again. My son pushed his way through a padlocked gate and was too excited to answer when I called him back, or perhaps he couldn't hear me over the tape's continuous loop crying, he's alive, he's alive, he's alive.

GARY YOUNG

The Fire Sermon

They came by night,
loosened her rope,
and took her into the hills.
There she learned
what it meant to be broken,
what it took to bear a load.

When the law finally caught up with them,
scavengers haggled
over the outlaw's blanket and boots.
They sold the horse to a carnival boss
who figured suckers would pay for the thrill
of filling the dead man's stirrups.

The traveling show pitched its tents
on the outskirts of town. And sure enough,
gawkers lined up, ready to ride.

When her notoriety faded,
as such things always do,
the showman built a tall, wooden ramp
to a platform high above a tank of water.
He cracked a whip across her back,
drove her up the scaffold
and chased her over the edge.
Next he covered the water's surface
with burning oil,
blindfolded the horse with a feed sack
and shoved her splashing
through the flames.

Once, maybe twice singed,

and the midway had a new attraction.
They paid to watch at first
but soon the showman found
that some would gladly pay more to ride.

Now the pink-eyed blind albino
clatters up the ramp by instinct,
muzzle scarred from kerosene,
flanks scabbed and knotted from cudgel blows.

She mounts the wooden tower
and plunges down through smoke and ash,
slips beneath the blazing surface,
disappears without a ripple,
taking one more pilgrim
through the fire.

*Diving horse acts have been around since the 1880s, and flourished as carnival and boardwalk acts in the 20th Century. Having a horse dive through fire is an invention of the author.

Legacy

Your eyes close where the horse
flames through the hoop head-on, three
riders totem on its back. One falls
for the crowd-fear of falling; one
thinks of air as a wing broken from her
like bread, like the word *star*
not shining, or the tree—its flight
stopped by a bird.

For the one who stays: motion
and the horse. Together they are
solving the distance—shoulder to arm,
hoof to mane. Borrow this: old
horse, ginger horse, horse amusing your
weakness for him. Garlands we earned
like a handful of flour.

Closer then. Not said. Horse
of our dreams, you carried earth like
a sky. He *was* the victim, even though *he*
said it, a kind of prosperity. "Again"
was not addressed to any woman.
The horse stumbled into his hut. Flames
from it. Shadows with their own bodies.
Once, just watching, he disappeared.
With us, he was less hopeful and meant
funerals just for the sake of ending like
everybody else.

Wounding the horse
was our danger. It wouldn't bleed
until we said goodbye.
The rider felt sorry and got off.
Goodbye, goodbye, we said.
I weighed almost nothing.

In the hut his voice had left
the choir. *I weighed*
almost nothing.

If I mention *you* this is not necessarily
a love poem, though the chance of this
is a conversation you are having
with the horse. Only the birds
keep us from flying. *I weighed*
almost nothing. I have left you
my horse.

Le Coursier de Jeanne D'Arc

You know that they burned her horse
before her. Though it is not recorded,
you know that they burned her Percheron
first, before her eyes, because you

know that story, so old that story,
the routine story, carried to its
extreme, of the cruelty that can make
of what a woman hears *a silence,*

that can make of what a woman sees
a lie. She had no son for them to burn,
for them to take from her in the world
not of her making and put to its pyre,

so they layered a greater one in front of
where she was staked to her own—
as you have seen her pictured sometimes,
her eyes raised to the sky. But they were

not raised. This is yet one of their lies.
They were not closed. Though her hands
were bound behind her, and her feet were
bound deep in what would become fire,

she watched. Of greenwood stakes
head-high and thicker than a man's waist
they laced the narrow corral that would not
burn until flesh had burned, until

bone was burning, and laid it thick
with tinder—fatted wicks and sulphur,

kindling and logs—and ran a ramp
up to its height from where the gray horse

waited, his dapples making of his flesh
a living metal, layers of life
through which the light shone out
in places as it seems to through the flesh

of certain fish, a light she knew
as purest, coming, like that, from within.
Not flinching, not praying, she looked
the last time on the body she knew

better than the flesh of any man, or child,
or woman, having long since left the lap
of her mother—the chest with its
perfect plates of muscle, the neck

with its perfect, prow-like curve,
the hindquarters'—pistons—powerful cleft
pennoned with the silk of his tail.
Having ridden as they did together

—those places, that hard, that long—
their eyes found easiest that day
the way to each other, their bodies
wedded in a sacrament unmediated

by man. With fire they drove him
up the ramp and off into the pyre
and tossed the flame in with him.
This was the last chance they gave her

to recant her world, in which their power
came not from God. Unmoved, the Men
of God began watching him burn, and better,
watching her watch him burn, hearing

the long made godlike trumpet of his terror,
his crashing in the wood, the groan

of stakes that held, the silverblack hide,
the pricked ears catching first

like driest bark, and the eyes.
And she knew, by this agony, that she
might choose to live still, if she would
but make her sign on the parchment

they would lay before her, which now
would include this new truth: that it
did not happen, this death in the circle,
the rearing, plunging, raging, the splendid

armor-colored head raised one last time
above the flames before they took him
—like any game untended on the spit—into
their yellow-green, their blackening red.

Inside the Church

Inside the church there was a horse and she knew it
inside the horse there was a cry all day
she kept hearing the cry of the day was the horse.
The run of the year was the horse pounding.
The clamor of hordes was one horse heaving
flanks lathered. The teeth bared
unhindered the horse's mane triumphant.
In wind even in no wind the horse whinnying
over the bowed heads, galloping over the grass.
The horse, nothing but land and the length
of the seasons flying. She found the horse prophesied
the horse she knew the horse of childhood
and of death, and of the life between them running.

Thoroughbreds

Blood flares from the nostrils.
The lungs, the enormous watermelon bellows,
are lined with it.
Legs conduits,
heartstalks that throb with each pulse,
each leap into air and two-beat thump
back on earth.
Their genes are a careful proposition.
They carry their sires like totems
in their names.
Their blood is as stylized as a strut.
Veins push out a nest of tubes to tunnel the meat,
branch like ivy stems beneath the drawn skin.
Nothing in nature reflects their taut poise.

In the boxes,
in the small rings with their necks enclasped by wreaths,
they skitter, coltish, annoyed.
On the track, they glide.
Fluidity comes with their lineage—
training sharpens the point.
In the dust and rumble of the furious brief loop
their purpose may seem blurred.
The curt whip speaks to them.
Their flanks are an argument with friction,
the structure of their haunches
an investment.
Robed in shining blankets,
they wait like fabulous emissaries from another world.
The heart lifts with their promise.
Windows slam at their start.

At the Stables

The stalwart bay, the roan. The furtive gelding in the
cottonwood grove.
A truculence emanating from beyond the tractor.
Out where the repairs expressed their profound
urgencies.
The shadows pooled around the trailers were a kind of
daunting weariness.
The dogs twitched and snapped at flies. The wind kept
touching off whirlwinds along the dirt road.
You could see where the chthonic met the eolian, but
you couldn't parse the needs.
The sky, in one way of speaking, "darkened."
But the ominousness was outside.
An unaccountable buoyancy swept through their bodies.
Not exactly a carnival of hopefulness, but the
malfeasance had been reduced to a foil, a minor
character with an eye patch and a slight limp.
"Oh happy day!" someone's radio music proclaimed, but
then the singers mentioned Jesus.
Today's happiness must be plotless.
Nobody wanted to think about when it began because
that put it in time and someone inevitably
would invent a story which would end, so they agreed
to turn off the radio.
But they couldn't stop the song that kept playing inside
their heads.
They recognized the linear, time-bound world-view as
their Euro-American inheritance.
They understood that each walked out alone among her
separate, culturally-determined fidelities.
One to muck out stalls, one to repair the tractor, still
another to mount the bay and ride out, oblivious,
under a threatening sky, singing without knowing it
"Oh happy day."

Amanda is Shod

The way the cooked shoes sizzle
dropped in a pail of cold water
the way the coals in the portable forge
die out like hungry eyes
the way the nails go in aslant
each one the tip of a snake's tongue

and the look of the parings
after the farrier's knife
has sliced through.

I collect them four marbled white C's
As refined as petrified wood
And dry them to circles of bone
And hang them away on my closet hook

Lest anyone cast a spell on Amanda.

Shoeing the Arabian

The farrier holds
the seventeen-hand Arabian's sinewed leg bent backwards between his own
stout legs and digs

the caked dirt out from the horseshoe, from its toe and heel calks,
until the soft hoof
gleams gray-white within the dull steel's U. He puts down

the scraper, picks up
a tong-like pliers, snips nail heads, pries the horseshoe loose, then off,
slaps it against leather

chaps to shake the last dirt free. He yanks the old nails out, trims the hoof
with sharp pliers,
a kind of horse-size nail-clippers, files the rough

hoof smooth
with a rasp. Hot work. The horse snorts, lashes its tail against
shiny chestnut

rump, gaskins, hocks to scourge and discourage the black
flies. This huge
beast shies, stamps, and doesn't necessarily want to be

shoed. The farrier
has to lean all his puny two hundred fifty pounds, back and left shoulder,
into the horse's

side to make him stand still. He punches the gelding's broad belly
to get him
to turn. My scrawny daughter in cream jodhpurs and black riding boots

DONALD PLATT

holds the horse's
halter, calls, "Whoa, Jasper, whoa!" and gentles him by tickling
his muzzle. The farrier

bends the Arabian's foot back at the fetlock,
puts the old, cleaned
shoe back on, drives the cut nails in with a hammer light

as the one I might use
to hang pictures, clips off the nail ends protruding through the sides
of the hoof. He slams

each nail head home by hammering it with a nail punch,
then places the hoof
on a foot stand. It's a round steel ball that fits inside

the horseshoe
and is mounted on a metal, two-foot stake. The farrier grinds the nail ends
down with his file

and oils the hoof. "You got to allow an hour to shoe a horse
right," he says
and spits. "It's thankless work." I think how much it's like

almost everything
worth doing. Each muscle in his arms aches from holding that impatient
foot still,

but to feel the ground thunder under the battering horseshoes,
to see the slim rider
give the horse free rein at full gallop and crouch over sweat-flecked

withers is enough
to make anyone stop dead and know life is a race horse that leaves
hoof prints for the rain to fill.

Robin Becker

Risk

The kildeer nested on the ground—
seconds from the horses' hooves
and the graceful arcs of the canter.
Each time we rounded the turn, she stood
over her speckled eggs (I could
see them from my horse's back)
and made a display
of her fierce white feathers.
How I admired her! Audacious
before the iron shoes!

Fools and Horses

His life was horses. Those who knew him
said this, whether or not they knew what
they were saying. What he always said was
Only horses and fools works, and a horse turns
his arse to it. Summer mornings, long before
I worked the routes myself, on trucks,
he would take me with him in the dark of 2 a.m.,
through a city gone silent while we slept.
In that quiet you could hear whickerings
from deep in the dairy stables—queer calls
out of a lost world of whinny and stamp,
of names that didn't quite fit the uncanny heads,
human almost, that bore them.
I followed him
up the ramp to his second-floor stalls,
along the row of hip-shot rumps—high haunches
he'd tap once, twice, and shoulder aside,
carrying feed into the stalls. Before daybreak,
he'd have them fed and harnessed, ready
for young drivers he had trouble trusting
even with tools hard as hammers—that careless
handling couldn't botch. They fetched the horses
one by one, drove them out through neighborhoods
waking to the tap of hooves, echoes you could hear,
back then, above machinery's rising drone.
Back
in the barn it would be time for mucking out.

***

Year by year, until the trucks, they'd plod
toward afternoon. Unhitched in the yard,
they'd come swinging in on their own—I couldn't
look at anything else. Heads down, traces slung
over the hames, they'd thunder up the ramp

Toward me, sweat-slick, saliva frothing their bits,
light pooled in their bottomless eyes—all that power
going any way it wanted.
                                        But they would head
for their stalls, stand arching their great necks,
blowing, as he took them out of harness, wiped
them down. *It's all money and we got none,* he'd say
as if to the sweaty flank he was wiping,
though I believed his words were meant for me.
So I listened, watched him closely—and the horses
in their loneliness, older by far than ours.
I stared hard into each archaic motion.

***

On shoeing days he'd set up shop downstairs
in the better light of open double doors.
Leather apron on, he'd set himself to keep
horses walking in our human ways
of cobblestones and pavement. He'd tap a leg
a time or two, lift it up between his knees
and hold it there, cajoling, cursing sometimes
when a horse wouldn't give him a leg or stand
there patient on three. He wasn't a man to use
the twitch, but he would if he had to.
The fat stink of frog filled the barn
as he carved it back, preparing hooves
for the iron. Then he'd heat each shoe and bend
the metal, careful it took on the right crescent—
a perfect fit with no luck in it.
                                        There still,
harness hung up around him, he is labor.
He hammers the shoes home, snips off nail ends
that drive through the horn, rasping them smooth.
The horse leans on him. Then they quarrel
like lovers in an ancient dialect, each
knowing just how far to go, both leaning
in different directions to go the same way—
the man bent over, backed up to the hoof,
the massive body above him held up, it seems,
by his knees, his hook-fingered hands—
companions in the traces of an old servitude,
a singular creature in their strangeness.

Horsebreaker

His mouth is raw from Copenhagen,
raw as the quick nerve
of the colt facing him,
raw like he's been eating the sand
the colt stands in nearly hock-deep.
He's up to his neck himself,
in debt for horses and pickups,
the births of children.
The schooling he can't make use of
lies scattered behind him
like pieces of rotten tack.

Here and now, on this place
back beyond the border of nowhere,
there is only the wind and noon heat,
flies and sweat,
and past the flat line cut by his hatbrim,
a wall-eyed colt tensed
to see what happens next.

– for Henry Shayne Miller

The Horse Tamer

Outside Montevideo,
Martin Hardoy enters the ring
and performs a sort of magic trick
by tying an unshod horse to a stake;
he vows to break her
not with force but by letting go.
I can't understand how this will be done,
the roan must know it's a type of prey,
its parallel eyes unable to see
the predatory gaucho who approaches
from her blind side,
letting his body lightly lean
against her shivering haunch.
If he comes from in front,
she retreats,
from behind, advances,
so attacking obliquely
he must keep the bridle taut until
her four shivering legs move as one;
then the braided rope goes loose in his hand,
his gift to her
a momentary absence of tension.
An hour later, he wraps a rubber tape
on her left foreleg
and gentles the horse to the ground,
the wildness in her eye supplanted
by a terrible confusion:
she's overcome and pretends to chew
without any food in her mouth.
I fear she will crack his skull
with a flailing hoof, but he feels no alarm.
Almost tame now, she turns her belly up,
like a zebra at the side of a lion
ready to die, entering a final calm.

Courting Terror

It was like riding a wave the way the gray Arab felt ready to slide out
from beneath me. In a heartbeat. Between two heartbeats.

Like any three-year-old at large in the world, the gelding rubbernecked
for the unfamiliar, giraffing for the ping of the blacksmith's hammer,

gawking to put sight to sound. Skittered like a leaf when the terrier
trotted past in a miniature horse blanket. Stopped stock still

when a car door opened, closed, then opened again—courting terror.
Just so my child's bedtime fear of snakes defies the evening's liturgy:

snakes can't get in wouldn't want to if they could besides
they're all asleep now it's winter. Just so I breathed the infant's lullaby

to the terrified horse: Bye baby bunting, daddy's gone a hunting—
though I was the least of his worries, asking him simply to put one
foot

in front of the other, the instructor urging more leg when I knew
I could feel the damn animal about to bolt.

Riding Lesson

I learned two things
from an early riding teacher.
He held a nervous filly
in one hand and gestured
with the other, saying "Listen.
Keep one leg on one side,
the other leg on the other side,
and your mind in the middle."

He turned and mounted.
She took two steps, then left
the ground, I thought for good.
But she came down hard, humped
her back, swallowed her neck,
and threw her rider as you'd
throw a rock. He rose, brushed
his pants and caught his breath,
and said, "See that's the way
to do it. When you see
they're gonna throw you, get off."

Horse Poetica

The one I rode in on. That mud-colored nag.
When he blinks his black eye bigger
than my fist, his eyelid's an upside-down
pocket. And the scrape, the spark of horseshoes
on dry riverbed rocks—every sound has a silence
tied to its tail. Or else it gets penned
up in the mighty barrel staves of his ribs.
Oh, but *staves?* That makes me
hear music. That tinny harmonica, that tuneless
squeezebox, the song we ought to know
better by now, but still follow for days
down a path that's only a path because
we believe it is. Now where'd our giddy up
and go go? My horse can't canter. I hop along.
We've been outfoxed. Farmed out and fenced in.
If we were given a chance, then given
a second chance, we'd both choose a paddle
and a boat and float. Soggy but saddle-less.
We'd both need new names.
Then new shoes. Meanwhile, we hang
a left at the one-armed cactus. There's another life
after this one, but it's just as dusty. Meanwhile,
we're caught in a crowd of cows and cowhands.
But they part for us, they part like the Red Sea
of beef. Then they get going. Then I get
the bit between his teeth. Then he bites.
Boy, could we use a minor catastrophe or two.
Let lightning like a lasso streak straight at us.

Sacking Out the Roan Filly

He found a mouse carcass floating in the drinking well.
Made him hellacious sick the same day he got the call:
missing roan trapped in the neighbor's corral. He put
down the phone like he'd never used one before,
like it was something dreadful, and pushed through
the back door to his pick up. Headed south, steered
with his wrists, his hands lifeless, his metal gaze hard-
pressed on the road. She saw him first and free-wheeled
inside the wooden hold of the lodge pole corral—
fancy, dancing, tail high.

"That's what you think," he muttered, hauling out
saddle, hackamore and rope. "Make no mistake.
This time I'm going to ride the hope out of you,
sink my spur into your strawberry hide until
your eyes roll wild and white. Snare you
with this lariat, then figure eight your two
hind feet. Sack and flap and hit and stick,
hobble, tie and trip you down, just to spook
you up one more time. You ain't never
going to buck me off again.

I'm going to shake and snap that burlap sack,
make you quiver like a bog in spring, throw
that blanket up and down like a bed sheet
in the wind. I'll stand in the middle and snap
the whip, make you come full circle, and again,
again, wearing deeper and deeper the limits
of your freedom.

I'll heave that leather saddle on your back,
cinch it tight, move up alongside your sweaty

neck, and, holding a handful of your red mane,
quick slip my toe in the stirrup while you stand.
There now. I'll be on your back, slick as can
be. At first you won't move at all. Then of a sudden,
you'll let out a bellow, put your head down
and bunch your legs tight and let go the Almighty.

Helluva lot of try. I like that in a cow pony,
in a fellow desert rat, a friend, who'll listen
to my dreams of that shiny girl who turned
me down, a ranch, a string of horses all my own.
No more buckarooing here, there for gas, a bunk,
and some spare change gone on boots and beer."

Once she quit he opened the gate,
held the reins in his hand like lace.
Let her find her pace, stood the trot,
his weight balanced over her shoulders
to save her for the long hours. The sun
hung low. In the meadow, big bagged cows
crooned. His white shirt filled with the evening.
She fixed her eyes on the distant hills. The scent
of sage was bright under her feet.

Riding the Black Man Killer

Spud said I couldn't ride
that ole black stud,
I said I could. And did,
legs wrapped like snakes
around his belly as he ran,
stone-pummeled by Spud
and Jimmie Ray, his owner,
to a full gallop down
the lane beside the cotton-
field, me ducking limbs
and hanging on for life,
hollering *whoa ole son,*
goddamn it whoa you hear…
Fear stuck in my throat
like a pecan, and my face,
mane-whipped I was so low,
was gray as cowpie left
out in the sun for weeks.
Somehow I made it, though,
and I was feeling proud
of myself as I rode back
at a slow walk to where
ole Spud and Jimmie Ray
was waiting near the barn.
I should've knowed they weren't
full done with me, not yet.
Next thing I know the black
is headed out across the field
and me bouncing like a cork
hit by a crappie, yelling fit
to be tied when I could
get breath enough. And then,

just as I get my legs
tucked up to throw myself
off that black devil, down
the road next to the field
comes a pickup, GMC I think,
and backfires like a joke.
The black lays back his ears,
pulls down against the bit,
and I have only time enough
to know what's coming. And
they do, sputtering like grease
in Mama's frying pan, a flock
of stars as big as moons.
It seems I landed flat
on my back with head square
in a fresh-laid pile of cow.
Spud says he figures I
was out a good five minutes,
maybe more, and that he was
plumb scared, allowing that
it was his rock done spooked
the black before he ever knew
what his arm was bringing on.
Funny thing, he says, was when
I come around I didn't say
a word, just lay there grinning
like some tomfool hound.
He still can't figure it,
and all I know is that
a dog don't fear no tick
he knows for certain is a tick.
And since the day I rode
that black man-killer, Spud
ain't ever said I couldn't ride.

Cowboy

During a time in my life
when I was trying to be a hip rancher
driving around in an old Ford pickup,
wearing jeans, stained Fry boots,
and shoulder length hair
under a crumpled Stetson
that shadowed a friendly grin,
a horse bit me.

I had come to see a lady
about buying something,
maybe a fencepost setter
or a Navajo blanket
or even a goat.
I was so involved
with making my point
as I leaned back against the gate
both hands waving
that I paid no attention to the horse.
All at once,
the horse was resting his brown neck
on my shoulder, square incisors
chomping through my shirt pocket.
"Lookin' for a sugar cube," the lady said calmly.
Sure that my nipple had been torn off
I sank to the ground
emitting a sound
I had never made before.
A piteous moo, the cry of a newborn calf
lost in the ravines.

moom, moooom, mooooom, ohhhhgod mooom

The lady laughed.
"What? You want your mom?
Here, let me get you a glass of water."
Before she got to the door
I was in the pickup bouncing down the road,
my Stetson somewhere in the dirt.

Hard Evidence

For the most part people don't
want to be told the truth.

The woman who called us on Elka, the three year old,
said she wanted something quiet, something
she could learn on. That mare's been under saddle
just a couple months but she's a solid citizen.
It seemed worth the woman's time to look.

Before she and her husband even got the car
to a full stop, they'd gotten an eyeful
of Fyfe-n-Drum, the two-year-old colt
tearing up the paddock, tail flagged over his back,
nine hundred pounds
of gleaming testosterone on the hoof.

Oh, we got her on the young mare
and she slopped around in the saddle
as we'd pictured she would, Elka packing
her around placidly like the saint she is but
all the woman could think about
was that colt. The stallion.

Drummie was for sale alright but we could see
they were greener than fresh paint and would be
in trouble with him in no time so we told them
he wasn't for sale *to them.*
Some folks are hard to help.
After the "no" on the colt,
they left in a huff, gravel sizzling out
from under their tires as they pulled onto the road.

No more than a month went by and
we ran into them at an auction. She
kind of nodded at us and turned away
to study her catalog. After the hammer fell
on the last lot she made a point of coming up to me.
Did you see the horse I bought? she asked
in a tone that said, *guess that shows you.*

Which horse? I asked. *Sixty-seven.* Yes,
triumphant was the tone. Sixty-seven
was a two-year-old stallion, sired by a horse
more famous than our colt's daddy, bred by
a farm with a name more famous than our name
and she'd paid one quarter what we were asking
for our guy. Least that's how she was looking at it.

Showtime is *a well-know sire,* I agreed,
then slipped in, *Did you notice how*
the handler had the chain shank run through
the colt's mouth to lead him? The look on her face
told me she was an auctioneer's dream.
She'd been the opening bid. And the closing bid.
Other people there knew more about Showtime babies
than she did. Showtime babies could be gems.
Or they could be black holes.
Unpredictable, unstable, untrainable,
Wasn't anybody there looking to bid against her.
The auctioneer hadn't missed that chain through the mouth.
He dropped the hammer and cleared that colt
on out of the sale ring while the handler still had a hold of him.

Soft-bodied beings like us humans sometimes think
a thousand pound horse tipped with rock-hard hooves
is formidable-looking but in their own world
horses are known to predators as delectable herbivores,
granola-munching hippies in a fanged and taloned world.
For horses, the primary rule of survival is:
run first, ask questions later. It's useful
to understand this about horses if
you're going to style yourself as a horse trainer.

When that woman called us next
the one thing we could give her credit for
was that it had taken nerve to climb on
with her even-more-clueless husband
holding the bridle. Not much know-how,
but nerve. A horse that is being held
so he can't go forward , can't go back,
has one other option which not unexpectedly
their auction stallion opted to go for.
When he got to Hi, ho, Silver height
the unfamiliar weight of a rider on his back
threw off his balance so now he was in
a freefall in the direction of the weight,
up and over till he sprawled flat on his back,
with the woman beneath him.

This isn't the kind of incident you come out of
unscathed. Her good luck was that she did
come out of it, with a broken back, but she wasn't
dead and they got her to the hospital
without paralyzing her. It was her hospital bed
she was calling from to ask us,
Do you want to buy a horse?

Seems she and the husband had arrived at
the conclusion they weren't ready for a stallion.
My husband paused. Not to consider the purchase, of course,
but to bite down the phrase *I told you so.*
When it comes to the truth, some folks require
hard evidence, and she'd come by her evidence
about as hard as she could.

Field With No Horse In It

I walked a long way trying to find a field my horse could graze.
The problem was, I didn't have much money, and horses
Cost a lot. I had an idea what my horse would look like: dark bay,
Heavily muscled, like the sheriff's horse I saw at the mall,
Little children circling to pat as high as they could reach,
The fat sheriff picking his teeth and smiling.
But the only field I could afford was far from all the others.
Many people could pay for horses, but they didn't like to walk.

The fields were arranged one in front of the other.
The first few surged with moving horses like schools of fish.
All the dappled haunches bore kicks and bites; the mares
And geldings threatened one another, ears clamped back tight.
There were lovely horses in those fields, but I didn't look
Too long. My horse wouldn't be scarred like that.
I knew how to take better care of a horse than most people did,
And I would prove it in good time.

The fields full of horses couldn't sustain a blade of grass.
There were too many hooves slicing the earth to slivers.
Someone had set out bathtubs for the horses to drink from.
The water in them was dirty, the porcelain stained with rust.
I was walking with a guide now, a woman who said nothing;
I didn't look at her long, but I was certain she was like me.
We walked along dirt roads rutted from long rains.
The red clay was wet and stuck to the bottoms of our boots.

Finally we came to a field without a single horse in it.
We paused at the closed gate. The final field was a rectangle
Of clover and lespedeza; those are a horse's favorite grasses.
A horse would be able to graze here forever as long as she
Was alone; when she used up one part she would pass to another,
And the place she'd grazed would be lush before she returned.
The field was fenced all around the way I knew and favored,

With dark-stained wood, the kind that's strong and safe.

This field was cheaper to rent because it was farther away.
It was eight hundred dollars a month; that was almost as much
As I made. I thought I might have to live in the field with my horse;
I didn't mind, but I had to have enough money
To buy the horse I wanted. I was worried, but I wanted the field
And the horse in it so badly I was sure I'd manage.
The field was lined with the tallest trees I'd seen, slender
With naked trunks like pines, but they dipped their heads down

Like obliging horses, and I could see they were not pines
But maples. The leaves were thick-fleshed and tropical; some leaves
Were ivory bounded in green, and some were the dark red
Of expensive wine. I jumped up as the heads started back into the sky
And picked leaves to keep and admire, one of each kind.
I held them side by side, and they seemed to become larger.
My guide hadn't seen the leaves close up before; she marveled
At their texture. I wanted to come back here many times before I died.

In my dream about fields and horses there were the strong colors
Of the earth. There were the contours of the human face
And the movement of animal bodies. I woke and knew right away
What I'd dreamed of. I thought about it all day; then I wrote it down.
I didn't have another method to find my way back to the field,
And it was the best I saw on my long walk; I'd still like
To watch my horse tearing up bites of clean grass
With a small sideways jerk of the head, getting close to the roots

The way a smart, happy horse eats, not minding a little dirt in her mouth
Because it's natural to her, and though she probably never thinks about it
It doesn't hurt anything, grass growing the way it does, spreading
From everywhere, right to the trunks of the tallest trees,
Where it has to stop because of shade, and those trees
Have never been chopped down, to be that tall, that different
From any you see out here in the real world, where people
Like to have certain things but don't like to go far to get them.

Ars Poetica: A Found Poem

Whenever I caught him down in the stall, I'd approach.
At first he jumped up the instant he heard me slide
the bolt. Then I could get the door open while
he stayed lying down, and I'd go in on my hands
and knees and crawl over to him so that
I wouldn't appear so threatening. It took
six or eight months before I could simply walk in
and sit with him, but I needed that kind of trust.

I kept him on a long rein to encourage him
to stretch out his neck and back. I danced with him
over ten or fifteen acres of fields with a lot
of flowing from one transition to another.
What I've learned is how to take the indirect route.
That final day I felt I could have cut
the bridle off, he went so well on his own.

Riding a One-Eyed Horse

One side of his world is always missing.
You may give it a casual wave of the hand
or rub it with your shoulder as you pass,
but nothing on his blind side ever happens.

Hundreds of trees slip past him into darkness,
drifting into a hollow hemisphere
whose sounds you will have to try to explain.
Your legs will tell him not to be afraid

if you learn never to lie. Do not forget
to turn his head and let what comes come seen:
he will jump the fences he has to if you swing
toward them from the side that he can see

and hold his good eye straight. The heavy dark
will stay beside you always; let him learn
to lean against it. It will steady him
and see you safely through diminished fields.

Contest

Neck arched
long mane brushing the rider's hand
the part-Arabian part-quarterhorse
canters by every day about dusk
Near the bridge the woman
on his back digs in her heels
Entices him to back-step
swivel and spin
Uses her whip to force him
across the bridge
and back again
Hooves clatter
on the asphalt and gravel
Every day he performs part
of what she demands
Every day they head homeward
her neck stiff with frustration
his ears pricked
tail swinging
head high

Giving In

In a fit of temper
I remove the saddle, uncinch
The girth that when tightened
Makes him cow kick and lunge
At me. I unbuckle the noseband
That keeps his mouth closed, take off
The martingale steadying his head,
The side reins posturing his top line. I unbraid
His black mane letting it fall
On both sides of his neck, let
His seal-soft ear fur grow, his whiskers
And jaw hairs go unshaven—the noise
Of electric clippers too alarming for his temperament.
I release his tail from its mud knot,
Toss aside gel pad and fleece saddle blanket,
Tear the For Sale sign from his stall door,
Remove my well-crafted ad from the classifieds.

I mount bareback without spurs
Just a short German whip
For encouragement. We exit the four
Cornered riding arena, saunter up
The drive leaving behind
Tight circles at trot and canter,
Shoulder fore, half pass, leg yield, attempts
At two tempi changes of lead at canter.
My feet free of stirrups, we walk through
The back gate into a sprawling meadow, his stride
Lengthening, his back warm beneath me where
Our muscles meet and finally

Read each other's every intention.

Coupled

The neck's crest bridges to the pricked ears.
The ears flick back when the neck rises.
I've read the loose-ring snaffle doubles
The hands' gestures to the horse's tongue:
Gloves mute their randomness, uncontrolled
Twitches of the fingers, blood's pulse.
I bought lilac nylon, suede-palmed to stick
To reins' leather slick with mare's sweat.
It lathers between her thighs on hot days.
Like today, as the video shows at home
In air-conditioning while I watch myself,
And her, working to learn. My techniques'
Flaws bewilder us both: the ears flick back
When the neck rises. The back hollows,
The hocks drive out behind, the lumbosacral
Joint drops forward flexion, and the touch
Of my legs to her barrel offends, as the ears
Tell, and the neck, which, when correct,
Arches along thc crcst's length, the thick mane
Loose to the left, lifting in stride, bent
Like the tall grass through which a bull snake
Roiled, once, at the mare's feet, escaping
The wellhouse shade where last spring it shed
Skin. Neither of us flinched. We're bold
From weeks of training's concentration,
So I think back years, to lessons, horse shows,
Abandoned hopes, my belief I laced
The talent, and know, now, decades late,
It was all wrong, including evaluation
Of error, and my life on top of bad riding
And worse guessing: I can't say I should've
Known but could've, since now, middle-aged,

Daily saddling the mare bought cheap
To relive old passions, ambitions, in secret
Dreams, I have gone on—gone and done it.
Sometimes, right. Her stiff side: right,
Meaning she is loath to stretch her left
But will, urged, considered, across the mowed
Bermuda pasture, mosquitoes choiring to feed,
Wood bees' stumbling feints, red dust, red mud,
Shoulder-in, leg yield, half-pass, rudiments
Of flying change, and my nights reading
And staring myself to sleep with remote control,
Slow mo, stop action, checking suspension
At the trot, why does she flirt her jaw, why fling
White lather, is the neck soft, or stiff, and which
Is wrong? Which goes round? Do I dare claim
We've done it right? Now that winning doesn't
Matter except alone, solitary ethic of pace,
Straddle, and afternoon light? I claim it
By the moment, where it lives. One night I read,
I must feel where each leg steps, not looking,
And next day did. Cantering, slow, hooves
Clocking spokes of a wheel. One night I read,
When you think you should take, give. Next
Day did: poured from suede palm, shoulder,
Sunburned, curled fingers, elbow's rusty hinge,
And the neck, chestnut, wet with honest rain,
Bowed to the bit, seeking touch through slight
Tension, chewing down air to meet metal
I could hold before her, floating: I won't betray
My joy when, between my calves, sides swelled,
And beneath my seat, back bounded like a doe,
Or ocean's wave, or love, of self, of rightness,
Balance, motion, everything. I'd say the world
Should've been there when I promised her that
Inch of space I'd plundered years and in obliging
Heart she returned the favor and gifted
Like a spring from earth's center: I'd say it
But the world was there, stretching snakeskin,
Bridging mare's footfalls everywhere, me
Mounted midst black-eyed susans, Indian

Paintbrush, one horsepower, dirt road west
Where pickups blurred, speeding, oblivious, wrong
As I'd been minutes before, and overhead both
Hawk and great blue heron, united in sky,
Gazing down, away, sailing like the sun
On high, and in my hands the clink of snaffle
Speaking back, soft, now, tongue, metal, forge
The rest of our lives worthwhile, soft, now, coupled.

To Rocket, a Riding Horse

You ought to thank the goodness of horses every morning.
–William Kitteredge

Rocket lies down in his paddock,
resting his cheek in November mud.
Rocket has never written a book,
has no care for God or politics.
His attention is fully focused.
That is why, when he wakes,
I will follow him out to the fences,
learning the space he knows,
and when the time is right,
ride him out on the wooded trails
where words begin and end in earth.

In a Long Line of Horses

Sweet tang of horse at dry edge of canyon,
steep tiny path descends, as subway stairs
descend through platforms in complex stations.
Clumsy, citified, never ridden a mare,
never been to a canyon of deep urban architecture
unearthed by celestial hands and turned to light,
man-made become god-made. God's maid I am,
thrilled to look agoraphobically down to the right:
drop to death immediate. "Don't lean, ma'am,"
the cowboy says. I straighten, of course,
and think with sudden pleasure of the animal below,
scratch her ears, and talk to her, though all
she loves is her chapped angel, the cowboy.
They lead hundreds into the canyon. We each enjoy
a superficial blue moment on her back. As pilgrims
we are not individuals in control. Her whim
to throw us may be her inner call. To trust
that she will do her work is our work
as we follow the stations of the canyon thrust
into our saddles against good city reason.
Where is the train? We are the train.

Riding to Work

On this 30-degree May Thursday morning
my buckskin's ears point south
into a southwest gust.
Ten miles from the bunkhouse
to the arena, in an hour
I'll be to work, although in fact
I'm working now, getting one ridden
before I get there,
where more horses wait,
eating alfalfa flakes in their stalls.

I follow fenced edges of pastures
summer grazed and fall fallow, cornfields
stubbled, irrigation-pivots still in the wind.
I tighten my hat-string under my chin, warm
in a flannel coat and chaps, loping
graveled two-tracks
on Kea, Lakota for frog,
an apt name as he shies at a rooster-
pheasant's ratcheting alarm, snorts
and almost hops from under me.

I watch for badger holes,
their dark mouths waiting
to swallow my horse's shins,
weave between low-hanging
cottonwood branches and cedars.
His breath growing shorter, Kea settles
into long-trot, his black legs eating
the ground, my body rocking
in the saddle seat, leather
creaking, the latigo sweat-stained.

In the quiet between gusts,
mourning doves murmur
and pick kernels of gravel from the sand
my gelding's hooves sink into, steel shoes
clinking the occasional stone.
As the sun breaks, meadowlarks stretch
wings above barbed-wire perches.
I guide the buckskin west, pink sky behind us
as we descend the slope of hills
into the last valley.
Along the county road now, Kea's neck
steaming in the sun-warming air, I wave
at a Suburban, a man driving alone.
I wonder what he's thinking, warm
in the car seat while my ass tingles
from denim on leather, my feet
in stirrups instead of pressing pedals.
He glances at me as he passes,
smiles, raises a single finger
from inefficiency's expensive wheel,

and we meet like this,
riding to work, a speed-limit sign
between us growing smaller in his rearview mirror and over my shoulder.
The arena not far now,
Kea's pace quickens—a clean stall,
water and hay ahead of him, the scent
of other horses like himself pulling him
like the rest of us
into the wind.

The Question of Remarkability

In the middle of the twentieth century
in the middle of the highway
from Fresno to Chowchilla,
through fields cut and bundled
like farmgirls' hair in summer,
up the porched shadebanks
of a pass that divides federal land
from big ranches, a '46 Ford pickup
pulls one horse in a slant-load trailer.

His head hangs out the window,
a whole room for a harness
swaying like a ballad at each turn.
He keeps still as foothills
gallop across his eyes.
He grazes on wind. A wheeled
gallery, more statue than animal,
more noun than verb. And as the truck
leans inland, the pastures study
this parody of the Pony Express.

All this could be a painting, but you
would lose the nuance of pavement.
Or it could even be a sonata, but you
might miss the scruff of mane
up the middle of his sloping back.
For some scenarios, words work
best, or simply to have been there,
whichever lasts longer.

Wet Land

Wapato is blooming this month, sagittaria latifolia,
"a round root the size of hen's eggs,"
favored as food by native inhabitants of Oregon,
once abundant around here.
Driving north I pass a pond full of Wapato
now blooming, the small white flowers
elevated on long stems
like spots of sunlight on shiny leaves.

Later, going south, I see the farmer
unloading drain pipe for the field at the curve.
It means he is going to put an end to the silver pools
that stand there in winter.
I know he is tired of farming,
wants to subdivide, build houses
at the bend of the road into town.
I feel a sigh of grief, thinking
I will no longer see that pond in winter.
The water will rush away
as if it were an unwelcome guest saving face,
pretending it has somewhere more important to go.

Once in the Wapato marsh I saw a red mare
standing in water up to her chest. Her neck arched
as she pulled wet weeds with her mouth.
I never go past there without hoping
to see her again, to see the red horse
up to her broad chest, mouthing weeds.

Signal Right

When the car breaks down
The world goes wrong:

Something suddenly
Makes right

Signals by hand from a Ford,
Something from the old days,

Something from getting things done
The way they'd always been done,

The way that works again.
How could we not remember this,

The wild riding of a spotted horse
One hand tied

To the horn of its saddle
The other hand up, waving

Then jackhammered,
The fingers of this second hand

Spread out, windmill-like,
This second hand, this third hand

The way a hand can look like so many
Moving fast, the fingers

Spread out strong.
The fingers too, they are a hundred

Fingers in that blur,

The hundred

Real fingers hidden
In every hand,

Every hand that tries
To point oneself from here

To where it is
We want to go.

The Back Way Home

Hours before another war, driving up canyon
under cold March sky, I spot a chestnut mare

nuzzling fence-wire, left hoof clopping time.
but no—caught in the mesh she champs

to break free, her mane rucked with cocklebur,
circle 13 on her rump like a Nazi tattoo.

As clouds break, the bluff bears a tinge
of rose. Near the creek

over a wind-stripped cottonwood, a hawk
circles on patrol. On a ship in the Persian Gulf

eighteen-year old marines light cigarettes, wait…
I stop, get out, kneel, whisper *Easy, girl*

reach through the wire, lock hands behind her
fetlock, stand. With a snort she lurches

free, shakes herself and whickering comes
to me. In the twilight she nudges my hand,

her eye as I turn to go transfixed
with dints of Polaris, that cold first flame.

After Work

I stop the car along the pasture edge,
gather up bags of corncobs from the back,
and get out.
Two whistles, one for each,
and familiar sounds draw close in darkness—
cadence of hoof on hardened bottomland,
twinned blowing of air through nostrils curious, flared.
They come, deepened and muscular movements
conjured out of sleep: each small noise and scent
heavy with earth, simple beyond communion,
beyond the stretched-out hand from which they calmly
take corncobs, pulling away as I hold
until the mid-points snap.
They are careful of my fingers,
offering that animal-knowledge,
the respect which is due to strangers;
and in the night, their mares' eyes shine, reflecting stars,
the entire, outer light of the world here.

Neon Horses

(Artist Martin Anderson built a series
of neon horses which appeared in fields
along the I-5 throughout Oregon.)

To come upon one, driving toward your lover
in the dark, the highway steaming
under four grooved wheels, the dry hum
of roadside weeds, cigarette smoke's
ribbon wisped out the open wind wing,
radio low, shadow of some small creature
careening alongside the interstate.

To look up and see one grazing in a field,
serene, calm as the moon in the severed dark,
bright hooves sunk in black nightgrass,
head dipped like a spoon to a pool of earth,
delicate spine glowing, blue bridge
arched to the stars, tail stroke throwing off
ghost light, empty haunch through which
the sagebrush, windswept, sways.

To see, for miles, its burning shape,
barest outline of throat, foreleg, the imagined
fetlock brushed in. The surprise of horse
held like breath, horse and what horse means
gleaming like a constellation, lineaments
of the true world: cowbird and sugar cube,
fallen apple, tractor wheel, torn wheat in its
worn treads, silo, hay, the baled sky, ruffled pond
from which geese, squalling, lift.

The after-smell of horse, rising, feral,
floating above the sorrel. The way night
knows itself with roses and thorns, buried edges,
knowing his arms are down there, electric, spread,
his jaw lifted to the the kiss on its way, depth
to be met and entered, full on his lips, moving toward it,
a still joy hovering behind the eyes:
as when the living horse is seen,
incomparable, massive, universe
of horse, too much for the mind,
only the heart's dark world can hold it,
crucible moment, muscle greeting muscle,
grass, gallop, crushed blossom, intake
of voltage, blue horse of the valley, horse
of dream, lit chimera distilled from liquid air.

Heat

My mare, when she was in heat,
would travel the fenceline for hours,
wearing the impatience
in her feet into the ground.

Not a stallion for miles, I'd assure her,
give it up.

She'd widen her nostrils,
sieve the wind for news, be moving again,
her underbelly darkening with sweat,
then stop at the gate a moment, wait
to see what I might do.
Oh, I knew
how it was for her, easily
recognized myself in that wide lust:
came to stand in the pasture
just to see it played.
Offered a hand, a bucket of grain—
a minute's distraction from passion
the most I gave.

Then she'd return to what burned her:
the fence, the fence,
so hoping I might see, might let her free.
I'd envy her then,
to be so restlessly sure
of heat, and need, and what it takes
to feed the wanting that we are—

only a gap to open
the width of a mare,

the rest would take care of itself.
Surely, surely I knew that,
who had the power of bucket
and bridle—
she would beseech me, sidle up,
be gone, as life is short.
But desire, desire is long.

Study for Two Figures

It is the year of the horse. The road rears against the horizon like the snow-dusted back of a horse. The sky roils with a thousand thousand skeletal horses. I kick over the porcelain teapot, you shuffle about the kitchen. We practice the eyes of terrified horses. *Like an unbrushed mane,* whisper your fingers in my beard. Dawn gallops against the windows. We sketch horses on the faces of playing cards. I'm dealt the pale horse of the north. You turn over the horse of knives, the horse of imaginary secrets, the colorless horse of equations chuckling wildly in the stable.

Between a Man and a Woman

They're driving west through quiet that oppresses,
visor low, wires of light spidering out the sun.
They do not speak.
They have not spoken for miles.

Between her vision and the afternoon heat,
the horses come,
ears backfolded, bellies tight,
and balance at the edge of sky, their silhouettes
astride this silence she could call home if only

he would touch her now, break into breathing
like so many horses rising out of the sea.

But the man does not see the horses.
He has focused on the yellow line,
held the speedometer at sixty.
planted his hands on the wheel at ten and two.

They pant like gods, the woman says.
Their blue backs shine, their hooves shine.
They seduce their own bones.
The woman closes her eyes.

How slowly she feels her way out of body,
how easily rides wave after wave
over creature ruins, over beaked outcroppings
and fossil poplars sinking
into all they have flowered of shadow.

And when she turns so utterly breathable,
no other air could inhabit his blood so well.

He would open his lungs,
he would say yes

yes to the rhythm of horses,
yes to himself possessed,
if only the road would stop rocking
and the distance dissolve.

Dusk coppers the gorge, powders the flanks
of sumac descending the draw.
And then she's dusk on the tongue,
light that flows free from his last glimpse of her
in the rear view mirror,
night wind consuming a sky without horses.

No Time for Virgil, No Time for the Horses

No time for Virgil, for the horses,
For light-spires through the undoing trees.
My father still calls from another city.
Everyone wants my love most of all.
And I leave the airport without you
Before the plane lifts along the concourse window
And its vapor trail crosses the others
Weaving over the exit I take east.
I hold the extra sleep with me all day long.
I think I will die of a sudden illness.
I dream I take you into me.
I dream I let the rope out.
Your heart is the same color as the woods
Rushing toward me with the jet's same noise.
I keep hold of the rope. Your hands are there, too.
We haul the heart in, through the bee-light spires
Along the path through the undoing trees.
The horses are sleeping and Virgil is blazing
In the thatched and matted field.

Studying Wu Wei, Muir Beach

There are days when you go
out into the bright spring fields
with the blue halter, the thick length
of rope with its sky-and-cloud braiding,
even the bucket of grain—
all corn-and-molasses sweetness,
the *maraca* sound of shaken seduction—
and the one you have gone for simply will not be caught.
It could be that the grass that day is too ripe.
It could be the mare who comes over, jutting her body
between his and yours. It could be
the wild-anise breeze that wanders in and out of his mane.
He might nip at the smallest mouthful,
but your hands' slightest rising—no matter how slow,
how cautious—breaks him away.
He doesn't have to run, though he knows he could.
Knows he is faster, stronger, less tied.
He knows he can take you or leave you in the dust.
But set aside purpose, leave the buckles and clasps
of intention draped over the fence, come forward
with both hands fully exposed, and he greedily eats.
Allows you to fondle his ears, scratch his neck, pull out
the broken half-carrot his soft-folded lips accept
tenderly from your palm. The mare edges close, and he
lays back one ear; the other stays pricked toward you,
in utmost attention. Whatever you came for,
this is what you will get: at best, a tempered affection
while red-tails circle and lupine shifts in the wind.
It is hard not to want to coerce a world that
takes what it pleases and walks away, but *Do not-doing,*
proposed Lao-tsu—and his horse. Today the world is tired.
It wants to lie down in green grass and stain its grey shoulders.

It wants to be left to study the non-human field,
to hold its own hungers, not yours, between its teeth.
Not words, but the sweetness of fennel. Not thought,
but the placid rituals of horse-dung and flies.
Nuzzling the festive altars from plantain to mustard,
From budded thistle to bent-stemmed rye. Feasting and
flowering
And sleeping in every muscle, every muzzle, every bone it
has.

The White Mare

I cannot be of two minds and ride
the white mare. Duplicities
with you affect my balance.
If I second-guess her footing,
I may confuse her gait
and make her stumble.
I relax against her body,
become less impressed
with my complexity.
You dismiss her as a substitute
for human attraction,
but she feels like a release,
an Arabian, bred for transport
across wastelands.
The white mare resists
what she doesn't trust.
I need to let you go.
When I find my seat
on the white mare, it's mine.

For This Long

For this many years
I've pulled my body
away from your body
like an old workhorse
plowing the fields, wearing
blinders, digging furrows
for the new seed.

How many rows I've traveled
only the sun knows.

The new ground I break
without you opens itself
invitingly to the rain
like a fresh grave
that I want to fall into
as soon as this work is done.

Counter Intuitive

As soon as you saw that I could move,
you caught the horse, examined his legs
for damage, placed the ladder beside him
so I'd remount without a saddle.

When the gelding spooked less, but again
and I managed to stay on, you said I'd gripped
with my legs when I should've released them
to get my seat, my balance.

You said it's counter intuitive
but true, the way the military trained you
not to turn your back on an ambush.

Later, I walked miles to relieve my jitters,
fear like anesthesia, hoped motion
would keep my body from stiffening.

As I saw you in my mind, riding bareback
through your field of rocks, brush, thorn trees,
the iron spike I missed in my spill,
I asked myself why I was trying to be fearless

as you, to prepare me for what enemy?
why the risks we take for pleasure,
as if desire were a mercenary
or the price on our heads.

Donna J. Gelagotis Lee

The New Filly

—Lésvos, Greece

The village boy jabs
his heels into the filly's
sides. She jumbles
down the street, her eyes
like dice. She is a gift
from his father, who also
"breaks" horses. I want
to take the makeshift halter,
lead her into the quiet
acquiescence of a neighboring
olive grove. But the years
have slid between me
and my legs, and
I am a Greek wife.
This would be
unusual. I lean
into possibility, my American
rhythms pushing me
to take on
the challenge. But, like
caution that floats
on a sea breeze, doubt
has come with age,
and reason. I see the filly
at nerve ends—
I know what it's like
to be at the beginning
of some cruel
transformation.

DONNA J. GELAGOTIS LEE

If caterpillars come out, the mares will drop their foals

We drop coins in the offering plate,
the g's from our gerunds,
a stitch in the sampler,
and nothing serious happens.
The money is freely given,
the word retains its meaning,
the fabric is not rent.

But every decade holds one April frost
and the accompanying plague of caterpillars.
You mustn't visualize anything pastoral.
No horses frolicking, frisky in sudden winter.
Think disease. Think spontaneous abortions.
No one can explain the cause and effect,
but no one who's buried
ten half-formed foals before breakfast
feels safe when the first bugs grace the leaves.

I learned on the farm not to question omens,
so when my husband hears God at three a. m.,
we listen carefully.
"If there are problems in your marriage,
there must be another man."
A faithful servant, this husband of mine,
he scours our house for clues.
Never one to argue with Saviors,
I harbor the words on my tongue,
there must be another man,
and embark on a search of my own.

Mesteños

(Mustangs of New Mexico)

The Buteo's rusty feathers hum across the open valley,
roots for a nest dangling from its beak.
It has completely disappeared beyond the strays
who are still chewing the sun out of each blade
and breathe against their own weight. They know
the fullness of being *and* the yet-to-be.
Their tails and manes waver
as they stand, holding down the true center
of the Milky Way.

On the ridge with the Bighorns jarring,
twilight cracks over their hooves,
then hides in the hot springs and among
the secret rock drawings. A white striped badger
rumbles and shimmies out of its burrow.
It has startled the shadow of the unclaimed stallion
joined to the mist from the waterfall, and the mare
with lips pulled back, sways
in the last light hunching under pines.

What Didn't Happen

This is the horse you couldn't catch.
He was a sorrel, a buckskin, a bay,
a paint, a dappled grey.

You should have caught him.
You could never have caught him.

He was yours. He wasn't yours.

He was in the wrong bar. He was in the far field.
You lost him because you hurried.
You lost him because you were slow.

Because unlucky. Because lucky.
Because you hadn't an apple.
Because it was apple time and he was glutted with apples.
Because sunshine spooked him.
Because it rained buckets.

That you carried a bridle, a saddle, a handful of oats—
none of it mattered.
Not boots or hat, not prayers, songs, tears.
The purity of your love didn't matter.
Your virgin heart. Your heart a whore.

And what if you had caught him
by the mane, by the forelock,
by one black hoof, one white star?
In all truth, here you are, horseless.
The bridle was beautiful, inlaid with silver.
But imagine, how far behind, riding,
you would have left me—
the thunder of hooves in your ears.

She Had Some Horses

She had some horses.

She had horses who were bodies of sand.
She had horses who were maps drawn of blood.
She had horses who were skins of ocean water.
She had horses who were the blue air of sky.
She had horses who were fur and teeth.
She had horses who were clay and would break.
She had horses who were splintered red cliff.

She had some horses.

She had horses with eyes of trains.
She had horses with full, brown thighs.
She had horses who laughed too much.
She had horses who threw rocks at glass houses.
She had horses who licked razor blades.

She had some horses.

She had horses who danced in their mothers' arms.
She had horses who thought they were the sun and their bodies shone and burned like stars.
She had horses who waltzed nightly on the moon.
She had horses who were much too shy, and kept quiet in stalls of their own making.

She had some horses.

She had horses who liked Creek Stomp Dance songs.
She had horses who cried in their beer.
She had horses who spit at male queens who made

them afraid of themselves.
She had horses who said they weren't afraid.
She had horses who lied.
She had horses who told the truth, who were stripped
bare of their tongues.

She had some horses.

She had horses who called themselves, *horse.*
She had horses who called themselves, *spirit,* and kept
their voices secret and to themselves.
She had horses who had no names.
She had horses who had books of names.

She had some horses.

She had horses who whispered in the dark, who were
afraid
to speak.
She had horses who screamed out of fear of the silence,
who
carried knives to protect themselves from ghosts.
She had horses who waited for destruction.
She had horses who waited for resurrection.

She had some horses.

She had horses who got down on their knees for any
saviour.
She had horses who thought their high price had saved
them.
She had horses who tried to save her, who climbed in
her
bed at night and prayed as they raped her.

She had some horses.

She had some horses she loved.
She had some horses she hated.

These were the same horses.

Sacrifice

I.

I will chew the bit, comfort in the bridle's pull toward
you. Wait for the zephyr of your hands along me.

Bend down to my great heart and imagine its
chambers, whispering blood traveling the veins.

Stamping a love song, I nuzzle the velvet envelope
My lips make, to the cupped hands you offer.

Your small fingers dart through the onyx river,
Braiding my mane; lean hard to my body.

II.

Untether the eucalyptus from its bird feet branches,
Cover the ground with its star caps, feather leaves.

Place my aunt, Maria, on the back of a horse, spindly
Legs firm as kindling, holding the belly of fire.

Let her head bow to the neck, the chestnut trunk
Of muscle, twitching; static air precedes lightning.

Hear the cadence of her breath, hooves asking their
Permission, and the intimate gesture, heel to rib.

III.

Chiron, oracle, healer, with equestrian haunches
And pensive expression, took to the night sky.

He became Sagittarius, asterism between Ophinchus,
in the west, and Capricornus, to the east. He sacrificed.

He gave his life to become our galactic archer, ruling
the hip, thigh and sacrum. Celestial arrow to human
spine.

What would I ask of him now? An astrologer's fine gaze,
the star's riddle: How? How can we go on this way?

Horse

On a metal table, a horse's heart and lungs.
I stare the slow miles down. July, the Rio

Grande's green tongue. Desert nights, crystal
animals, —a silver throw of stars. Constellations

stalked us: Love's incredible velocity
standing still. The left ventricle's giant balloon

still filled with blood: a rushing in my ears, wind
through juniper and sagebrush, on red rim

rock a clattering of hooves. *Will you, will you,*
I said. The coarse mane and straining neck,

the frantic whites of the eyes. The *Sangres,* snowy,
astonished us, as we were to each other, always close-

up & far away. The left ventricle courses fresh blood
throughout the horse's body. The right ventricle

sends blood to the ochreous lungs. Canyons sleep
in our straw hearts. Breathing is what saves

us. Anonymity lives in that rust-turreted land. We
made up new names, places without destination. I

once said *I love you.* Somewhere those words still
stand, a ruined adobe chimney. History changes easily

when people talk too much, or are simply struck
speechless. The skull's stark white light

frees us. Now I want to push my hands into each
of the heart's great cavities. My hands are heavy

& red with the earth. The horse is a great table
that holds and carries us over the land, selflessly.

The Sorrel

Walking at night, blood and bone
coaxing flesh down a country path,
I come across the fenced-in sorrel
grazing in a light-green field
so lit by the moon it glows
like wheat, and stop to call her name.

But I have nothing to give, no
sweet thing except my hand in her mane,
my voice in her ear. Even as clouds
drag their long darkness over the field
I call and wait, wanting to feel her
living skull, her warm breath blowing,

nose nudging my hand for more, still more.

The Horses

Every night now
for a month
I have run away
to the blue lake
where the wild horses
come to drink.

I talk to my clumsy hands.
I scold my feet.
I hide
and watch the horses,
calling their names softly,
names I invent.

"Here, Thunder Cloud!
Here, Swan Neck!"
The first time, they run away.
The second, they snort
and drink quickly,
twitching their ears.

Now they stiffen,
lift their necks
and look at me.

In the moonlight
the white coats appear blue
and the bays shadows.
In the bushes
I stand perfectly still.

My hands pry
the branches apart.
I take a step or two forward,
my skin silky, quivering.

Horses

I brace my knee against
one side of the lifted bale
and tug at twine until
it bursts and loosed hay
tumbles from the high loft
over the bowed heads of horses
waiting in the barn's shadow.

In dream, the red one stands
over my bed, wide-eyed and quiet,
though with her mane afire.
Or galloped across quick fields,
it is her neck that sweats
beneath my hand, her sides
heaving between my thighs.

GREGORY ORR

There Are Two Worlds

Perhaps the ankle of a horse is holy.

Crossing the Mississippi at dusk, Clemens thought
Of a sequel in which Huck Finn, in old age, became
A hermit, & insane. And never wrote it.

And perhaps all that he left out is holy.

The river, anyway, became a sacrament when
He spoke of it, even though
The last ten chapters were a failure he devised

To please America, & make his lady
Happy: to buy her silk, furs, & jewels with

Hues no one in Hannibal had ever seen.

There, above the river, if
The pattern of the stars is a blueprint for a heaven
Left unfinished,

I also believe the ankle of a horse,
In the seventh furlong, is as delicate as the fine lace
Of faith, & therefore holy.

I think it was only Twain's cynicism, the smell of a river
Lingering in his nostrils forever, that kept
His humor alive to the end.

I don't know how he managed it.

I used to make love to a woman, who,

When I left, would kiss the door she held open for me,
As if instead of me, as if she already missed me.
I would stand there in the cold air, breathing it,
Amused by her charm, which was, like the scent of a
river,

Provocative, the dusk & first lights along the shore.

Should I say my soul went mad for a year, &
Could not sleep? To whom should I say so?

She was gentle, & intended no harm.

If the ankle of a horse is holy, & if it fails
In the stretch & the horse goes down, &
The jockey in the bright shout of his silks
Is pitched headlong onto
The track, & maimed, & if later, the horse is
Destroyed, & all that is holy

Is also destroyed: hundreds of bones & muscles that
Tried their best to be pure flight, a lyric
Made flesh, then

I would like to go home, please.

Even though I betrayed it, & left, even though
I might be, at such a time as I am permitted
To go back to my wife, my son—no one, or

No more than a stone in a pasture full
Of stones, full of the indifferent grasses,

(& Huck Finn insane by then & living alone)

It will be, it might be still,
A place where what can only remain holy grazes, &
Where men might, also, approach with soft halters,
And, having no alternative, lead that fast world

Home—though it is only to the closed dark of stalls,
And though the men walk ahead of the horses slightly
Afraid, & at all times in awe of their
Quickness, & how they have nothing to lose, especially

Now, when the first stars appear slowly enough
To be counted, & the breath of horses makes white
signatures

On the air: Last Button, No Kidding, Brief Affair—

And the air is colder.

Horse Madness

1.

means fury; means heat.
    From *Hippomanes,*
in Ferry's rendering
of Virgil's third georgic:
is slick with froth; is blood-
lipped; is spring-wild.
I see it in your eyes.
The horse is meant,
    like us, for madness.
It must be held in halter

lest it rear or run.
    It must be *scanted of*
leafy foods come
spring, to make it lean,
make it less familiar.
These things Virgil knows.
Yet it may run or rear
or with alarm
    betray your presence,
despite your care.

The eyes go everywhere.
    The eyes are orbital, animal;
they reflect both worlds.
So *Jackanappes-*
on-horsebacke
—weed we hold
as common marigold—
wraps a sun inside
    its petal before
the sun starts down…

2.

Their eyes were my clock.
Thus the oval eyes
of goats and sheep
turn rounder as the day
goes down. Turn round to see,
in thirst, in pain or panic,
what gallops near, whatever
holds itself away, grinding
in the brooding dust.
What makes Virgil

so compelling, beyond
the grace of verse, is
farmer knowledge.
Thus the shepherd sings
he finds his likeness
in their eyes; his judgment
grows of patience, as
practice grows of prudence.
As goats deserve
no less than sheep deserve...

3.

Means burning-in-the-
marrow; means as-they-
rush-into-the-fire. Meaning
all of us. I look at you
and find—what? Mythology,
song. Thus slaughter begins,
among the bullocks,
when bees are lost
and must be raised again.
The nose is stopped

(who devised an art
like this?) and the body
beat until its innards fall.

Then—with marjoram—
a ferment. Then the offal
seeds with bees, and up
they may be gathered.
    Meaning madness
is its own mythology.

The horse begins
    to tremble. The body
shivers; nor whip, nor reins,
nor wide opposing river,
whose rising can
bring down mountains,
may hold one back. I see it
in your eyes. Means
    the face I see is not,
my love, my face.

Alphabet of Ordinary Horses & Yellow Light

Rothenberg's wild running horses:
How memory multiplies: its fissures, blue-beige
landscape
Of the muted hide, or fields of tall corn, swaying
In the wind off lake Erie, the summer rain, drenched &
dazzling
The light broke. The broken light.

~

And your hair. Mary Magdalena's sopping hands.
For what sentence, the Romans rode in galleys,
The Technicolor chariots of fractured hot rodders
along the Isle
Burn the asphalt into adverbs, detritus & debris, ice
yellow

As ice icicles outside the paint factory, the Kool-Aid
yellow
Of my father's hand.

~

Light of this room, the shapes our bodies shade,
Manifestos of mercy. This insomnia, certitude,
Napalm, this burning of the hands, your uncle's war
crimes
& regrets
Of never giving. The mouth's Os, he told us of that
painted horse:
I wept right there, the horses pulling from the body's
grief,
its brass & blur:

~

To sieve, the verb shifts, running into ran, afterwards
only
Absence: hips half tilt, lips pressed, eclipsed:
The moon argues as if Allah's eye. It is the absent who
is blessed.
For varicose we claim to climb,

Windswept along the lake. This you I enter as if
running, the light
That breathes:

~

Your scratchy voice on the line: *I am calling you with the*
Tasman Sea
In my hair: In your wild horses, the Tasman Sea.

Horses of San Marco
Venice, 1989

Above the Basilica's archway,
stoneleaf,
Corinthian columns
and Romanesque frieze,
four bronze horses
turn their heads toward each other
as if they would speak.
Their mouths are open,
eyes set apart, manes shaved
like the war horses of Greece. Breastplates
encircle their arched stallion necks.

With someone I love,
I watch them high above
under the blue alcove of stars.

The Venetti took them
from Byzantium,
to mount on San Marco.

Mid-stride, they pause,
each lifting one slender knee,
and face the piazza
as if come from their stable
to see what caused
the commotion below.

Nine years ago
in New York I saw them
with someone else that I loved.

I wondered then:

Did the sculptor know
where grass grows
rich enough
to feed muscles like these?

I wanted to leap
onto one of those broad backs,
ride him away at a gallop.

Many with stolen loves
have traveled as far as these horses
on the plain of the sea.

Is the muscle of the heart
ever strong enough?

The balcon
darkens into shadows.
The horses are still there,
however,
on their pedestals.

They will keep lovers of horses
in their gleaming eyes.

*Four bronze chariot horses, stolen from the Hippodrome in Byzantium in 1204 and mounted on the Basilica San Marco, became the symbols of Venetian political and religious freedom from the Emperor of Byzantium.

Floating Farm

On summer nights
the horses sleep standing in the fields.
Their stalls are so empty your dream sweeps
like a good groom into the vacant rooms
to check the flooring of wood chips,
the salt licks attached to the walls
like magnified amulets.

Bales of hay cinched
at the waist fill the loft like tawny packages.
Saddles rest in their stands
like swans asleep on the pond.
And released from its duties
the scoop in the grain bin
is the ghost of your hand.

The horses are sleepwalking
in their designated fields.
Before dawn they'll drift—
one sleek shoulder at a time—
to the paddock, to the cool stillness
of the stable, while your dreaming lips
make the syllables of their names.

The Country for Which There Is No Map

You're asleep in the cabin
but I'm too tired to sleep.
I walk out to the sand road, hear
the creek sweep across the rocks
and the leaves rattle. Passing over
the fence, I catch
the scent of lavender leaves, break off
one and crush it
between my fingers. I turn and see
the horses, their skin
twitching in moonlight. They come closer,
bow their large heads.
One nuzzles his moist nostrils
into my palm. His breath
is so hot, I want to cry out,
but I've gone too far into the meadow
for anyone to hear me.

Invitation

Near dusk, the memory
of your body rises to me
while I'm pushing back and back
the hoe in the garden.

Sweet pepper plants shiver
as I weed around stems.

Marigolds spit pungent
yellow when I snap off
their dried blossoms.

I see your stocky body
shadowed in my door frame, and
your voice, full of accents,
makes my body open
every cell to its calling.
Please, say "horses" again.

Don't worry, all the children
are in bed, and my husband
is traveling for the business.

So, we're alone, honey,
in my garden. The neighbors suspect
nothing. I am a shadow to them.
Don't be afraid. Step into the darkness
before the timer my husband installed
on the back porch trips
and makes the flood lights blaze.

Horses

It is age it is what it is
Mouthful of grand little horses spilling

Who has not been cruel to them
All those pictures
In books for children
Watercolors and paper maché I can't throw out
Gallopers and trotters and windblown posers
Bedded down on straw the beautifully lame

A clever pair said in French in a bar forget horses
I watched them speaking to a handsome
High-achieving group and said nothing
For years I tried to mouth their language

There are on cold nights behind the tavern men
And women who can blame them with pencils
Wishing they were someone else

How little the hole in the sky
The stars who have followed orders
All evening in the morning need
To escape

Let's you and me my great great darling let's

Open Secret

Living with an open secret
knowing only
to expect the ordinary
knowing that nothing else
can happen but the ordinary—
knowing that the days
will soon make everything known
knowing that a slip
will soon make everything known
knowing that the secret will someday
make itself undeniably known
knowing that some morning soon we will awaken
to see in the field beyond our open window
a horse waiting that we have known,
from the beginning,
has always been there,
waiting.

Equuleus Moonrise, Wukoki, 1999

Without garden they woke to impulse, were
poorly suited to surfaces that shunned
their strides. If it was cold, they exhaled storms;
if it hailed on them, they stormed back cutting
themselves, cutting in half the night they let
pass beneath their gait, only to join it
again transformed, no less inhospitable
as any underworld of our making,
thunder cells of first steps retold in the
painted skies of their skin. Saddled without
rider, moonrise blinding Cassiopeia's
Chair before another turn, we say now
that the horse followed us to the ruins,
that crater-scarred worlds shifting in haunches
as she walked were ours, that four winged fruits, wing-
like bracts of saltbush, were radiant as
if she knew what we in our telling
never arrive at. We lay where roofless
walls opened to the sky, where the dead were
buried in floors, perhaps the bones of a
child holding us in place, row upon row
of stones ending in stars. She had come so
far, this mare who lowered her head into
fields of one seeded fruits that do not split.
Winds went on sharpening rock back to earth.
As if waking for the first time into
our lives, we were luminous, honed with her,
and into this world, we woke as strangers.

Surrender

Sometimes the light, a horse,
gallops into the room
and demands you surrender.
It paws the floor, snorts,
and so you rise out of the low-lying
cloud of the self, the half-dreaming
wakefulness we call love,
and into the cool air of the real.

It shakes its mane impatiently,
rears and kicks, its beautiful body
demanding your attention,
pushing its way in. Not
that you're afraid, not exactly.
But it shines straight into your eyes.
And though the heart is small
and cramped, barely large enough to suit
your own wants, you retreat into a corner,
make do with less. The only
possibility when the world lifts its head
and light pours from its back
in quantities enough to drown you.

Two Horses

Two horses
standing on a rise
have just broken
a cast of night,
are a severity
of shoulders.

The light cannot
believe itself.

It can only follow them down
into a swale,
among the redroot,
the nimblewill.

Just Because

We were in the foothills
of the Sierras, as though in a movie,
as though we had planned it that way,

riding bareback in the late afternoon
with a breeze behind us
and our horses gentle and without guile,

and even the six vultures
around the dead calf we passed
edged quietly away unfurling their wings

and the sidewinder under the rocks
shifted slightly into the shade
and the sound of the hooves through the grass

was like water all around us,
the smell of horses and sagebrush
as I had always imagined

and if someone had hollered
buffalo over the rise
I wouldn't have been surprised

because the clouds were drifting
on a long trail west
and the rivers of my desire

could have been flowing anywhere
we were because we were
in that kind of day, miles

from nowhere and in open
country because the wind
has been taking us easily

in any direction and our horses
were sidestepping mound and burrow
because even our words

among scorpion and thorn
had been falling all day
in just the right places.

On Horseback, Hell's Gate Canyon, October

for Kimberly

We ride past basalt columns, ascend
a cow face to top an outcropping
above the Snake and sit there, and watch.

Here is the topography of desire: a sky heavy
with grey smoke, the blue and ancient river,
unrequited; the rogue, stiff bunch

of thistle and sage, brown, curled coneflowers,
and across the stream the accumulated green.
All those oppositions that pull toward a center.

Like the pleated hills of the canyon, distance
pushes away, pushes past an irreparable edge.
Yet here we are, two long-time lovers on horseback,

relics to a belief, putting the pieces together
that creation could not. Constancy a thing
like a slow horse plodding along the veins

that bighorn and cattle cut through rock.
Trust like giving the horse his head
to feel his way over stony rubble,

perilous going, getting there.

Gypsy Freedom

Gypsies weave halters
from horse hair so horses
can control themselves.

At eighteen Django Reinhardt
put his soul into a guitar.
An enclosed wagon

is a traveling bedroom.
A man and a woman
can love each other

without speaking. A sandbar
shows up for the low tide.
Losing two fingers

doesn't have to end a career.
A bridge helps guitar strings
cross the North Sea,

and the singer remembers
the next verse. Nostrils
are not the only way

to breathe. Horses gulp air
whether they gallop
or drag a stone boat.

Woman and Horse on the Beach

A milky overcast, fresh breezes. She rides
all afternoon. Dismounts; rubs her cheek
against a chestnut muzzle, stations her horse
on the stretch of sand just above the tideline.

She lays saddle and boots on rock,
hangs her clothes on the juts and roots
of a beached eucalyptus,

then plunges naked
through the icy surf of the shallows;
in the ocean's astringent green-and-white marble

swims off the echoes
of her sweaty gallop.

The sand draws sunrays down
through high fog, cossets and coddles them.
Its weather counters the crisp air.

The horse waits
without a blink
without a sound.

She rides the breakers to shore,
tosses herself dripping, face up,

flat onto the warm sand, her head
back between the horse's forelegs,
arms flung out. If she opened
her eyes, she'd see his head
framed by sky.

The horse keeps perfectly still, perfectly
silent. His patience supples and
mellows like heart grain.

The Photograph

of a horse by the ocean. I found it on a bedside table.
On the table
is a glass of water. Who took the photograph of the
horse
by the ocean? The glass filled with water throws
light on the walls. Why is the horse
by the ocean? The photograph—no I should say
the snapshot's black & white. Often
I take it from the drawer. I say photograph
because it's old. I always make sure there's a glass
on the table. I pour water in the glass
then start looking. The horse is white with black
spots—an Appaloosa?
The mane blows in wind as it turns its head
back from the ocean. Often
after looking at the photo I need to
sleep, because it's so old, and in the photograph it
appears to be
snowing. Waves like tomahawks
chop at the water's surface. In my thirsty sleep
the horse gallops across the ocean. The horse is a house
filled with holes, but I am safe in its looking.

Swimming the Mare

If we were lovers we would enter
the water this way,   skin-on-skin, the salt ridge
on her back dissipating, my flesh on her flesh,   heat
   singing
the tips of the blades of grass,
the mare's belly's a wet copper-kettle as we dip into the
   black of the pond
her mane frothing up between my hands.

Surely there's some prayer to St. Godiva, patron saint of
   chocolate and decadence, the what-will-the-neighbors-
think toss of both our manes, our pissy attitudes solved
by chocolates rustling in their sexy wrappers or the
   plunge

into the water. Maybe this is the prayer: the heat
   whispering   *climb on*
The water whispering   *come in.*

Tess Gallagher

Close to Me Now

Through low valley mist
I saw the horses
barely moving, caressed flank
and forelock, the dip
of the back. Human love is a wonder
if only to say: this body! the mist!

TESS GALLAGHER

Horses in the Cathedral

Outside, the Palio beats
into rock-pocked streets.
Hot jockeys seize stallions'

wet necks, spread thighs, clench
ribs, whip, spur, strike, pray
to praise the gentle flesh of Mary.

Throngs hoist tambourines,
banners. The fracas blasts,
the inferno drives my love

and me toward stone, inside
the Duomo, to realign along
its ribboned pillars and squares.

Ninety seconds the stallions streak
the scallop of the Campo, I rein
you into the nave, circumvent

the stretched face of the Baptist,
sterling relics: limbs and hearts,
scarlet scarves of the *contrade,*

riders' helmets, intrepid trousers.
Vapor ticker-tapes from the candelabra,
stars glitter the dark of this high house,

lions hold the pulpit.
Midway along the tombs
of bishops and cardinals

you *shhh,* strip shirt and shorts;
without a nod to the hood-eyed
apostles in the altarpiece, the popes'

heads crowning the colonnade,
expose yourself greedy and starved.
While the horses lap the Campo,

we kneel on cooling marble, roll,
tattoo into skin the illustrations
embedded in the pavement:
on the vault of your hipbones,
Abraham raises his knife to Isaac;
below the rose window of your mouth,

Moses strikes a spring from rock;
over the transepts of your arms
serpents slither up fish-tailed nudes;

in the niche back of my knees,
a thin-ribbed she-wolf suckles
a boy who mirrors your grateful glaze.

As the wild circus pulses under the sun,
we skirt the finish, heat the stone,
and above you, my craven angel,

over your unruly parts, in the dizzying
dark—shoulders, flanks, withers, legs—
my mane thrashes, untamed.

Canela

for MVR El Corazon

Caminamos juntos en el Mercado
Tus cuatro pezunas, mis dos pies.
No necisito ninguna cuerda, porque
Quieres seguirme por
Las calles angostas.

Te compro una manta,
Una manta para tu espalda,
Una manta de flores,
De hilachas,
De sangre y plata.

Ven conmigo, mi cariño,
Te doy esta manta, para
Mantenar tu corazon, para
Calentar tu cuerpo oscuro,
Tu cuerpo de humo y canlea.

~

We walk together in the market,
Your four hooves, my two feet.
I need no rope, for
You want to follow me through
The narrow streets.

I buy a blanket for you,
A blanket for your back,
A blanket of flowers,
Of threads,
Of blood and silver.

Come with me, my darling.
I give you this blanket
To protect your heart,
To warm your dark body,
Your body of smoke and cinnamon.

Loving Horses

for Grayce Davis

Yellow aspen. Quaking leaf. Metal barn creaking.
Dust like rain against the roof. What could be better
than a horse dreaming in a sunlit stall? The heave
of chest, the nostrils flaring. The head carving light
into shadow and deeper shadow. The sheen of a horse's
coat
is a form of weeping, the form weeping takes
when it hears the solitary cry of the flicker
in the fog-softened morning. The cry of the flicker
which is the word *tear* lengthened and brought to bear
upon the meadow's longings, the longings we bring to
the meadow.
Which are the same longings we bring to the horse in
the dawn.
The eye seems bottomless. Fetlock and pastern seem
designed
more for flight than galloping, tendons taut as the bones
in a bat's wing. The bats which veer across the barn's
mouth
in the dusk, feeding on the flies which feed on the
horses
which feed on the hay scattered in their outdoor runs.
Yellow aspen. Quaking leaf. Metal barn creaking.
Dust like rain against the roof. What could be better
than a horse
galloping with horses in a rain-freshened meadow?
The young women lean and listen to the soliloquy of
hoofbeats.
In a gallop, as we first saw in Muybridge's photographs,
all four hooves are off the ground at once. *Walk.*
Working trot. Extended trot. Canter. Gallop.
Count strides to the fence. Fold. Take the fence.

Sit up. Gallop on. It is thought that the horse,
because it cannot see immediately ahead,
must remember the jump it jumps blindly, guided by the rider's
hands and seat and legs. And the rider must look past the jump,
head up, to keep the horse's energy moving forward
so that of the three—horse, rider, spectator—only the spectator sees
the actual jump as it is jumped. Which is a metaphor for life,
the way this moment I am in, this moment I am trying to be in,
does not exist until I am in the next one. The *nextness* of the fences—
the way a man who is leaving his wife for another woman
can no longer see the wife he is leaving. Or the way the child struggles
with the piano concerto until she begins to work
on the next, more difficult, concerto which makes the first one
easy to play and filled with something like joy
where before there was only agony. Which reminds me of an afternoon—
It was the son's birthday, and the mother invited the father
to a party at the house she lived in with her new lover. The father
brought his current lover who spent the afternoon measuring
the distance between herself and the ex-wife, between the father
and the wife's new lover. These were fences that needed jumping
at a full gallop, and she could only see them
when she turned her head to one side and then, when she
needed to jump, they would have already disappeared. *Dad,*

my daughter might say if she were watching over my
  shoulder.
Why do you turn everything into a lecture? The poem
is about horses and horses are about themselves.
Yellow aspen. Quaking leaf. Metal barn creaking.
Dust like rain against the roof. The horses stomp and
  sway, shift their weight
from leg to leg. *So handsome,* my daughter says. We are
  sitting in my Jeep,
leaving the barn on an afternoon on which I'd struggled,
in a counselling session, to explain how I had tried
desperately not to fall in love with the woman
I had already fallen in love with. It is late afternoon, the
  sun is setting
magnanimously over the Jemez Mountains, and her
  horse, Codeman—
half muscular Hanoverian, half elegant Thoroughbred—
  has come out
to dip his light-sculpting head into the water trough.
  Look at him, Dad.
Her voice is hushed, almost a whisper. *Just look at*
  him.

Clemente's Red Horse

1.

People think I'm crazy—
Nobody else saw the red horse.

They saw only the same horse,
The same beast they had always seen

No matter how hard
I tried to explain.

This carving of a red horse
I hold in my hand,

I made it from memory,
I made it from having seen

A red horse one morning
Remarkable in the distance.

Red—the horse was this color of red,
Bright and near to fire,

Not the simple brown color
That can sometimes turn on itself,

That pretend-red.
The horse was red

Not before or after this moment,
But it was red at that moment I saw it.

The sun rising shone
A particular light on the horse.

It made a different horse in its place
As it stood and looked at me.
That light made the animal red,
Red on the inside and outside both.

Red was the only way I could see it
From then on.
The horse itself, which was brown,
Was lost to me soon thereafter.

2.

But the red *horse-of-the-moment*
Lives still.

Where there had been one horse,
Suddenly for me there were two,

But in the same space.
The horse was unexpectedly bigger to me

Though it had not grown.
I hold some of that horse now in my hands.

People think I'm crazy—
Nobody else saw the red horse.

They don't want to hear about it, they say.
They think it has nothing to do with them.

They don't have time.
They're busy with something of their own, busy

Thinking about the yellow tree
They have inside themselves,

Even after all these years,
The tree that turned butter yellow,

Once, in their childhood,
Yellow altogether one moody dusk,

A sudden color they never forgot.
A yellow tree

Or a shimmering, old-orange hillside—
They each have something.

I have not seen their secrets,
The same way they have not seen the horse,

But I know they have them.
I carved the red horse

To show them what I know.
They only pretend not to recognize it.

3.

They shake their heads
As if they don't know what I am talking about.

But a red horse, it stops you.
It makes you laugh, at the very least.

It stops you from moving along the street
The way you had intended.

It makes you think, *that's impossible,*
But you are face-to-face with it.

These moments aren't only the sun's doing—
Other things conspire as well.

The moon, too, more than once has given me
A luminous gray house,

A house not my own but in the same spot,

Making where I live seem twice as big,

Just like the horse,
My one house suddenly two different houses.

And the wind, too, lends itself to this work.
The wind has bent the world,

And taken away the weak parts—
It makes me close my eyes when it blows

But I have seen it. The stars, too,
The way they move around in the sky—

They're up to something.
I don't know what. I don't know

More than to paint a horse red, finally,
And understand that I live in many places here.

People think I'm crazy.
Still, they don't go on for too long.

We argue about the red horse.
But the red horse, there it is.

Red Horse

His last day an old man whittles
a wooden horse to fit in a child's hand, whittles
a horse from a chunk of the high desert, stains
its coat mesa-red, speckles its back like a pheasant's,
adds a bit of hair for mane and tail,
gives it to his grandson who now holds

this horse shaped by his grandfather's hand,
in his hand, and he slips out early, this boy,
and finds you, a real red horse, likeness
of the carving, where you wait on the freshly
powdered plain. Ice haloes around
your hooves. The boy climbs on your back,
one hand still clutching the wooden horse.

Moss-soft bed of your nicker, just before you
carry him through the Ponderosas, tall, thinks
the boy, like horses, and he hears stones
gallop down cliffs as a blueblack herd
thunders above, even piñon smoke, to this boy,
is scented like horses, and shadows hover
in the shape of horses. You bear him down
steep trails past the family's sheep, a good ride

and the boy knows that when he goes
to the places you are not, red horse,
into the fullness of his life and into
places where this place is not,

he will keep close the wooden horse,
your likeness shaped by his grandfather's
hand, that he might call you,
that you might take him back,

back to the place where he began.

Late Summer Fever

for Graves Truesdale

The breath of the pregnant mare was coming in gasps.
She stamped her hindlegs twice when I walked into the
barn.

I remember crossing four of Hervie's fields that day
to watch the colt being born;

past the sheep that ran in circles all day long,
cowbirds gathered in the ash tree by the barn,

small as flies from where I stood,
coils of electrical fencing, the smell

of ammonia & fire: how she bucked when I got too
close, shied wildly,
& then her thigh muscles rippled as they shivered open
& forgot me,

a coarse, golden static suddenly blazing the haydust.

Once, as a boy, they put me in
a bathtub of ice
to break my fever.

The bird with a tail of so many bright colors, that
whispered its heat into my ear,
was my only friend. Not those tall shapes,

moving so far above me, but a blue ripple,
I was born with a caul on my head

the shadows of birds passing across the surface of my
stomach.

& then it appeared, as though drifting: a tiny, half-
formed, blue face,
recently undrowned from its birthwaters, almost
human.

I felt so small as a ripple once the ice had melted,
the ice that gave its form to my heat…

& the mare shifted, & pushed, a black muscle rippling
as her colt eased down through several human arms,

down there where my long, black hair floated
like the silk of a horse's drowned mane.

Snuffed tongue of my fever still licking the inside of my ear,
lay there like driftwood in the straw for the mare to lick,

worn smooth by a current.
And it stood for a moment in the August light,

on thin legs that buckled to one side, then folded at the
knees
as the mare began to lick its head.

Licking its last heat from my forehead—no,

all we could think to do was cut & tie the cord anyway,
that was my mother's hand.

Struggled, turned blue, lifted a crinkled, pink ear, & its
chest
swelled just once, then fell,

what I remember is my hearing, suddenly blotted open
as they pulled me up into the screaming of cicadas,

under some blind weight, an invisible blue palm pressing
  down,
the oaks, lashing like breakers to a sudden calm,

& my temples were born again, as the grass
rushed away in a single ripple from the barn.

& the other horses shifted & stamped in their stalls,
the ash tree tossed open in the wind & began to breathe.

& the air filled with that small death,
the way the smell of rain fills a forest before it breaks.

Through the cracked barn-door you could hear it,
breath for breath across the yard—& then the colt

pulling itself out, still folded, blind, root & glazed vein,
slab of its side half-swallowed, I gasp,
                                        as if drawn from water.

All they could think to do was leave me there,
lit by chaff on the floor.
                                        In the dream that keeps coming
  back
in the shape of a barn, I'm breathed out over water,

my heart dancing like a small flame on the surface.
I'm lifted

& set back down, into a body, in a barn.
& then the colt coming out crippled,

limb for bent limb, I try to lift it; I'm folded,
then opening, then rising up slowly

like haydust, like nothing at all into the stillness,
the heavy light of late summer.

What Happened to Me

A boy rides a horse after school
On a warm day and clear
And on one day he does not hear
The call, one day does not come home.
The day is not less usual,
Not different from any other,
That particular day when now his mother
Cannot coolly bathe him, or comb
Or kiss his face, his hands, cannot
Fool this boy so easily about things.
The day is not different when he brings
Home nothing, though his hands are full.
On a warm day and clear
A boy rides a horse after school.
He is a small boy still
But the horse is big.
The world is there and this
Is its animal, and this,
His stepping off, is the getting on
The horse of the ground that will take him.

The Rope

From Picasso's *Boy Leading a Horse*
The William S. Paley Collection

A naked boy
leads a blue horse
across a desert.
The horse, wild.
The curve of her neck
proclaims it. The boy,
the cork color of the sand,
the horse, a chiaroscuro
of the sky. Each figure
locked in the outline
that summoned it
out of the surrounding
immensity.

The boy faces front
gentling the horse
on a rope that isn't there.
It used to be there. The horse
feels it around her neck.
The boy holds the other end
in his hand. He does not pull.
He loves this filly. She has
a girl's eyes. Her forelock,
her mane, a wash of blue
rising—a dawn color
untouched from the first
pure swath. The boy
has big feet, solid feet.
He knows where he's going.
The horse prances, back hooves

nothing but a blur of joy.
They have been together
a long time, coming
for a long time. When
they find you, they will walk
through the walls of your house
and change everything. You too
may be sacrificed.

Kaspar Hauser

"I cried and said horse, horse,
because my feet hurt so much."
Kaspar Hauser (1812-1833)

Or consider the wordless, like the foundling
boy who rises from a hole in the German
earth in his sixteenth year knee-less
as a cheap doll and gropes toward Nuremburg,
a wad of ribbon and a blanched and sanded
toy horse in each hand. For the first time
he witnesses the difference between day and night,
his arms crossed to guard his eyes from the sun.
Every one he meets he meets for the first time,
but just to speak is to groan or weep
apology, to whisper *Ross,* the word for horse
the man who locked him up dropped in his ear.

When horse is the obliteration of the world,
he begs for a hole where horse means longing
for a horse, or thank you for this ribbon.
Horse is both the music from a peasant's wedding
and the laughter, horse the sadness
of a lame boy too weak or scared to carry
a toy over the threshold of a foster home,
horse the pain of all walking, and walking an awkward
compromise between falling down and standing up,
horse the last word he whispers before the pain
of talking faints him to sleep. Horse is even
that last shadow lunging, the dagger
that cleaves his heart like a plaything, like a child's
hand, like the pearled neck of an Arabian,
Kaspar thinks, bleeding to death. Something to stroke,
something to dress, something to call by a favorite name.

Sonnets to Orpheus 1:20

Rainer Maria Rilke

Dir aber, Herr, o was weih ich dir, sag
der das Ohr den Geschöpfen gelehrt?—
Mein Erinnern an einen Frühlingstag,
seinen Abend, in Rußland—ein Pferd...

Herüber vom Dorf kam der Schimmel allein,
an der vorderen Fessel den Pflock,
um die Nacht auf den Wiesen allein zu sein;
wie schlug seiner Mähne Gelock

an den Hals im Takte des Übermuts,
bei dem grob gehemmten Gallop.
Wie sprangen die Quellen des Rossebluts!

Der fühlte die Weiten, und ob!
Der sang und der hörte—, dein Sagenkreis
War *in* ihm geschlossen.
Sein Bild: Ich weih's.

~

But what can I consecrate, master, to you,
Who taught every creature to listen?
My memory of a day in spring,
his evening, in Russia—a horse.

The gray came out of the village alone,
around his front fetlock the tether,
to be by himself in the fields that night.
And, oh! The beat of his curly mane,

on his neck, to the jubilant rhythm

of that rough, that tether-obstructed gait.
How the springs of horse blood bubbled!

He felt the call of the distance—and how!
He sang and he listened. Your mythic ring
was closed *within him.*
                                        His image—my gift.

Zephyr

So he rode into crone-cold Berlin
on a gallant wind,

rescuer, eager-to-serve savior,
and the starving denizens

of a ragtag precinct,
ambushed his horse!

In the war's last gasp and moan,
only fledgling soldiers

of the Third Reich remained
to march into the city of stone eagles

and defend it—a downcast city
already minus

fuel and bustling automobiles;
so cannons and horses

were commissioned. Eighteen,
an ardent equestrian, he was given

just one brisk day
to fashion a viable troop—

With onerous horse-drawn cannons, imagine,
they sallied into forlorn

street battles in Berlin:
Scattered heaps

of teenaged cavalrymen skirmishing
at the gates of Hitler's city;

jerry-built bases posted
in the middle of barraged streets:

Now he stresses the word *Hitlerjugend*
making his close-listening,

truth-or-bust daughter shudder.
After dinner

and his relished pilsner,
he recounts for her

the ire and clamor, the pallor
of an empty-bellied Berlin,

the brash cries of the ravenous citizens,
at first pestering,

then menacing, rampaging—
his regal horse, Zephyr,

burnished with the name
of the god of the western wind,

his magnificent ally, reduced
to meat and aroma,

by the hopeless maws
of an unmoored crowd—

Gutted, fed-upon, forsaken,
the overturned horses

of his makeshift, teenaged battalion
spilled wine, spilled

scarlet and vermilion

on the blasted sidewalks of Berlin—
And the other utterly-believing,
street battling boys

under his futile command?
Lost to him forever in the pell-mell

tumult of defeat,
the ransacked aftermath,

the ensuing juggernaut
of dazed refugees from the east—

Six decades and yet
this garish splatter

and marauding grief,
the memory of a purblind,
match-lit faith in the Führer,
remain trenchant, at-the-ready,

the sweet memento of Zephyr's stride,
the brindled beauty

and unforced prowess that seemed
so just, propitious—

As if from a rust-flecked watering can,
an old man's fluent tears,

bracing as a cavalry
or an ambush:

so much to choose from, daughter—who can say
what they're for?

For an Olympian wind, a zealous rider, a boy still
undividable from his horse.

The Last Horse Alive in Mother Russia

As Interpreted from a Photograph, 1943

The last horse alive in Mother Russia,
Grazing through the ashes of Stalingrad,
Is not listed in war statistics, in frontage made
To Dar Gova. Nor does history, unforgiving,
Remember plowshares before they were swords.

Yet the horse was there, a furred ellipsis,
Nosing the ribs of gutted shops, her tail an icicle
Chandelier, shale smoking blue beneath her hooves,
In a forest of chimneys, the slag that remained
Of a city collapsed like a punctured lung,

While the mare continued her dotted line,
Past flame-haired children and smoldering grain,
Past bricks and eyes all focused skyward
In the position of the damned,
Beneath the ice that laced her spine,

A fever burned and vapor rose, her chipped hooves
Buckling on the Volga's brim,
Near the tractor factories with splintered gears,
Near the frost-pinched fingers of the camera man,
Who was seeking signs of a relenting god.

And there, the horse's bones unlocked,
As she rested her muzzle against the rubble,
As a soldier's vodka spilled from her veins,
As the camera bulb popped
Then froze her limbs in the act of supplication.

And she became the end of the ellipsis of war,
Where the heart bursts forward
And joins the rest.

Salute

Dawn upon dawn, my blond
warrior father's whereabouts,

a fierce morsel in the mouth of a sphinx;
for sixty fogbound years,

not a word and then
a key-cold message from Russia:

Father's remains
had been recovered and interred

in a resting-place
for fallen Germans.

Month after abrading month,
my diligent mother had mailed

a tin-kept sum to ensure
the gallant burial of luckless

soldiers lost abroad,
then spurred me,

with her dying breath,
to solve the mystery—

Suffused with the titan birches' beauty,
dressed in overdue

atoms of grief—
my mother's apt charity

miraculously repaid—
suddenly I witnessed,

past my father's terse marker,
two white unhampered horses

saunter from the haze-wrapped woods,
and halt—

their riffled manes
dazzling as epaulettes.

And after a strict, bygone calm
that the breeze-swept stallions lowered

like an unbelievable drawbridge,
I clutched my shawl, remembering

Mother's captivating,
laissez-faire laugh,

as she claimed Father so loved
his saddle and his ambling bay,

God must have given him
the soul of a centaur—

Then the pert white allies
vanished into the haze,

the wind-tugged woods—
Dawn upon dawn,

and the hush after the kudos
of their trumpet-clear hooves:

Silence is the keenest salute.

Detail of the Four Chambers to the Horse's Heart

1.

Listen. The last time I saw my father
alive, he spoke of horses, the brute geometry
of a broken team in motion. He tallied
the bushels of oats, gallons of water
down to the drop each task would cost.
How Belgians loved hardwood hames the most.
Give them the timber sled at Logging Camp
any day, the workable meadows in need
of leveling, tilling, harrowing, new seeding.
We could've been in our dark loafing shed,
cooling off between loads of chopping hay,
the way he carried on that last good day.
With the proper encouragement, he said,
they would work themselves to death.

2.

Drifts of snow up to their hocks and knees,
the team struggles. They want nothing more
than to droop in the breath-warm barn,
to fill both cheeks with the chopped timothy
of August afternoons, to muzzle trough water,
then rest. Nothing more now than to rest.
Snowflakes alighting on their hot withers
vanish. The sledge so laden with slush and ice.
They snort, toss, stamp and fart to keep blood
thrumming through their bodies, heavenly
machinery in sync with work and weather.
Because the driver, my father, chirps and barks
in a barely human way, they labor.
The work will stop when he says so.

3.

Breaker of Mustangs and Broncos, saint
to all things unbridled, you knew cancer
(like the roots dismantling your culvert)
would have you drawn and quartered.
The stallions whipped to sunder limb
from perishable limb. Divided, the evil
in the body loses its power. The fallen
horse, for example, you saw trampled
had disappeared overnight, scattered
across acres by coyotes or not as dead
as you thought. His harem of mares
soon another's. You were often called
a man even then. Startled in every direction,
those horses almost touched the ground.

4.

So much can spook a horse when the world
comes alive: an unlatched gate the wind
knocks, a pine knot popping like a shotgun
in the campfire. If blinders fail to block
all fresh deadfall along his usual trail,
he'll snap the trace. Now loop a rope
around his upper lip to put a "twitch" on.
This, somehow, settles him down more
than the creak of doubletrees, the routine
caress of your currycomb, the molasses
that glues oats in hunks of giddy bliss.
Given sweets, any horse will follow you.
Whisper what you want to this one.
Never question that disquieted heart.

I Was Thinking About That Horse Talking

My father never got over the laughter he heard
While watching from above the gurney, like a dream,
His dentures fall from his gaping mouth.
One rescuer, my father later called *a punk,*
Even went so far as to say,
"He won't be needing those anymore."

As a child, my father was raised moving slowly
Across the heat and snow of Arizona deserts.
My grandfather, a German immigrant,
Laid iron rails, and miles later
Supervised other men laying rails,
Driving spikes, for America
And the Southern Pacific Railroad.

The children—One daughter and four sons—
Were said to keep rattlesnakes
For pets. They were said to hang the shed skins
On saguaro cacti at Christmastime.
My father said this to me when I was a girl.
He said that at night, they—the children—buried
Themselves, except their faces, in the desert sand
Like horned toads: to hide from Geronimo
And to keep warm.

He once told me a secret:
The quarter-sized scar that remained ivory
On his tanned upper-arm, happened one night
When he refused to bury himself;
An arrow shot silently through the dark
Into his stubborn skin. He said he didn't cry
Then, couldn't tell anybody

Afterward, for fear of the lashing
His father would give him, or worse yet, for fear
Of the pain it would cause his frail mother.

He told me not to tell, and I haven't until now.

A week before my father's last heart attack,
He called to tell me he was going to sell his horse.
It seemed that while out riding in the mountains that day,
The *damned thing* kept trying to cross over
Lookout Ridge and head toward the cemetery—
This, despite my father's lashing. *What good's*
An old bag of bones that won't listen to you,
He asked me.

I was thinking about these things last summer,
Nineteen years after my father's death,
As I hiked alone, in the Black Rock desert of Nevada.
I was thinking about that horse talking
To my father. I was thinking
About the stories my father told me—stories
I never told anyone else. I was thinking these things
When I came upon a long twist of wild horsehair,
A tail apparently knotted up so tight it had to be shed,
Left there, draped over a spiny sage. I touched
Its weathered strands, its brown gray
Coarseness, as I listened for the words.

a mamaist Bold Venture

my horse belonged of course to my grandfather Morton Schwartz
gone all these years I never even met him
my horse I ride in my dreams is black one night, white another
he sometimes nuzzles me awake
my horse I've seen in photos and books but never in real life yet is
growing more real to me with each day
my horse is bold and loves adventure, shying not a whit from life nor
a whit from death
my horse has won races and was crowned champion more than once
my horse carries me high in the saddle and quickens me like a pulse
when he sees me hiding, he trots me out into view
when I'm in need of rest, he himself becomes my nest
my horse if I fall presses me on, encouraging me
my horse if I lose control guides me safely into my truth of things
my horse likes to lick my neck
I am afraid of my horse sometimes but that doesn't stop me
my horse is a clean animal who ruminates and sings the sweetest
music my ears will ever hear
wherever I go my horse is there with me and I, I thank my grandfather always
for my horse is bold and free, he crosses the waters
splashing in the waves of his destiny

My Father's Horses

I see them everywhere,
And my dumb lips like thin snails
Trail over their own shimmering,
Wet. I see them,
And my lips are the felt wrappings tied twice
Around the legs of an oak table.
Their heads in blue light.
I see them with their nostrils,
Chins tucked into chest,
Into the black armoire,
The beautiful brass latchings.
I see them from a window—
The carrots boiling there below
Raise their rough steam
Like the stableman's two hands.
These are the horses of summer lunches.
The knotted, now unbraidable hair in its dust
And McCrery's Cream Cheese in a plain brown box.
I see they are actors.
Imported from Sweden,
They read the dark Neruda in blond sweaters.
I fall from their laughter;
Lips pulled back from teeth.
I would race them to be naked,
Pull the black sweater
Off over my head,
My invisible haunches quivering.

Meager Intruders

Sometime in the middle of the night,
a horse found its way into the hallway
and chewed the doorframes raw. In each
bedroom there was a sister trying to sleep,
and each paced her room clad only in the rude
shadow of the gnawing sound. Finally one
slender girl, older than the rest, pushed
her door out and, ready to yell, saw the horse
standing in skeletal sorrow, gouging wood
from the wall with stark teeth in a bony jaw.
She thought for a moment she could
feed it her hair and give it new strength.
Then it saw her and jerked with fear.
She tried to touch its velvet nose
as it backed desperately out of the hall,
banging its hocks on the walls,
splintering baseboards with long hooves.
Just before it could turn away,
she hooked her bra like a halter
and looped it over one flicking ear
as it ran lonely into the briar of night.

Farm: A Family

Father was a horse broken by his uncles, whisky-fed,
white star freckled.
Mother was a bird, flapping worm beaked, knocking her
nose on the trees.
Grandma was a mare, horse head frowning, long gray
hair twitching under flies.
Tie that Stag up, tie him to the bar! Order him a heart
with a twist of lime.

Mother was a bird, flapping worm beaked, knocking her
nose on the trees.
Father bucks. Father bucks Mother. Father bucks all
three ponies fathered.
Tie that Stag up, tie him to the bar! Order him a twist
with a heart of lime.
Father was a horse broken by Mother, ridden on the
beaches, salt licked stomped.

Father bucking. Father bucking Mother. Father bucking
all three ponies. Fathered
Sister was a cow, still in a field, breasts full of heavy
cream.
Father was a horse broken. Mother ridden on the
beaches, assault. Licked stomped
Brother was a mule, more brawn than brain, kicking
back-turned shins with glee.

Sister was a cow so still in a field, breasts full, heavy
cream.
I was a sheep, ebony and shaved, exhausted from
jumping off cliffs.
Brother was a mule, more brawny than brainy, kicking

back turning shins to glee.
Grandpa was the farm, hearse in the barn, saddled the same, raced natives to the grave.

I was a sheep, ebony and shaven, exhausted from jumping off cliffs.
Grandma was a mare, horse head frowning, long gray hair twitching under flies.
Grandpa was the farm, hearse in the barn, saddled the same, raced natives to the grave.
Father was a horse broken by his uncles, whisky-fed, white star freckled.

Phaethon

All day you muck the horses' stalls in heat
that jellifies your arms, your knees, your brain,
and turns the whole group ornery in its pen.
The chestnut bites your shoulder. The broodmare spills
your beer. And twice, you swear, the cribber foal
lets go the wood to call you one dumb fuck.

Later, after sloughing off the stench
and drinking Lone Oak by the light of late-
night *Mr. Ed* reruns, "Ed Goes to Vegas,"
"Ed the Appleholic," you stumble to your dreams
to find your father's fiery stable annoyed
by your gawking. They toss their manes as if to say,
We know you're no Apollo. Ditto that.
You grew up down the mountain, not in Delphi,
a rag-doll driver with paper chariots
and reins of twine, incapable of handling
dead ringers, let alone these thoroughbreds.
You've been bucked, kicked, and railed by your own trainer
who stood over you like a statue you saw once,
greening, glass-eyed, looking through you to fields
diminishing beyond, and to the horses,
always the horses, then straight at you,
into you, the kid who shovels shit, and saying
as he did to Rilke, *change your life,*
or, *do you want to be a serious rider or what?*

A bored child, you'll beg to get your wish, just once,
and when you do and view from those temple gates
a violet dawn and the eagle's mountaintop perch,
you will know well the weakness of your hands.

And so too will the horses, the leaves you scorch,
the sacred rivers that freeze shut from your distance,
and the god whose rods of thunderbolts will not
be spared on you. Yet you beg, the dream being all
you see: the shiver of the great beasts' shoulders,
each sunstroke executed perfectly,
each heavenly turn familiar as the fields
you've plowed below, where your audience will stand,
shield its eyes, and comment on the weather,
mistaking you for a god, a prophet, your father.

While Currying a Gelding

My fault, he said when
the gelding balked

the fence and tossed me.
Not pain but my resistance

exposed me as one who
might know him.

Currying, our fingers touched
opening

his past: All I know
is horses

and how to kill.
In the first melee

when half-tracks
scored Budapest's cobbles

he filled bottles
with grain alcohol, petrol,

whatever he could find,
stole his cousins' undershirts

to twist into wicks.
Father shot, brothers

rounded up; how he got out,
got to Far Hills Stables

is a mystery he wouldn't
reveal. As if he were

a Percheron
who shied from no burden,

he said, I carry
my father's name.

At the Races With Jan

Sligo, Ireland, anniversary of our father's death

Here 6-year-olds read the forms,
place bets, and win.
Serious as bankers, they argue odds
and head for candy racks outside
the Quonset hut where we sip stout.

It's you we carry in our eyes, you
our gambling father who used to
phone illegal bets to Rudy
the man with no last name,

you who sees the pack and one
horse edging through, the jockey
yelling, whipping as you'd say
to beat the band,

into the last furlong—
the ground shakes in our spines,
sun pokes over clouds then slips
behind Ben Bulben as for you

Henry Reginald out of O'Reilly
our pick Kilgarvin
noses first across the line.

The Measure of the Year

A canoe made of horse ribs tipped over in the pasture.
Prairie flowers took it for a meetinghouse.
They grow there with a vengeance.

Buck posts float across the flooded swamp
Where my father rode in and under.
Different horse.

He held her head up out of the mud
And said how he was sorry
Till they came to pull him out.

We found the white filly
On the only hard ground by the south gate.
He said she'd been a ghost from the start and he was right.

We covered her with branches.
There were things he had the wrong names for
Like rose crystals. Though

They were about what you'd think from a name like that.
He told us somewhere on Sand Creek Pass
Was a crystal that spelled our own initials

And we should try to find it.
We walked through sagebrush and sand currents, looking.
He said pasqueflowers and paintbrush

Wait till Easter to grow,
Then they come up even with snow still on the ground.
I thought I'd seen that happen.

White Lilies in a White Vase

—Easter 1998

Back from the stables, I sit on the porch swing,
unstrap my half-chaps, untie my paddock boots.
My shoulders remember before I do and roll forward.
I see through the window five white lilies
in a white vase. My mother's gift. Each Easter
she sends them—cold beauty in a colder month.
One year since I rode with Francie—bigger sister,
one of four, the brassy one, bright and funny,
a laugh like a horse's whinny and just as sudden.
We walked out across the still-damp pasture,
she on the chestnut gelding, I on the thin Arabian mare,
gift of my husband, chatting about weddings—
Leah's at the Dallas Country Club, Giselle's
in the state park in Fort Worth, Carmen's
wild dancing until dawn at Chubby's Bar.
All of us married now to circumstance. Even
Francie, first to fall in love, last to marry.
Married to barrel racing for eighteen years,
she traded her saddle for a guitar, then
her guitar for a degree. She had restlessness in her
the way a horse has running. In Amsterdam
the year before leaving Smith, she pursued
a thin blonde boy from Cleveland. A writer,
he called himself, taking a break from Harvard
to see the world. Hitchhiking across Europe,
she told me, she awoke one morning somewhere
in France. She poked her head out of her sleeping bag
and looked out on a field of lavender stretching
to the horizon, a pale blue mist floating above it.
In the cool morning her shoulders heaved
and for a moment she didn't know how she could go on,
nor knew how to say what she was feeling.

The boy she would marry two years later
slept beside her. She felt completely free,
full of hope. Anything was possible and that
terrified her. Such beauty! and she saw,
she said, what must have killed Van Gogh.
Lavender, blue mist, cool breeze, the eastern
horizon's white lip. All of it before her.
Then it was gone. One year ago,
we rode out together across this ranch.
Quail flushed from the underbrush; a hawk
circled above us. Everywhere, blue flax bloomed.
There is no explanation. Today, down
by Sutter's Creek, I think I saw what Francie saw.
Then the moment passed and where the beauty had been—
an infinite loneliness flowed through me
like the faint fragrance of a dying lily.

for Francie, 1956-1997

The Ribbon

We earned them
by completing the course
without error,
by showing the best form
at the walk, trot, and canter.
Blue, red, yellow, and white,
the ribbons fluttered
from the horses' bridles
as we trotted
proudly from the ring.

Each night before sleep
my mother removes
from her blouse
the piece of black fabric.
The dark threads
have started to fray.
In the morning
she will pin it to her dress
and everyone she meets will know
she has completed one life
and entered the ring
for another.

My Mother's Tango

I see her windows open in the rain, laundry in the windows—
she rides a wild pony for my birthday,
a white pony on the seventh floor.
"And where will we keep it?" "On the balcony!"
the pony neighing on the balcony for nine weeks.
At the center of my life: my mother dances,
yes here, as in childhood, my mother
asks to describe the stages of my happiness—
she speaks of soups, she is of their telling:
between the regiments of saucers and towels,
she moves so fast—she is motionless,
opening and closing doors.
But what was happiness? A pony on the balcony!
My mother's past, a cloak she wore on her shoulder.
I draw an axis through the afternoon
to see her, sixty, courting a foreign language—
young, not young—my mother
gallops a pony on the seventh floor.
She becomes a stranger and acts herself, opens
what is shut, shuts what is open.

Your body'd gone

silent. *Unresponsive* was the word
paraded around. I, crossing your arms,
felt my own muscles itching to uppercut—
to unsmug them right out of their lab coats.

You settled on another salvation:
site of stable dust, sunlight, a wheelchair
of height and twitch. A horseshoe nailed
above the entrance, luck-side up.
My bones ached irony—*Hope Corrals.*
A valuable operation, under-funded.

We took you on a Tuesday afternoon
like this was beginning. No naiveté of morning.
None of Sunday's goodbye nonsense.

We, your reluctant attendants: sudden believers.
Shasta, and Tunstall Sue, and Westward
approached, bent their heads, soft mouths
to your quiet oat-filled hands. Westward
was everything as he brushed his mouth over your hair—
as no one moved to smooth— knowing
this gift of tangle and moist was more
than years of us crossing, uncrossing.

Ascent to Shasta's back— the *certified*
disabled saddle. Your beautiful, overmuch
helmet, and that slow gait of horse and rider.
A cycle punctuated with the tap of hardground hoof
and your *here now, here now,* encouragement
I'd swear was meant to guide us.

Buckskin Horse

At the grocery check-out stand I remember horses
love carrots. Back at the produce section, I pull a bag

from under the pile where they stock the freshest
produce.
I want the horses to love me. The buckskin gelding was
foaled

thirty years ago on a ranch in Texas when I was sixteen
in a California city. In this corral in Marfa, we hold our
heads together

and breathe each others' breath. Horses do this to
remember
one another. His black muzzle bumps my cheek as I lean
in close,

inhale his carrot sweet breath, pale earth, seasons in
motion,
and hope the breath he pulls from me is not so filled with
sadness,

or the cloying odor that comes from uncertainty. I rest
my head against his neck. When I sat in the room with
my mother

in the quiet of her dying, I inhaled her thin breath.
Her inhaling and body were so slight.

I was the buckskin horse, hoofing the pale earth.
I was the buckskin horse, the color of dry grass.

Afterwards

My mother died and days fall like water
into themselves so I go outside and walk
the pasture. By now it's dusk, air cooling
down into the scruffy grass.
My camera is ready and I plan
to catch the colt on film
with his big knees and ears like carpet.
But horses are so curious
about people, especially or maybe only
when the human is very silent and still,
the way we are inside after a death.

I try to focus the camera, the colt
snuffles my arm, the lens is misting
and each time I move back
so I can hold him inside the frame
he stands for a minute until I get very quiet.
Then he comes right up to my face
with his velvety muzzle
and sniffs the camera and clouds the lens.
He can't quite manage his long legs yet
but his eyelashes are fair and his mother
is heedlessly grazing along the fence
so why not trot after me? A woman
who will scratch him all over,
this woman moving through
the drowning light with nothing
better to cry about.

Plato's Bad Horse

I wanted Plato's bad horse,
not the good one, set on discourse and decorum.
I wanted the horse that pulls toward
the radiant face of the beloved.

He takes the bit shamelessly:
a great jumble of a beast, thick-necked,
bleary-eyed. He is, we are expressly told,
the mate of insolence and knavery.

The good horse, upright and clean-limbed,
boasts an aquiline nose, a milk-white eye.
He will drench the soul in penitential sweat,
take the teeth out of intemperate desire.

But Plato's bad horse is part scapegoat
and part ox. (I'd seen oxen tremble in unison,
and then, bellies to the earth like improbable
mice, creep forward in a liquid movement

that unseated marble slabs.)
Only after much bit-yanking and plying
of the whip, will the sight of the beloved
bring the bad horse to his knees.

•

One off-season, my mother stabled two horses:
they were both bad, and consequently,
drew the phantom chariot of their desires
evenly over the field, the Indian paintbrush,

the half-rusted fern announcing the stone wall
that ran beside the woods. She herself had become
misshapen with desire: she wanted to keep living,
like the roans—
She found delicate work for the fingers
along their parsed necks, little stopping places,
elaborate as the fretwork of a flute,
That maintained in her the ability to dwell…

And this is how my mother left me, her hands
offering solace to those difficult beasts
whose existence slipped my mind even before
they were dispatched to parts unknown.

My memories have become too blurred
to be of use, like horses that cannot be ridden.
Like my mother's roans pulling in tandem
to join the halves of what I still don't know.

Fragment

May I present my grandmother, the
human burr. Wind's a cappella in her ears, the
tears in her eyes twin comet tails.
  A ditch gapes. This—she thinks—
will be her last moment. Notes,
despite her terror, the teasels growing there.
  It's a grave for running water only,
hers still cigarettes away. Not for years,
not till I'm born, and live to hear the tale of
Maude. Not till she's shown, then
saved for me, a set of Limoges plates. (The mare
beneath her clears the ditch,
clatters over a bridge).

Each plate depicts a different flower,
their edges scallop, lively with gold.
Bone china. Her face might be
made of it, too. Fired at the moment the giddy
mare went awry. Many are Maude's moods,
and wear the ribbons of whim.
  Ruth: my grandmother's name.
Maude: the mare's. She's dapple grey or
liver chestnut, she's fifteen hands or seventeen two.
Scar, no scar below one hock,
rough-gaited or water-smooth. Set to
fences, she comes under, or stands boldly back.

Fences. They're running parallel with one.
Oh, one/one/one/one/one each post a
white-hot second. Amidst this blaze
Maude veers; Ruth sees a man, red-sweatered, distant.
  He waves. Did he wave? Idiot, already gone.

They're headed home; were Maude's route
pedigree, it might read as follows:
Short Cut out of Steeplechase by way of No Control.
Ruth ducks low-hanging branches: they're
flat-out through an orchard, grazed
limbs lobbing apples in their wake

The Limoges? Intact. I'm setting places for dessert.
Plates for eight thudding softly down on mats.
The painter knew her stuff: here's asters
stiffly maned, sweet peas in deshabillé,
an orchid's brazen invitation. And blood will tell, they say,
I've grown as stubborn as the woman
clinging to the creature
destined to best her iron will. Ask her son who sired me
if this is not so: he's had to endure between us,
like an anvil between blows.

If for a moment you try to envision
survival as aura around the body, you'll
see Ruth low on the neck of the mare, and brilliant,
brilliant just now.

Refugio's Hair

In the old days of our family
My grandmother was a young woman
Whose hair was as long as the river.
She lived with her sisters on the ranch
La Calera, the land of the lime,
And her days were happy.

But her uncle Carlos lived there too
Carlos whose soul had the edge of a knife.
One day to teach her to ride a horse
He made her climb on the fastest one
Bare-back, and sit there
As he held its long face in his arms.

And then he did the unspeakable deed
For which he would always be remembered.
He called for the handsome baby Pirrín
And he placed the child in her arms.
With that picture of a Madonna on horseback
He slapped the shank of the horse's rear leg.

The horse did what a horse must
Racing full toward the bright horizon.
But first he ran under the álamo trees
To rid his back of this unfair weight,
This woman full of tears
And this baby full of love.

When they reached the trees and went under
Her hair which had trailed her
Equal in its magnificence to the tail of the horse
That hair rose up, and flew into the branches
As if it were a thousand arms

All of them trying to save her.

The horse ran off and left her
The baby still in her arms,
The two of them hanging from her hair.
The baby looked only at her
And did not cry, so steady was her cradle.
Her sisters came running to save them.

But the hair would not let go.
From its fear it held on, and had to be cut
All of it, from her head.
From that day on my grandmother
Wore her hair short, like a scream
But it was long like a river in her sleep.

Then

When she was a girl and he was her horse,
she would lie on the grass at his feet (which she

would have been careful to call his hooves)
summer days, and he would take up the grass

in his teeth, his great yellow, beastly teeth,
even the grass mingled with her hair,

teasing her as if he would bite her hair,
though he never did. Standing at the barn door,

he would rub his long nose down her back.
Once, after a yawn (listening to her with her silly friends),

he closed his jaws around her arm
and shook it, mildly impatient as a husband.

And if you had asked her then, What is love?
she could so easily have told you.

From Dread in the Eyes of Horses

Eggs. Dates and camel's milk.
Give this. In one hour the foal will
stand, in two will run. The care then of
women, the schooling from fear, clamor
of household, a prospect of saddles.

They kneel to it, folded
on its four perfect legs, stroke
the good back, the muscles bunched at the chest.
Its head, how the will shines large in it
as what may be used to overcome it.

The women of the horses comb out
their cruel histories of hair only for
the pleasure of horses, for the lost mares
on the Ridge of Yellow Horses, their white arms
praying the hair down breasts ordinary
as knees. The extent of their power,
this intimation of sexual wealth. From dread
in the eyes of horses are taken their songs.
In the white forests the last free horses
eat branches and roots, are hunted like deer
and carry no one.

A wedge of light where the doorway opens
the room—in it, a sickness of sleep.
The arms of the women, their coarse
white hair. In a bank of sunlight, a man
whitewashes the house he owns—no shores, no
worlds above it and farther, shrill, obsidian,
the high feasting of the horses.

The Rising

The pregnant mare at rest in the field
the moment we drove by decided
to stand up, rolled her massive body
sideways over the pasture grass, her spine
a latticed gathering of bone, curved ribs
visible between the groaning, hanging pots
of flesh, her muscled haunches straining,
knee bones bent on the bent grass cleaved
astride the earth she pushed against to lift
the brindled breast, the hidden architecture
of the neck, the anvil head, her burred mane
tossing flames as her legs unlatched in air
while the back legs buried beneath her belly
set her horny hooves in opposition
to the spongy earth to right themselves and rise,
a counterweight concentrated there, and by
a willful rump and switch of tail hauled up,
flank and fetlock, the beast who seized herself
and rolled and wrenched and winched the wave
of her body that was the grand totality of herself
to stand upright in the depth of that field, all
in an instant's passing. The heaviness
of gravity upon her. The strength of the mother.

Membrane

A foal emerges from the womb.
I stretch back the white
membrane veiling his nose.

He breathes first breaths,
his nostrils straining.

My child, I say, warming him
with my towel, feeling him
kick thin tissue off his legs.
His hooves flash their unhardened
fingers, scraping softly in straw.

I do not wash my hands
before sleep; instead,

carry the smell of birth
to my bed, wrapping myself in
the folds of thin sheets.

Praise Be

Eleven months, two weeks in the womb
and this one sticks a foreleg out
frail as a dowel quivering
in the unfamiliar air and then
the other leg, cocked at the knee
at first, then straightening
and here's the head, a big blind fish
thrashing inside its see-through sack
and for a moment the panting mare
desists, lies still as death.

I tear the caul, look into eyes
As innocent, as skittery
As minnows. Three heaves, the shoulders pass.
The hips emerge. Fluid as snakes
the hind legs trail out glistening.
The whole astonished filly, still
attached, draws breath and whinnies
a treble tremolo that leaps
in her mother who knickers a low-key response.

Let them prosper, the dams and their sucklings.
Let nothing inhibit their heedless growing.
Let them raise up on sturdy pasterns
and trot out in light summer rain
onto the long lazy unfenced fields
of heaven.

Filly

Hard heat of noon.
Mares lie on the grass
beneath willow trees.

But the filly born in the spring
has morning in her veins.

She arches her neck, leaps and kicks,
gallops up the hillside
pounding thunder out of the ground.

At the top she pauses,
then plunges back down.

The valley flows from her knees.

Appaloosa

In spring, when the earth turns
to food, and the mares thicken
with what they have kept hidden
through winter in their bodies,

and between her legs weeks early
the sac grew
of the thin bluish milk that is the first need,
in the last days

she'd come reluctantly, if at all,
to the wooden barn, preferring
the other heavy mares for company;
and when the time came withdrawing

even from them somewhere
she knew, to the hardwood valley
of the pasture, the bay of slag fence, wherever
she had chosen

to do what must be done.
And did it, alone,
working her mute body.
I understand little of this,

except that once
I was young,
that it did not seem mysterious
but love, an ordinary duty, to follow her

track through the mud and the milkweed
path down, chest-high, to the stream-bed sump–land
where I could hear her,

bleeding. A night had passed,

and the ripping,
and the crying out: now she stood
bending to him, the pure form,
licking the film from his eyes, a little

fearful. He curled across the wide vervaine,
an Appaloosa colt—
though the mare was chestnut, the sire high bay.
Such things happened,

Appaloosa:
how an ordinary pair
makes a strange one, born strong but
roan through the chest, clear-starred but

stippled white through the haunch, and
striped hooves, and blue eyes.
Those days
farmers drowned them, made mares refuse them;

hell-to-break, pepper-minded, wicked clever—
impossible to predict, or to breed.
Or if they do, two of a kind,
the colt is normal

but trouble. Broken, they run like fire.
I watched him almost-sleep, the first I'd seen.
She muzzled Necco wafers from my pocket;
we watched him breathe. He watched us watch.

Three days, my father
took the animal. So I never learned
what happened to him
that he was strange,

and marked fire in an older world,
and unprofitable.
My father never told me, and I never asked,
and I was afraid.

Childhood and Then Some

1.

Feeding horses to sugar cubes
necks crane as they melt
across the fence in easy groans.

Wind takes the sunhat off,
straw light light, and you feel yourself
lift for just a moment.

2.

Losing count on the slow way
to a chocolate-chew center.
Your whole mouth taking in, consoling
consoling the record-lost tootsie pop.

Clang of the dinner bell.
You drop the spoon, look away,
leave it lying prone-open and dirt flat
next to Rowan's ditch-bound tracks:
a processional of hoof and shudder.

3.

The hat is gone. Light.

Little girls and horses

In the burning grapefruit grove you decide never again
to speak
with someone you love. Because they're dragging. Or, as
I like to say,
your money where your mouth is loosey-goosey. Flawed
and wonderful,
asking repeatedly: So many thousands of offerings?
Bullshit
you're not looking at that willow tree, I said—and
vice-versa. Like some old
horse-mentor, careful to be extra-respectful because he
was strange enough
to square away a table. And you'll do it too—selling and
breeding
as lovers and judges—and as a teasing bounce—
why to me right now you're so short-lived. Why you're
slipping through
the window to the mercies of the world.

Horses

Gae and I evolve into the Palominos, Gold and Goldie.
We hang out near the stables on the Los Angeles River.
From behind the high wooden fenceposts we ache for
  them. They are always shoeing us away and we aren't
supposed to be this far from home. A dollar to ride
for an hour, way too much, and they won't let us ride
anyway with out an adult. Carrots,
horses like carrots. Old bread. Sneaking sugar cubes
her parents use in their coffee to their big mouths, lips,
  teeth. To lose a finger would be worth it.

One day we watch a man break a horse. He takes
a two-by-four and brings it down with all his might
  between it's ears.
"That'll teach you who's boss!" We can hardly make it
  home for the shock and rage. "There's more female
hormone in the testicle of a stallion than in any other
known tissue," Mr. Walker says when we get there. And
says again and again whenever he catches us as Gold and
  Goldie.

Our legs and arms grow into the four long legs
and our ears grow pointed and long under our
  lengthening manes.
My nostrils flare to hers, she bares her lips, we hang
our necks around each other's. Our backs arch, our tails
start growing, we prance and neigh and paw the air, then
gallop past the old men, explosion
    of horse!
We leave them in our dust. This is not pretend. We are
horses trapped in human bodies. We are horses from
  deep underground,

from the elaborate ongoing civilization under the earth
that's superior to this one but what this one is supposed
to be.
We belong to a wild herd that escaped a century ago
from the Spanish Land Grant Ranchos and the Mexican
War and the Indians,
that hides by day in the canyons, that comes down the
river beds and roams the Basin at night. Even now a
horse sometimes escapes from the County Farm at Ran-
cho Los Amigos or the Hollydale stables
and runs the LA River bottom.

Not shoed, bridled, or saddled. We can't walk, we can
only trot. We trot and gallop everywhere, we whinny,
we scream.
We're wild horses in the hills of Nevada. We're involved
in elaborate dramas rescuing and freeing horses from the
glue and dogfood factories. We cry,
we die, we discuss endlessly the evil
of hurting and killing and eating horses. We trot down
the dogfood aisles of McCoys, hide as much
horsemeat as we can in the ice cream freezers,
we love you horse is our prayer, we know you're still
alive in there.
We follow the Kentucky Derby news longing for next
May, who will wear the roses?
And the Santa Anita and Tijuana racetrack news. We
love Willy Shoemaker.
But why aren't there girl jockeys? There aren't many
men who weigh only a hundred pounds, there are lots
of women who do.
We will be the first girl jockeys.
Did you know Man O War died of the 1918 flu? Or
some famous race horse.
We try to figure out how to find out for sure.
We hear about Sea Biscuit.
We will grow up to be stable girls to help them escape.
Everywhere horses are abused, it is wrong. Wrong.

Pegasus, the winged horse, flies in the sky at gas stations

all over LA. Horsepower! A car is a horse with wings.
A stallion
is a girl with testicles. A girl is a horse in her soul.
Pegasus is the winged horse of the Muses, born of sea
foam and the blood of the slaughtered Medusa. Pegasus
is Medusa's son! Ooh, we love that. Medusa,
Chief of the Gorgons!
A hideous or terrifying woman.
There were three Gorgons with serpents on their heads
instead of hair
but Medusa was the one that was mortal.
She'd been a beautiful maiden, especially famous for her
hair, but she violated Athena who always takes the
father's side and so transformed her hair into serpents
and made her face so hideous that whoever set eyes on it
was instantly turned into stone.

We look up chimaeras, gorgons, and sea monsters.
I read the Bible about the Four Horsemen of the
Apocalypse,
Conquest, Slaughter, Famine and Death
who appear on white, red, black and pale horses
typifying the evils of war. I'm praying nightly now
about the Korean War. Our horses are about the female
hormone in the testicle of the stallion, yes, but not as
in the cliché about girls. It isn't about sex, it isn't mas-
turbation, it's pure energy. Pure love. Identification
with all captive spirits, with the oppressed, about saving
the horse,
our selves, from bossy, jealous, brutal men.
From our fathers.
The horse is freedom. The poet
Milton said Medusa is the unconquered virgin.
Pegasus is the son of a virgin like Jesus!
Pegasus' father was Poseidon, God of the Sea, this is why
the horse in Greek means wave,
what is meant that he was born from sea foam.
Medusa, like Mary, was a virgin mother. Gae and I
will grow up to be unconquered virgin mothers.

Daddy gives us permission to dig as deep as we can
in the far west corner of the backyard, at the head of his garden
not far from where my bloody things are buried. We dig for the horses. *Yet earth contains the horse*
as a remembrance of wild Arenas we avoid, another poet wrote. Gae and I aren't avoiding the wild Arenas,
we are seeking them.
We dig deep in the ground, to huddle with, in the protection of, to race
with horses, safe from the adults. A winged horse
sprang from the murdered blood of Medusa, we understand exactly what that means. We dig into my sprayed blood.
We don't have flying dreams. Our horses gallop inside
the earth. Sometimes
I'm digging for Korea.

"Let me see if you're a woman yet, Lu," Daddy whispers.
I'm a horse, Daddy. You don't know it but I'm a stallion, unconquered.
Goldie leads the way over the back fence into the Beaver's back yard.
I, Gold, will follow wherever she leads. Pegasus
is spray from my blood spilt to the ground
when Daddy split me in two. Wild horses
could not drive Gold from Goldie. What was the name
of Lady Godiva's horse, Daddy? Who was inside
the Trojan horse, Daddy? *Far back,*
far back in our dark soul, D.H. Lawrence wrote, *the horse prances.*
Mama read *Lady Chatterley's Lover*
at night with a flashlight under her orphanage blankets
while the U.S. Supreme Court debated banning it.

Who's inside the Trojan horse, Daddy?

The Beautiful

The back of a colt is not for riding
but this small horse of yours, so red, with no
white socks or star or blaze, with whiskery lips,
so obviously fast and careful of his rider, this horse
let me.
We went bareback of course and bridle-less
out of the stall, out the wide doors of the barn
into the dust of the yard where the tractor idles. From there
we had a look around and chose the gate, him
arching his neck, sidestepping
at my word.
          We reached the fields
there to jump the ditches and run and run until his mane
stuck out.
He ate clover with the cows; we saw the coyote and a bull
and walked through yellow hay unmown and belly high,
my legs swishing through it, his hooves knocking
sparks from stone.
                    When we swam the green eye of the cow
pond
his shoulders moved under my hands and then
while he lunged I slid and only held his tail, and then
to see the owls we went among the cottonwoods.
In a clearing there he nosed the ground and knelt
and rolled. And then

for a sugar lump he brought me nicely home.

I was a child but convincing even so.
Question after question didn't shake me.
Your outrage didn't strike me as a likely thing.
But finally I had nothing more to say.
How much less of you I thought
for punishing a lie so beautiful
it told you everything.

Saturday Matinee

Gene Autry galloping hard on his pony,
in black and white, the ground and bushes gray,
toward gray mountains under a gray sky
where white clouds drift, hooves pounding
in the small theater as I sat forward
in my seat, my heart in my mouth with envy,
with longing for freedom, for Gene Autry,
the boy beside me sliding his hand over
for mine, the odor of popcorn in place

of sagebrush, and I saw myself inside
that movie, black hat on my head while
I rushed after him, my pony dapple-gray,
my hair long and blown back by the wind,
galloping so hard but upright western style,
a real cowgirl, and the hand in the theater
like some kind of insect I was brushing away,

My body wanting to rush after my mind—
away from that kid in his button-down shirt,
away from the white clapboard houses,
the dark deciduous forest on the edges
of town, the asphalt, the street lights,
and my father forbidding me to go
to the movie while I sobbed, sobbed
for love of Gene Autry, for love
of the wide open west, of horses
and galloping, for love, for love.

Blue-Eyed Horse

Can you imagine how Strawberry picked the trail. How
  Thunder
followed Strawberry and Tanka followed Thunder. Their
  discovery of the deer-trail

and sisters, picking themselves up and saying,

for the sake of their integrity,

the dearest things. Grass from underneath a river—
  draws itself out—
it doesn't have to but it breaks

the visitor-sisters. Breaking, even if
he doesn't need to, the trail or the sides of Thunder's
  mouth,
making her tender. Foaming white

up the horses' staircase. Fire-red mouth

and red nylon reins. We tricked her out of her pity—so
  obviously
that men were ashamed. She was in no hurry for
  anything and we ran
her up the canyon to arrive
more completely with the others. Coos,

pleasure that left me vulnerable. You could see
why we called her fucking gorgeous and (this is
  important)

how it would be difficult

to love someone who'd tell me not to play around with a thunderbird.
Who trusts me to carve out something

that I'd started a while ago or so
explains fidelity by a horse out the canyon—I try

to arrange the memory. To be nothing
like the grass beneath the river that will not compel us.

The Horse

At first we didn't see she had become a horse,
dark mane ruffling in a breeze, luminous brown eyes

watching our games of tag and blind man.
We'd pretended so long to be horses, chestnut filly,

appaloosa and sorrel, whether
it was wither or shoulder was no big deal.

She waited, nosing the grass,
laying her elegant head along the fence rail

as if sighting down a barrel into her old life.
Her old life, the life we galloped through,

kids, skipping into houses
and when summer ended, school,

band practice, football. My brother said,
"Ignore her." Fret of her head

like a "yes" or "no," stamp of a hoof.
She had a way of turning when happy,

trotting down the path to the open field,
her powerful legs suddenly loping, rolling her

through the high brown grass. Her brown coat
shone in the sun. In rain

she stood beneath the orchard trees,
her forelock hanging in her eyes.

"She'll come around." My brother hummed
and turned his head. "Act like nothing's wrong."

And the following summer when I saw him
standing with her, shivering his flank

to discourage a fly, I guessed he'd been right
all along. Nothing was wrong.

I leaned over the fence
to toss them June apples. They crunched

and drooled, shaking their noses
because the flesh was so sour.

Black Beauty

For two years at least
Shirley Kipps and I were horses—
you could tell by the way we walked
tossing our manes and jangling our bits.

We trotted with our chins pulled in
then galloped aggressively
stomping the leading leg
till the soles of our feet hurt.

I was Black Beauty of course,
whinnying softly when the boy
(whom no one else could see)
came to me with a pocketful of sugar;

Shirley was Tiny—
sometimes a lowly carthorse,
sometimes even a donkey
kept as company for Black Beauty.

Sundays we would lope along the ridge,
clouds scudding, sea sparking,
and I would buck with joy
while Tiny trotted stiffly beside me

never arguing when I said
her red browband was tacky,
never threatening to kick or bite
until the day I made her pull a plough—

then she looked furious,
bared her yellow teeth

and galloped across the golf course
her shoes wreaking havoc with the tenth green.
Years later in Chinatown
I thought I saw Shirley
pulling a cartload of vegetables,
a little lame on the near side.

Her long ears drooped liked Tiny's
but when I turned to greet her
she twitched away a fly
and cut me dead.

First Love

i Changeling

I always felt I didn't belong,
born into the wrong pack, a changeling
left by immigrant fairies, trapped on the boat
when Pop came over from England.

They wilted in the delirious heat;
wings and spells soaked with sweat,
they confused their magic.
Or maybe they stole just the right seed
of an idea from my mother's stock—
a sturdy girl with legs
made to swing over a horse
to teach them to survive. Not me.

Flabby, prone to sneezing fits, I was useless.
Only at Gran's I learned to be at home
in this elastic skin,
stretched to snapping point, keeping my feelings in.

Then one summer when I was thirteen
a family appeared on the neighbouring farm.
"Hobbyists," Gran said, "not serious.
But nice. They sold their shop in town."
One child named Clara—the type I should have been.
Older than me, but crazed with loneliness,
any kid would do as her apprentice.

For three whole weeks she had me to herself.
We fed her cheeky bantams,
skinned our knees climbing stunted wattles,

chain-sneezed together, collapsed with laughter
watching piglets, farty little beach balls,
latching onto teats as long as fingers.

Then there were the horses.
I went wild with love and fear.
First she dinked me on her ancient pony—
twelve hands three—back like a slippery dip.
Next she showed her champions.
I stood in awe as she worked them both:
walk, trot, change diagonal,
watch that lateral movement. But the canter—

when they rocked together,
muscles quivering in harmony,
the dust rolled up in sympathetic clouds—
the mists of time—and she became a Centaur,
girl and animal fused,
feeling what she could be in her bones.

ii First Flight

Horses perch on their toes – their hooves –
always ready to flee. Tasty prey,
a meal for wolves, any sharp-toothed predator
that harried their ancestors
still hunts them in their genes.

Even with bellies full on a grassy plain,
they're ready to take off and at the gallop
hang suspended for an instant,
four feet in the air.

I plucked titbits like that from books,
hungry for whatever made me worthy.

One night Clara called late.
"Turn up at 5 am.
Time for your first ride out before it's hot."

I dressed in jeans, biked over.
She'd saddled up already before dawn.

I'd trotted round on Sam, the quarter horse,
the smaller of her two,
and sat a lazy canter.
Goblin Mist, the thoroughbred,
her great grey hope, was only for herself.

We walked them out into a world
that dark had gentled, stroking every outline.
The horses, fresh but easy,
stretched their noses down,
nuzzling at the green fuzz left by sheep.

Air was flavoured with a hint of wattle.
Cockatoos rustled from the gums
to peck at bits of chaff.
The flies were dopey,
no anxious whirring yet to cut the quiet.
When we reached a bend in the path
Clara said, "Shorten your reins"
and suddenly fired ahead
as if a hungry beast were on her tail.

Sam knew what that meant
and leapt, a heartbeat behind,
like a second rifle shot.
Together, we sliced through wind and dust

but Clara dashed ahead,
flattening on her horse's neck
till once again she and he were one.
Then "Go" reared in my brain.

I urged Sam on, embracing him,
fingers in his mane, and laughed.
"Okay?" Clara shouted back.
My blood so loud she must have heard.

Stretching out, the two of us,
this natural way of being *we,*
balanced on his neck so he could fly—
that was it—this being *we*—

a streamlined creature we became.
We, I felt, *we,* I breathed,
losing all control and zooming forward
we, two yet one, *we* flew as one

all four feet in the air,
racing Clara for no prize but speed
till the world blurred but we were clear—
galloping into being here.

I was in love with Clara and her horses.

Now I knew how I could survive.
We we we we drumming out the infinite,
each perfect second of it.
I was terrified alive.

Why Young Girls Like to Ride Bareback

You grasp a clump of mane in your left hand,
spring up and fall across her back;
then, pulling on the wiry black hair
which cuts into your palm and fourth finger,
haul yourself up till your right leg
swings across the plump cheek of her hindquarters.

Now you hold her, warm and alive, between your
thighs.
In summer, wearing shorts, you feel the dander
of her coat, glossy and dusty at the same time,
greasing up the insides of your calves,
and as she walks, each of your knees in turn
feels the muscle bulge out behind her shoulder.

Trotting's a matter of balance. You bounce around
unable to enter her motion as you will when the trot
breaks and she finally waltzes from two to three time.
Nothing to be done at the trot but grab again that mane
that feels, though you don't yet know it, like pubic hair,
and straddle her jolting spine with your seat bones

knowing that when the canter comes, you will suddenly
merge—you and that great, that powerful friend:
she, bunching up behind, rocking across the fulcrum,
exploding forward on to the leading leg, and you
digging your seat down into the sway of her back,
your whole body singing: we are one, we are one,
   we are one.

Horse

"It's all about the orgasm, you know,"
my friend in Physics 102 pronounced.
But it wasn't:
it was the thick sweetness of fresh manure,
the wet slide of hay slick under my boot.
It was the horse's rump, good for slapping,
and the stomach shining gold and oiled
after I would brush and brush.
The velour muzzle resting warm against my neck—
"But *riding* it," Amy persisted on about
what everybody knew of girls and horses
while I saw my first barrel turn:
the three-year old was water underneath my skin,
he bent to any move I made, however small.
Flawless obedience. And then the final figure eight:
he swooped around the barrel,
his body slanted so steeply to one side
that I smelled the hoof-flung dirt
and knew at once it was a perfect turn
and what if I would fall
and what if I would never catch my breath?
So if that's what my friend meant,
then, yes.

Summer Horses

When the sun nails itself to the field
and the barn kneels in the heat,

what else could we do but leave saddles
unlifted and take our mares to the river?

We ride bareback down dirt roads single file.
We don't weigh much. It is July 1975;

our bodies have not yet suffered
and our minds are still neatly folded.

Rumps drip sweat as they take their
measured steps. The horses stop to drink

but we urge them deeper, so they stumble
in, giving ragged moans when the water

takes their weight. We glide, cold river
swift at our hips—life bright in loose

time, under formal tall trees,
three girls given and received.

Why Shy and Gawky Girls Will Ride

You get to sit.
The horse goes first.
Both hands stay occupied with reins.
No need to hide your two-legged lope
or mute your nickering
if any kid's in Marta Miller's yard.
No need to shake your own hair as the mane.
There is a mane,
a thick strong clump you get to hold.
and ears will flick to hear your voice
no matter what you say,
though language is
your hands and legs and never
looking down. Higher, faster
than any laughter,
or photo Marta Miller takes
of you sopping wet, full frontal
in droopy cotton underpants,
a dopey grin that drips with trust
after running through the sprinkler
in Marta Miller's yard,
which is another reason why
shy and gawky girls will ride
and why, years later,
when Marta Miller's husband
ran off with his lover,
you didn't mind, though you did have
feelings for her son and daughter,
especially the daughter
who was still too young to ride.

My Life as a Horse

There was a time, before breasts,
before blood flowed, before boys' bodies
made me too aware, when I was a girlhorse,
a shiny black filly with a lilt to her gallop,
dressed in a blaze and two pairs
of white stockings.

My friends Kathy and Nan
were horses too, and we vaulted
over stone walls together, our manes
floating like silk in the breeze.

We straddled branches, urged ourselves on
with whips of peeled willow,
neighed, and pawed at the macadam
with hooves that rang like iron.
We were clover thunder together.
We were stampeding magic.
We were sweaty creatures
no one could understand.

Then my friends got real horses
and didn't need to play, occupied
by gymkhanas, the North Salem Hunt Club.
and the beautiful palomino and bay,
whose muzzles felt soft as down
against my cheek when I nickered to them
in the tongue of our ancestor, Eohipppus.

I carried on alone for a while,
galloping down Keeler Lane to the school bus,
whinnying at horses confined in their paddocks,

tossing my tangled braids fiercely,
until it got too hard by myself
and the ways of horses dissolved
like the first bloodstains
I washed from my jeans in cold water.
I was a girl.
I wore a Teencharm bra, and boys
were suddenly the only thing that mattered.
But sometimes, when I am out running,
or see a horse alone, she comes back to me,
that long gallop of rippling muscle,
that pretty filly, that girlhorse,
so silky and unencumbered
by the laws of the body.

Girls and Horses

I remember Emily Evans
in third grade, the first
of the riding crop girls, galloping
through Red Rover and Dodgeball,
ponytail bobbing to the gait,
her flanks constantly lashed
by an applewood sapling.
And how she whinnied,
big yellow teeth and velvet muzzle
curled as she called to other horses
far off in the fields along Mansfield Avenue.

Boys stepped back
away from the speed and intensity
of Emily at full gallop,
unconsciously aware that something
was happening before their time.

The girls fluttered as if exposure
was here, and they might step in it.

In Junior High, rich girls
with velvet hard hats and their own horses,
strode impeccably on the grounds
of the Ox Ridge Hunt Club
in smart jodhpurs and well-shined
always-new boots, and their hair
smelled of money.

Emily and I went to Major Self's,
a place of blue uniforms with red stripes
lining the legs, uniforms of cavalry

and caissons.
We had to march for half an hour
around the ankled dust of the indoor ring.
Complete with privates to captains,
we were close-ordered and right-flanked,
and snapped-to; perhaps an effort to turn us
into men before we mounted the horses
and rode off into our own sexuality.

Our parents hovered, seeing dances
and low-cut dresses on the horizon
and the hot blood of summer nights.
Gangly boys began to call
and we giggled in corners and kept diaries.

Our parents desperately praised our
blue ribbons, but the horses were losing
to the inevitable march of hormones
and one by one we began to drop off the horses
and into kissing games and going steady,
slow dances, closely pressed bodies.

Emily galloped on, still full of horses
and tack rooms, heels pointed down
in shined stirrups   until ninth grade
when she had an affair
with the social studies teacher:
her parents flamed with betrayal—
her innocence and her horse-days
behind her at last.

Bareback Pantoum

One night, bareback and young, we rode through the woods
and the woods were on fire—
two borrowed horses, two local boys
whose waists we clung to, my sister and I

and the woods were on fire—
the pounding of hooves and the smell of smoke and the sharp
sweat of boys
whose waists we clung to, my sister and I,
as we rode toward flame with the sky in our mouths—

the pounding of hooves and the smell of smoke and the sharp
sweat of boys
and the heart saying: *mine*
as we rode toward flame with the sky in our mouths—
the trees turning gold, then crimson, white

and the heart saying: *mine*
of the wild, bright world;
the trees turning gold, then crimson, white
as they burned in the darkness, and we were girls

of the wild, bright world
of the woods near our house—we could turn, see the lights
as they burned in the darkness, and we were girls
so we rode just to ride

through the woods near our house—we could turn, see
the lights—
and the horses would carry us, carry us home
so we rode just to ride,
my sister and I, just to be close to that danger, desire

and the horses would carry us, carry us home
—two borrowed horses, two local boys,
my sister and I—just to be close to that danger, desire—
one night, bareback and young, we rode through the woods.

*The Sugargap Node of Ranvier**

1.
Sugar, glorious sparked synapse of a mare—
your clairaudient episodes, those quick
hinges
to another world full of aural nettle,
of gadflies' iridescent scratch,
unset me. Once to a bramble
of puncture,
dye berries, of blooming juice red wet red my oxygenated
poppy spots:
all blood scramble like vine,
like screamchild in sun.

2.
Next, the scar-clank of hail, the clatter happy iron roof:
a canal to glazed eyes, your spook
charge to mudtumble embankment.
A Black Margate—
you were a skin shine changeling of water torque
and hook. Harness flail, and again, ears snapped
to sound
past storm, fissures of light open signals
decoding up
lash dot vertebra.
A cranked angle at nightfall.

3.
Next, blank. Urban. Gutters funneling sky, memory
for horses. Life an XY axis text acid base
nerves shrinkwrapped to cocktail forks nerves sheathed
like chicken wire. Gaps happen.
In this youthfright I missed
that muscle twitch you sensed
a wearthin noise oncoming:
the future's
foxgrab at
exposed lines.

*node of Ranvier: a gap in the myelin sheath of a nerve

Queenie

What was a horse but a colossal
machine that sped away with me, so
finally I hung by one foot from one
stirrup and bounced along the gravel?

I'd thought I knew to make her canter
but I was dragged and scraped over
the country road, not thinking, feeling
This is It, nothing ahead for me but hurt

and blood and ugliness—Who was that
Queenie, graceful chestnut giantess,
retiree from a circus, rescued
from the glue factory or saved from

being horsemeat by the kindly father
of my friend Janet, what deliverer
of knowledge, that she—so soulful when
her huge teeth snarked an apple from my hand—

could, in one instant, catapult me,
a dauntless child of ten, from that morning
to this day I steer our car across a bridge
to your hospital, this brutal day I need

no brilliant doctor to tell me what comes
with the terrain, to say there'll be no one to
lift me from the ground, to carry me to
the stable, to bring me uninjured home.

Horses

What I wanted,
what I thought I wanted,
was sinew & bone
made of wind.

Every letter to Santa real or metaphorical
was for a horse.
Color didn't matter but size
did and a wild look in the eye.

This would be my gallop
on the great steppes of life.
The haven of its back, where a girlchild
so closely harnessed,

could lie easily and be carried
into once upon a time.
Yes, I'd heard about Lincoln Steffins
and the barn full of shit,

how with all that, there must
be a pony. I would willingly dig.

I would tie the horse
in my small yard
to the tether pole, or the horse chestnut
worthy of the village smith.

I would ride it to school, to the library,
envy would paint me as I rode,
invincible, an animal that big,
bigger than my mother;

quiet, reflective, patient
    as my grandmother.
My mother could not afford a horse
    she told me. This was true.

An easy out for her,
no dissuader for me.
There was always God.
    To keep me away from boys,

Mother signed me up for riding lessons.
    Whoa. Horses
were much bigger than I'd imagined.
    Their teeth were yellow

and their jaws strong. They would
    step on toes and kick out
at mysterious angles with their hard back feet.
    They would reach against the bit

and eat forbidden grass and roll
    with their saddles in the mud;
they would arch their backs and buck
    and they always headed for home.

Horses, it seems, were not what I wanted.

The Horse

My best friend's mother took me riding with them.
Janie rode Prince: a brown and white stallion
of princely mien. I got Stinky:
a small, blue-eyed, mean gray mare;
perhaps because it wasn't far to fall,
but perhaps a judgment on me.

Stinky was a disobedient horse,
reducing the advantage, to a beginner,
of her road-hugging construction.
They gave me instruction how to run a horse:
pull left on reins to turn left, both to stop,
et cetera; but this cut no ice with Stinky.
She lunged forward,
and brought her right hoof down hard
on Janie's mother's foot, breaking many bones.

I was thus relieved of association with The Horse
till teenage envy led me to seek out
equus caballus again: to ape the in-crowd girls.
I signed up for riding lessons.
The owners of the stable where these girls
stored their private horses
saddled me on Della, their oldest, slowest,
most swaybacked horse, whose belly hung
almost to the sawdust; and who broke
from the circle of much younger children
(my idols off galloping through the park)
to ring-center to release a flood of urine
as if that swag of gut was filled with nothing but.
She peed and peed and peed and peed
for an adolescent's eternity; with me aboard,
dead-center of attention, on display, trapped,
in my last adventure with The Horse.

Los Caballos

At Cuevo de los Caballos, straight-backed girls with tall
  black boots
circle on their horses in the Spanish heat. I watch them
from across the street, their backdrop the Mediterranean.
I was born an asthmatic, allergic to animal dander and
  never was able to have a pet, except for a turtle named
Henrietta and Gabriel, an angelfish who jumped out
of his tank to his death in the prairie of our living room
shag. I wondered what it would be like
to cuddle up to something small and alive, to feed an
  apple to a goat
without worrying about being licked, my hand sure to
  swell to the size of a baseball mitt. I sat behind the
  circus tent, because I couldn't breathe inside, watching
the elephants being hosed down. I was especially
mesmerized by horses and drew them obsessively in my
notebook. I detailed the leg muscles
and learned how to shade and shadow on snouts.
I sometimes drew Lady Godiva, her hair like a dress,
swirling and meshing with the mane of her horse.
When the fair came one autumn, kids lined up for pony
  rides and a woman, like the teacher at Cuevo de los
  Caballos, stood with a rope
tied to the pony's reign. I watched my sister and my
  friends,
one by one, put their foot into a stirrup of the pony's
  saddle, then be hoisted up by an adult. The woman
  led the pony in a loop
as parents clicked their cameras. I'm sorry, my mother
  said as I begged to get on. But I cried, I kicked, and
  somehow she relinquished. She put her long gloves
  over my hands.

She wrapped her scarf around my face, covering my mouth
and nose. She pulled my socks way up under my jeans
so that my skin wouldn't get anywhere near the pony's.
I felt like I was entering heaven as I swung my leg up over
the saddle,
but then everything went black. I woke up
in the emergency room, plastic tubes in my nose,
my hands and arms covered by a red rash. My mother
looked guilty. My sister, bored, used to me landing in
the hospital,
sat in an plastic chair, coloring. After their lessons,
the girls file out of Cuevo de los Caballos into Smart
Cars and Peugeots,
their mothers waiting with bottled water. I snap
the horses with my digital camera, using the zoom.
I gave up sketching, getting too close, when I was a girl.

Girls Who Love Horses

Not caring I have guests, the tailless cat
Begins to have her kittens. It's her first time;
She's plainly puzzled. Spasms rippling her
Spotted flanks, she lies down, gets up, then half-
Canters across the bathroom floor, a black
Unpunctured water bag protruding.
It's my first time, too, as midwife; holding her,
I'm yelling for vet book, towels, plenty
Of old newspaper; meanwhile, kitten number one
Squirts out, squirming, still attached inside
Until the cord breaks. Soon placenta follows,
And mother settles down to eat it, still
Slow to lick clean her baby. But she does,
Finally, deftly, while the guests watch, saying
They need to go, will call later for a nose-count.
The next contractions bring kittens with extra-
Long umbilicals the mother won't bite off.
On the phone the vet says, cut them, save her
The work, and I'm about to when a slight tug
Yields more cord. Then more. It oozes out, limp,
Bloody, while I just stare, open palm full of kitten
And gut, scissors poised above it. Five minutes
To the vet's office, the kittens in a cardboard box—
Dr. Guilloud finds more defects I didn't notice:
The tiny forefeet set on backwards, cleft
Palate, hare-lip. I leave three kittens there
To be put down. At home the fourth—born first—
Seems strong and nurses hard; in days, he's dead
Too. I've tried heating pad, bottle nursed, tube
Fed: no use. Mother cat hardly notices.
She's come in heat again.

***

I was one of those girls who grew up
Loving horses, but now I can't afford to ride,
My small house rings with birdsong, barking
Dogs, my own shouting for order, which never
Comes. I might be called eccentric. Friends,
No doubt, say so, if kindly. But I know what I loved.
They don't know that sometimes I go to horse shows
Just to see girls ride. They sit straight, hair pinned
Under black caps, the slightest shift of weight,
Nudge of calf, significant, a kind of love letter
Suggesting control, as, I suppose, all love letters do.
When I was twenty, my art professor asked me
If the saddle made me come. He said the horse
"Quite consciously" symbolized father or phallus.
But what I loved in riding was the animal
Trusting me. To other people, I was nothing,
But the horse obeyed—so I came to know control,
Quietly, like something stolen, as it must be,
By dint of wit from a greater force.

***

The litter of defective kittens died
Suddenly. Not so the foal, born crooked-
Legged and stunted, to Elfin, the bay mare,
Twelve years ago. His twin smothered in the sac
As the mare kept laboring, alone at night
On pasture. I saw his body, long, straight legs,
Coat redder than dried blood. The womb was crowded
With two in it; the chestnut, perfect, larger,
Took all the room, pushed out first, died without
Breathing. His bay brother followed skewed
And lived. Bottle-fed, he grew slowly, gave up
Growing at one year for no discernible reason.

His tracks lived on unevenly in mud
The May sun dried around the bar; for months
The drought reminded me of what I'd lost
For good: he was the last colt, the grown horses
Already sold. I'd sit on stacks of lumber once
Intended for a fence, and smoke—no hay
Inside now, it was safe—thinking I heard
Hoofbeats, spilled corn, my own heart beating.

***

For girls who grow up loving horses,
There is no hope. Nothing will break you
Of love for power, yet for small things, new-
Born colts on stilt legs, you have a soft heart
And a fine touch. Your whole life, you take in
Strays, building your hungry empire, ruling
Whatever loves you, if love means to follow
On padded paw, answer commands in your voice
Only. Young girls are indulged in their passion.
It's thought to be a "phase." But they don't grow
Out of it. When at horse shows I watch girls ride,
Their eyes trained sharp ahead, strong hands set—
Or "soft" if they have talent—I believe, as they do,
They're immortal. Then I remember,
I lived through that, it's gone. Horses belong
To other people. I feed the cats, change the paper
In the parrot cage, fall asleep on the sofa.
I don't have everything I wish I had.
I have enough. But it wouldn't hurt
If some things mattered the way they had:
The "give" in the fingers, the wrist held straight.
And knowing—knowing, *now this matters.*

Omeline

Give me back the smell of Omeline
as I'd open up the burlap sack
and scoop my hands into its sticky sweetness,
my horse stamping impatiently from his stall.

Give me back those afternoons,
stretching out between school and dinner,
when I'd climb up on my horse's back
and we'd go deep into the oak and redwood forests
on the old roads, cantering wherever we could,
and I'd forget where I ended and he started,
and we'd just move through time.

I remember how sometimes I'd take lumps of molasses
from the sweet grainy mix, and suck on them,
before I'd spit them out,
amazed that something that smelled so much like
  cookies baking
could taste so bitter—then I'd watch my horse
nose deep in his grain, snorting with pleasure,
swishing away a fly or two with his black tail.

How gladly I would walk back down that trail
to the stable, the full bags of grain, my horse,
and being ten years old,
not knowing how much I could ever want this back.

Ardor

On Ardor's shelves, instead of books lived a herd of tiny horses. She would visit the shows, choosing only white stock, because whites were among horses the wildest. When she came home in the afternoons, she would find a colt, his hooves over the edge, or a mare's mane dreadlocked from brushing past branches. Sometimes the thuds of the horses' hooves would wake her in the blank moonlight of her apartment.

Riding the horses was out of the question. They would not be ridden. Sometimes this made Ardor angry and she would resolve to sell them, the colts first, away from the mares. Or sell all the mares, leaving the stallions to go insane. Sometimes for days she would feed the horses nothing. One win-ter she went so long that their ribs turned to grins and the flesh around their tails collapsed. But she relented. She always relented, carrying them buckets of feed which honeyed the fingers which after-wards she would allow them to lick, feeling the rough warmth of their tongues.

Among the horses, Ardor loved one stallion most. He reared above her, his eyes rolled back, his hide wet. Every rope she looped towards him would slip away, its oh turning smaller and smaller as she pulled it in. Once he'd allowed her close enough to smell his breath, which was hot and redolent with sweat and the sweet weight of the clover she'd planted for him on the shelf.

One day Ardor met a man. She brought him home, cooked him lobster purged in wine, made him a salad deeply green as grass. After champagne, he removed her blouse, lipping each button free. He slid the zipper down her skirt. They slept. What woke them was the silence, the empty shelves, the shards of white china, everywhere on the floor.

Sonnets to Orpheus II:4

RAINER MARIA RILKE

O dieses ist das Tier, das es nicht giebt.
Sie wußtens nicht und habens jeden Falls
sein Wandeln, seine Haltung, seinen Hals
bis in des stillen Blickes Licht—geliebt.

Zwar *war* es nicht. Doch weil sie's liebten, ward
ein reines Tier. Sie ließen immer Raum.
Und in dem Raume, klar und ausgespart,
erhob es leicht sein Haupt und brauchte kaum

zu sein. Sie nährten es mit keinem Korn,
nur immer mit der Möglichkeit, es sei.
Und die gab solche Stärke an das Tier,

daß es aus sich heraus ein Stirnhorn trieb. Ein Horn.
Zu einer Jungfrau kam es weiß herbei—
und war im Silber-Spiegel und in ihr.

~

This is the non-existent beast. They did
not know that it did not exist and so
they loved it anyway—gait, posture, crest,
down to the very gaze of its still eyes.

True, it did *not* exist, but since they loved it,
a pure beast came to be. They always gave it space,
and in that clear, bright space that they had saved,
it raise its head a little, scarcely needing

to be. They did not nourish it with grain—
just with the possibility of being.
And that endowed the beast with such great strength

it grew a frontal horn—a uni-corn.
When, in its whiteness it approached a virgin,
it *was*—within the mirror, within her.

Out of School

In our narrow strip of wild, at any season,
though early spring, when you've begun to notice
the hard leafed grasses and low myrtles
that have been green all winter, is when they're likely:
two girls on horses, with so much bobbing and digression
around what wind has downed or rain deepened
that you have to slow, yourself, to be sure of their heading.
It's a first love, I'm told, something like boys with dogs,
shier, though, more determined—with so strong a privacy
I can hardly show, meeting them, such broad friendliness
as between strangers on a March path,
and far from town, is endurable.
If it's sexual, as they say, how huge the obliquity.
Those outsize eyes. I can't tell: crazed, kind?
The dark, deadbolted mountain of a body.
Does a man look that way? I suppose I do,
and yet in a tale or dream, the breathing house
everyone else walks into, but that you, weakly at the door,
thunderous, soundless, fail at entering
would be your own body, wouldn't it, that, the next
  morning,
hopeful, or mildly resigned, and half forgetful,
you might feed, cluck softly to, take for a jog?
Your riding on unutterable—something—
between seasons, on no path at all, near dawn,
with a friend who may or may not stay a friend?
It is the thing to do forever, I want to tell them,
meaning I have learned nothing all these years, nothing.
Which is true for an instant as I stumble
through the sudden give (snow yielding) of a white door
into a morning dense, like a house shut up for winter,
with leaf odor not yet coalesced as leaves:

into my life again, inviolate, unwished for.
But nothing is something. I could tell them—
since they think it's revelations they are waiting for—
how many of them time never will reveal.
If we diverge, with only a nod, towards what is coming,
only my silence meaning, if it can,
the world is as much yours now as it ever will be,
well, no one young could believe it—
though with our distance widened to a shout,
wavering again, I wouldn't mind stopping to hear
any voice, even my own, whisper that spring
is again unthinkable, again mysteriously clear.

Results of the Polo Game

The young boys forget about cars awhile,
saunter carefully casual to touch the lathered shoulder,
wait for the sweet monotony of walking the wet ones dry.
The ponies are tough and tired and friendly,
walk docilely for a hundred different hands
around the circuit of cities and grass.

The young girls love easily:
the sweet smell of the silken coats,
the immense deep moving of hidden muscle,
the fumbling soft lips, the fine bony heads.

But the boys are slower, reluctant to react
to the uncoiling of this unfamiliar love.
They carry the smell in their nostrils for hours,
stronger, stranger than perfume or gasoline.
In bed before sleep they walk the wet horses,
the heads still loom at their shoulders,
their fingers curve to the sweated leather.
There is the neck to touch, to arch with the arm,
comparisons to make: a thousand pounds of power
held by thin reins, the alien metal in the soft mouth.

The thighs ache to curve around this new body.
There is confusion about the meanings of love,
embarrassment at boundaries that will not stay put,
ambiguous language that always leads to lust:
the curves, the shine, the power, the deep sweet smell,
the capturing, taming, gentling, the moving together.
The girls already know. Their thighs are open.
It is a satisfactory substitute, this love.
The boys, in sleep, run a hand through the thick mane,
lay their faces against a shining shoulder, and decide.

1961: Santa Rosa

At Circle C Ranch I had my own horse
for the week. *Sugar.* A mountain with legs
and a five point star to his forehead.
Without a show of turquoise and tooled boots,
the working ranch gave a city boy something
of The West, through knowing what will spook
a horse, or that a comprehending
ear tilts before there's rain. *Sugar* was young
for his size, measured by hands
instead of feet which I took on faith
because it sounded like something
out of Sunday School, like using hectares
instead acres. And each of us
was shown a saddle blanket, to smooth
it flat so the wool won't hurt like a knife.
I followed along.
I was trainable. I stopped calling a horse's coat
his fur after a ranch hand told me different,
feeling sorry for anyone that stupid—
up to age ten.
One afternoon I just stood watching *Sugar* flinch
in the shade, unmoved by the flies I hated.
Then, in a rodeo on the last day
we entered the barrel race and came in Third.
I remember thinking *Boy, that's all right.*
And everything was.

Cherry Blossom

Little boys aren't supposed to play
with horses, and even though I asked
every Christmas for Cherry Blossom—

the yellow one with the pink mane,
silver star on the left flank, pink
princess crown on her head—

I was given army men and footballs,
and I had to borrow my sister's toys
to play 'herd in the wild by the river.'

I do watch football now although
my girlfriend knows the rules better
than I do—she teases me about it.

But I've subscribed to *Horse and Rider*
for two years now, and although I don't
like all the cowboys and ropes, I

like the lines of the horses as they
stretch into a lope across the grass,
a free filly is more beautiful than

the sunset she runs from. I might yet
look into riding lessons—I wonder
how expensive they are, and if
they let you run free.

CHRIS DRANGLE

My Pony Pete

He had a wide-brimmed face
That veered to the left.
When you asked him a question
He would nod perceptibly
In no particular order.
If Pete were a flannel shirt—
He would have been
The best flannel shirt
A missing button or two
Only adding to his greatness

Big Jim

Born of a mold, he was as large as a man
in an action-figure set; his mane I'd touch
for luck was the same fur I applied to his coat,
dark brown and shaved close, with tiny ponds
of baldness where the stick-glue dried too soon.
How he'd dance for me on all fours, or two
hind legs, or no feet at all, shaking his tail feathers,
and how I yearned to say words like canter, and post,
even lope; instead, I'd whisper, *heel,* and *play dead,*
then *giddy up* while he was still lying down,
and off he'd go toward the curtains and blinds
I'd raise to show him the world of the Barbato's
only two horse-lengths away! *That's their wall,*
I'd say, *Easy, boy, that's their swatch of grass.*
I took him to the water and made him drink
from the hand-sized holy water font at our door,
and there I bathed him as well. God,
he was such an animal, all sweat and energy,
finding in our reel-to-reel the tape for his legs
after a hard race or before, and in the styptic pencil
ease. When my brother suggested putting him
out to stud, I drove my brother away, using
the whips I used in the stretch—the thick ends
of palms—and the spurs of my own fingernails.
And it was true he never slept, for often
I would find him standing in his gelded way,
upon a blazer I never wore—his eyes not there at all.
I had forgotten them. If my father spoke of horsepower
in crankshafts, or lifted his belt to stop our horsing around,
I'd take Big Jim in my hands and hold him up like a chalice,
letting him transform into the real thing, not the symbol
of horse but horse itself. And we'd ride from the attic

to the cellar where he'd find skittish waterbugs
that would give him a scare. He was not of
the animal kingdom, I had to remind him, but kin
to the wooden horse of myth, kin to something
stuffed. And yet, we'd kiss that way you see horses do,
the side of his long face against my cheek,
and never once did I, in rage at his faults, threaten
to send him to the rendering plant, never once mention
the word glue after applying his hair. And now where
has he gone,
in what long meadow does he ride, having been lost,
lo, these many years? And who am I without him
beneath me, without his hair under the comb of
my thumb? Was he perhaps put down years ago,
and to this sad requiem become a sod? If only I knew,
if only we could ride one last time, his horse's head
and mine pointed toward eternity: *That way,* I'd yell,
that way, big boy, you go, up, up and away, hi ho. Gone
Big Jimminy, all plaster, all horse, from fetlock to bald spots.

A Memory: Austin Country Day Camp—Horseback and Swimming Lessons

When I was nine my life was trail rides
and laps at the pool. The water turned me blue,
the stamping, snorting horses made me quake,
but in Texas, unmanly fear won't do.

Each day a new mount and I knew
someday I'd draw wild *Ricochet,*
the screwy, wall-eyed mare who shied
at gates. Sure enough, she bolted when I

tried to force her on to the track,
a demented bullet, gunning down
the rows of barns, me the burr in
her blanket, sticking to her jolting back.

Miss Rosy, whose laugh we loved, though
she smelled of chlorine and had skin
like harness leather, came running when
she saw, yelling, "Get her head up!"

Haul her back! Get her head up, boy!"
And I stood in the stirrups and pulled
mightily with puny arms and joy, joy,
Ricochet did her Trigger bit, pawing

sky with wicked hooves, and then halted.
Miss Rosy called me hero, claimed
I'd bossed that spitfire. I got over the shame.
I got over wobbled-legged fear.

On other mounts, in a comic way,
I was thrown. But I grabbed the pommel
and hoisted up again and did not pray,
but watched for that twitch of ear. God knows

I didn't master women or self-doubt.
Horses, calm or mad, taught that one must,
even if just nine, be alert for doom.
So I check the wind, don't trust in trust,

know that gates can open to a dreaded place.
Still, there was Rosy's wet shining face—
just arch your back and float. Her lips firm
when she jerked the cinch—*tight, like this.*

Horse

The first horse I ever saw
was hauling a wagon stacked with furniture
past storefronts along Knickerbocker Avenue.
He was taller than a car, blue-black with flies,

and bits of green ribbon tied to his mane
bounced near his caked and rheumy eyes.
I had seen horses in books before, but
this horse shimmered in the Brooklyn noon.

I could hear his hooves strike the tar,
the colossal nostrils snort back the heat,
and breathe his inexorable, dung-tinged fume.
Under the enormous belly, his ------

swung like the policeman's nightstick,
a dowsing rod, longer than my arm—
even the Catholic girls could see it
hung there like a rubber spigot.

When he let loose, the steaming street
flowed with frothy, spattering urine.
And when he stopped to let the junkman
toss a tabletop onto the wagon bed,

I worked behind his triangular head
to touch his foreleg above the knee,
the muscle jerking the mar of hair.
Horse, I remember thinking,

four years old and standing there,
struck momentarily dumb,
while the power gathered in his thigh
surged like language into my thumb.

Work

Although constructed of the most up-to-date, technically
advanced elements of woven glass,
carrying messages by laser pulse, the cable the telephone
men are threading down the manhole
has exactly the same thickness and tense flexibility and
has to be handled with the same delicacy
as the penis of the huge palomino stallion I saw breeding
at the riding school when I was twelve
who couldn't get it in so that Charlie Young the little
stablehand had to help him with it.
How more than horrified I was that Charlie would touch
the raw, unpeeled, violet-purple thing,
thinking nothing of it, slipping between the flaring,
snorting stud and the gleaming mare,
comely and lascivious, who, sidling under now, next year
would throw a mediocre foal, soon sold.

The Lie

Never daring feed
the tall roan mare
fenced next door,
I saw without seeing
the look he wore
before he screamed—
my little brother, bit—
and grabbed the hand
to steal us past
the widower's porch
where suddenly
the old man stood,
yelling we were warned.

And I shouted *lie,*
cried the old man was mean,
called him dumb,
the only words I had
to say it wasn't fair
no one had explained
how terrible quiet
then loud could be pain,
and later wouldn't admit
I'd held my brother up,
mute as I remained
it wasn't the widower
nor his horse
that put us up to it,
yet how could my brother be
guilty of his fearlessness,
let alone me
my innocence?

Horses like Gods

I was told not to touch
the horses until I knew
what I was doing.
They could injure or even kill you.
Thoroughbred machines.
Muscles you could see ripple.
Living machines I had to learn
how to control. I proved
I could take a harness
and lead one around.
I knew simple tricks:
turn your back
and the horse would come closer,
wave your hat and make it stop.

For months I labored alongside
a man twice my age,
a horseman his whole life
who forgot simple things:
where he left the gas can,
to the shut the barn door,
or lock the gate.
He once left me alone, sitting
on the fence, while he took the truck
into town to place a bet on a race tip.

Each morning we walked horses
to the paddock. On the hottest
day of the summer, the horses spooked,
stood up on hind legs, lifted us

off the ground, an awkward dance,
human marionettes mastered by horses.
We glanced at each other off the ground.
He smiled at me. The waltz lasted a few seconds.
We loosed them into their field,
snorting, heads held high.
We leaned on the fence, sweating,
drank water from the hose,
sprayed the horses, left them shimmering
in the field like two gods.

On Human Maps

Rather brilliant horses swirl in the field.
They are green and orange and blue,
some variegated like the petals
of tulips or irises, some striped
like national flags.

They kick up their heels
as if they are dancing the polka.
They braid each other's manes
with their mouths, weaving in ribbons,
color added to color
in unpredictable ways.
Russet and blue, for instance. Mauve and red.

They are proud of having no riders,
gather burrs for each other's backs
to make sure. They are aware of being
fenced in, that their pasture is a square
on human maps, but they pine about it less often.

When these horses race in enormous circles,
their ribboned manes flying,
their tails dazzling brooms,
to the human eye their field
kaleidoscopes, glints like a gem.
But they have no notion of this.
They run for themselves only.

What they see from inside their brilliant horse bodies
are clouds low over mountains,
then spirals, triangles, jagged lines carved in rock,
finally, the slow light of solstice swelling a cavern.

And then they are trance horses, their sharp hooves
weightless as their bodies fade into the branches
of trees or among the rocks of a stream.
Some roll on their backs in the clouds.
Others become flying squirrels, spread their sails
in the damp air of forests.

And when they return to their pasture
their souls are supple as wine-filled bagotas.
They become ordinary again,
even flinging off their brilliant skins
so that lupines, poppies and lobelia
spring up at their feet.
But these horses continue to glow.
And they take the wild grasses
into their mouths lovingly.

Peter A. Nash

Windy and Fawn

In moonlight
the horses wander side by side,
mother and daughter
passing in and out of black pine shadows,
occasionally snatching a blackberry bramble;
they nod their heads
as if discussing something of immense significance.

On summer mornings
they roll in warm grass,
legs waving in the air,
and then like Great Danes lying on their bellies
they survey the world with mild faces
and pointed ears.

I'm not sure that I could do it.
I mean, live in a field with one of my sons,
standing beside him,
eating from the same flake of hay
pulling burrs off each other's back
or hunkered down under a maple tree
shoulders touching in the pattering rain,
coats dripping, while chickadees click
in the hedges.
We'd probably be
at opposite ends of the pasture,
looking over the fence
giving little speeches.

But my wife, Judy—
put her in that great green room with our daughter Hana—
I can see them galloping around, whinnying,
laughing at some crazy thing that a raven said,
their big yellow molars glinting
in the bright light of early afternoon.

Red Rock

I

Granddaughter, sixteen,
says she's going elk hunting
with her other grandpa,
spending opening weekend
camped in Utah mountain country.
They'll be riding horses, hers never
around guns, but she's not afraid.
She can handle him.

I've just ridden the bus
with a cousin, fifty, who told me
of her knee replacement,
the accident at eighteen
riding horses with her dad.

Her horse was flighty,
his wasn't, so they traded.
She only spurred him
one time, only one time,
and he went straight up
in the air, his head rearing back
into her face and chest,
breaking her teeth,
saddle horn cracking her ribs,
foot catching in the stirrup,
horse dragging her
halfway to the river,
tearing her knee to shreds,
seven surgeries from eighteen
to forty, at forty a new knee
made of plastic and titanium
attached to severed leg bones,

three-inch-long spikes
driven into marrow.

My cousin's front gate
is adorned with hardware
they've removed over years
of upgrades. The gruesomest,
she says, were bolts that stuck out
the sides of her leg to fasten
a brace on with wing nuts.

II

She can't be mad at that horse
anymore. It was killed by a semi
coming over the hill where her dad
and her brother and the hired man
were bringing Herefords down
from summer pasture,
truck plowing through cows,
throwing them like stuffed toys
off the edges of the highway,
cows and a truck barreling into
men on horseback,
knee-wrecker mangled
beyond recognition,
hired man killed, my cousin's dad
game-legged til the day he died,
her brother still limping,
winters affecting them both,
her metal parts and his
absorbing cold like a tooth ache.

III

Granddaughter's horse
isn't flighty. She's taught him
to be steady, trained him
for barrel racing. Named him
Red Rock, his face like a Hereford.

Says he won't buck when the guns
go off. Trusts him, her grandpa,
her indestructible teenage body.

She'll ride the crest of that hill
where cows come down from
summer range before the hunt,
their red bodies fat and matted,
white faces bobbing and swaying,
their exodus followed by guns, men,
and horses, one red with a white face,
carrying a small-town girl who learned
how to ride in 4-H. Nothing like
my cousin on her Idaho ranch,
who's been riding all her life.

Nothing like me, whose horse-riding
never got past leading my little sister
under a too-low apple tree branch,
scraping her off the horse's back.

Nothing like my brother-in-law
who went hunting with friends,
bagged a buck and strapped the head
on a pack-horse, antlers jutting out
from the saddle, spooking the horse
to a frenzy, no one able to stop it
from running, rolling, gouging its sides
into gore with the horns until
my brother-in-law had to shoot it,
last time he's ever picked up a gun.

But Granddaughter won't be spooked.
No leading her under low-lying branches
or trading for a mount she doesn't know.
If that horse of hers is true to his name,
she'll weld herself on him like moss to a stone
and come home with a story of her own.

IV

Here's the story: *It was just me*
and my grandpa and my cousin CJ
who's nine. First thing we had to do
is wade across a creek on horseback.
Grandpa led the way on Rex, going slow
to stay dry, but Red Rock jumped in
with a splash and soaked my grandpa.

Then we started up the muddy hill,
but it was slippery and Red Rock laid down.
We tried rocking him up with his saddle,
but he wouldn't move until Grandpa
whipped him good. Meanwhile, CJ
got on behind Grandpa, too scared
to ride the horse Grandpa brought for him,
the one everybody calls Black but CJ
secretly named Moonshine, because
Moonshine wanted to RUN up the hill.

On the way back, we went out around
so we wouldn't slide all the way down.
Got stuck in the trees a few times,
came out on a cliff. A grouse flew up.
Red Rock tends to shy, but he shied
uphill, thank goodness, so we didn't
fall off the cliff. Then we had to skirt
a hillside of loose rock, and I begged
my grandpa to let me get off and lead
Red Rock, but he said no, you stay on.
We made it back. Didn't see a single elk.
And I was glad we didn't. I was living,
I was happy, I was ready to go home.

Kate's Horses

Horses horses horses…
The whole country of France
but your photographs
were all of horses.
Horses standing, horses grazing.
Horses rolling, running, rearing.
Old horses with their ribs showing.
Young horses nursing.
Horses nose to tail
swishing flies.

With the confidence
of one thirteen
you told me about horses:
mares and bays,
blazes and stockings,
how to measure with your hands.
From pasture to pasture
Each horse—
a fresh reason for being.

Lance Larsen

Neighing Horses Behind My Right Shoulder

The colt nuzzles her mother till a chorus of painted
shivers passes from teat to purling mouth,

as if the sky itself had speckled their Appaloosa
backs with blessing. Are they less true, these ponies,

for being bendably hollow, gestated the same wet
afternoon in an aging plastics factory in Taiwan?

Toy horses: all day, through three states, across
the plush blue of backseat upholstery, my daughter

has galloped them. Now they sleep touching noses,
and now they swim through air—Pegasus times two

times seven shades of apricot violence the setting sun
lays in our laps. What are these neighs that nicker

through the car but anthems we sing to falling dark,
to galloping air? *Thank you, wind. Ride me again. Amen.*

The Tryout

For Hannah

She sat the pinto pony,

Whose tail was a tattered flag,
Whose coat was unshorn wool,
Who had bucked one off,
Bolted on another, backed up, and balked.

Her feet still, toes to the trees that lined the arena,
Hands the slant of a church roof,
The reins squeezed, not tugged,
Words softly cooed.
She rose from the saddle,
Touched down and rose again,
Like kisses on a child's forehead.

Horse in Shadow

for Grayce, again

Cold, the wind that riffs through the west end door,
sounding its low moan, grieving the moment's passing.
And cold the nose of the near-black gelding,
where he stomps once in the glistening darkness,
the gentled night. My twelve-year-old daughter,
stiff in her jodhpurs and boots, removes one glove
and reaches a carrot toward the shadowed head.
"Good boy," she purrs. "Good boy." *Good boy,*
who'd bucked and lurched, galloping hell-bent
at the corrugated wall, whirling until he'd launched
her from the saddle into the dust-dazzled air.
"Good boy," she says. And he *is*—furious teacher,
unendurable bliss—because she *says* he is, loyal girl,
good friend, forgiver, profferer of carrots, wielder
of whips, tiny commander in her wafer-thin saddle.

Gallup

The day before she turns five, Amy hears
the doctors speak of her galloping heart.

The stethoscope has pressed its hard cold coin
into her chest. Air empties from the room.

When she is alone, she listens for the horse
that gallops in her ribs, for hoofbeats in her blood.

What she understands is this: tomorrow
they will sleep her and peel apart the fence

against which the red stallion beats tattoo
and let him out. Then her heart will canter,

walk an ordinary, one-two gait.
But she wonders—will he run into the sky

without her? Will his wild mane tangle in clouds,
and his hooves spark a starfall beyond the moon?

She sees an empty saddle on his back.
When they open the gate to let him out

(this must be the secret), she will hold on—
she will gallop too.

Blackberries

On Society Hill Road I stop
My car at the gate to Sandy's
Stables and pick blackberries.

My daughter won't mind.
She'd rather stay on Ravada
Than gather berries she won't eat.

I eat more berries than
I put into the pail.
My fingers turn purple from the juice.

I work my way to the center
Of the bush where, lying coiled
In thick grass, a copperhead waits,

Shading itself from the midday sun.
I am not surprised. I know
Some grief always waits

At the heart of sweetness, the light.
I leave the snake alone, move
To another bush, and fill the pail.

When I pick up my daughter,
I learn that a cottonmouth
Bit a stable girl on the shin

While she emptied a load of manure
Behind the barn. The horses listen,
Their eyes alert, their ears cocked.

They scrape the ground with their hooves.
They roam from side to side,
Nipping each other's flanks.

Wind rises and rain comes in big drops.
We drive under a blackberry sky.
A tornado chases us home.

Right of Way

Under chestnut braids
blood pools on asphalt
around my daughter's ears
that do not hear
the siren's scream or
her pony's struggle to stand
on splintered bone
or
my ringing phone.

A Short Poem about the Long Poem

The lyric poem then is
that moment in which you realize
your daughter's horse has
stepped into downed wire
and will surely panic,
your cherished ten year old inalterably
aboard one thousand pounds
of instinctual terror.

In that suspended moment, the lyric
lets you off, releases you:
burned with the memory to be sure
but freed, loosed
in the space the lyric leaves
for the silences to speak.

The longer poem by contrast
requires you to stay mounted;
to watch her face
as the mare bolts, to pound
after her as if you could
control, rather than only
uncover over time, what must
come next: the mare racing riderless
and the still form curled
where it fell, nested motionless in the grass.

There is, you know, a desire
to remain with the unresolved
moment: the mare nearly
to the horizon, stirrups akimbo
as she runs and the reins

blown out, empty; there is a
desire never to ask
the only things that matter
for fear of what the answers might be.

The long poem asks
you to dismount
and go to her.

Today at Camp

Today at camp
Blackie reared and plunged
Into the ring while still
Tied to the fence. The rail
Gave. The board broke. My
Daughter tried to calm
The horse, was reaching
For his halter when
The wood let loose like
A windmilled punch—slammed
Her down. The counselor
Shouted: Get up. Get up.
She did. Rose on colt-like
Legs from a cloud of dust.
The fence was mended.
Her wounds were cleaned. And when
I tuck her in tonight
I make a bedtime story
Of the day she toppled
From the grocery cart
When she was just a year.
She laughs when I describe
The horrifying thunk
I heard when she hit
Ground. I laugh too
From this remove, remembering
The doctor's words when he declared
All is well. The baby's well.
Remembering, again
I gather in my faith
Enough to say goodnight.

No White Horses

Over the ring's oval,
leaving u-shaped smudges,
casting a shadow thirty hands high—
my daughter, riding a white horse,
seems distant as sunset.
A rim of gold traces her profile;
gold, the flanks of the old horse
patient under her
light, bobbing form,
gold in the tail's loose curtain
closing before dust and flies.
She's explained to me
there are no white horses—
equestrians use other terms
more descriptive and less pure
        the mare I have called white
        in this poem
        is technically a grey
and I exasperate her exactness,
because I'm no horsewoman
and I forget. Still, the mare—
        for all that she is grey—
glows no less at sunset
with a beige powder clouding
and rising into gold against
the reddening, and darkening, sky.
Sun draws a bright finger
down my daughter's hair: unruly, vining—
down her back, over the mare's
rump, tail, haunch, hock;
gold dustclouds ascend past
my daughter's boots, her knees

her own trundling rump as she learns to post.
        A mist of yellow separates me from
        the small girl and the white horse
that is neither white nor grey
but gold.

Without Ceremony

In two weeks nothing will change
except this currant bush tinged with blossoms
and acidic fruits. It's about to become a shield
for the burnt husk of an old-growth cedar.

You'll pick up your want ads and call
about another horse.
I can picture a thoroughbred straight from the track
nuzzling grain and alfalfa,
drinking from a chipped porcelain bathtub.

In two weeks nothing will change
but the moon, swollen like viscera,
plural as an organ the body doesn't know it has yet.

A slender girl,
you'll stand at dusk, with your hard breasts
and flat stomach, and I won't give this
poem to you, or listen to your recite
Hebrew words in a place beyond nerves.

Instead I'll wrap something pretty
and put it into your hands.
The animal you love will stare full on
at what it can see:
two peripheral scenes
cut by a dark swath down the middle.

Wild Stallion, Point Reyes, 1977

Sky and sky. And after sky, a space flight's integers
  of wonder. And after: visionless distance
more penetrating than this headland, its sea-cliffs
  rampant with the wind's scrawls, the ocean
foaming ashore, awash in its slow eternity; distance
  that is itself impenetrable; that is,
useless, except as furthest backdrop for this wood
  where he walks beneath stanchioned redwoods—
wispy beard, backpack snug to his shoulders, the path
  opening on more path, on the promise
of expanse, his dream of the west a dream of revelation.

Behind him: the Greyhound's hum, hitchhiked rides
  from Famine's End to Tamalpais,
those cult recruiters who approached him on the Wharf,
  their lies nearly alluring; further north,
a Renaissance Fair where he picked from motley crowd
  that friend who took him further back—
concrete yards of apartments, row houses, malice
  of voices through a bedroom wall,
haunts that flowed with smuggled beer, boy-talk.

Here is hunger of vision, livid under the trees'
  spidered canopy; as now, from somewhere
up the path he hears the rhythm of hoof beats growing
  louder, dithyrambic. And it flashes
past, ashen, its mane driven behind as it gallops
  toward granite boundaries, scrub-pine,
windscape, crashing sea. There, too, he'll stand
  dumbstruck, wanting to carry it
with him, wanting to leave it behind—his life.

Why the Horse

After our boy died, she was necessary:
bugged-eyed, underfed, ribs like lath.
And her ears pinned flat
against her head. We didn't know

this meant danger, a red flag
as on the beach where Portugese men-of-war
landed their flotilla, or the diamondback's rattle,
or the siren's wail as clouds folded

themselves and wind reared
and rooftops bucked off.
We didn't know,
necessary thing she was,

that wildness does not approve
the halter, the lead, the longe-line, the coaxing
no matter how gentle.
That first time,
she pulled the rope hard,

the nylon melting calluses.
She reared to strike front hooves
down. Necessary as she was,
I dodged the tumult, tried again,

and, again, this time was awarded
the hip-pivot to kick.
Round and round, the mare and I danced,
one step away from disaster, one slip

from what might have been necessity

for those closest to me, wishing death
upon themselves, wishing dust
as beneath the mare's hooves.

The mare had stood her ground before,
against others who did not need her.
That black horse worked me hard,
her stampings a heart knocking,

her flicking tail impatience,
her bolting as from invisible fear.
She worked death out of me.
And I stayed with her, stayed

with her, stayed with
her until she calmed to my singing, my humming,
until she plodded behind me, head down,
hoof-steps making their relaxed impressions,

and wild things made their necessary peace.
In the same ring, with the same enemies.

Sam Witt

Black Pony on a Bank of the James

Simple blood & mass, simple machinery—
acres downriver from the paper mills,

head curled into its own long shadow, decorticated
& grazing...

stopped by the river long enough to say your name:
Knucklebone, empty, porcelain head.

Stopped breathing long enough dead child to say your name:
when your faces are washed from me in a grassly painful rain,

Mouthful of White Powder & *felt you,*
pulled from me into its black, cideling eyes

for their small, reflected sunset blood to thin,

running at the corner with tears of rheum, & dew,
that the light lay down its tiny eggs into our eyes,

& feed you, with the other palm pressed
to the pony's gently swelling side,

for a long time listening to your empty grazing in the river's echo,
& hish...

Once, as kids, in an orchard, before dawn,
you stroked the flashlight beam across a pony's dwarfed,

powerful back: his side was rising gently, falling, then rose,
like a giant wineskin stretching its seams through that circle of five,

rolling a waterdrop down his hide,
& I stepped back into you, a tiny, human spark from your hand

suddenly going out in its eye, & we both inhaled,
but the pony didn't wake.

Of human beastliness, I sleep in my feet,
a handful of sugar: a muzzle-kiss: a smoking thumb

lifting its luscious neck now when I approach,
such gentle breeding that I walk in my walking sleep,

a black gelding with its left ear torn & healed.
I step forward, I stop myself, a hand on its swelling flank.

I too am a starveling, all five stomachs half-full.

I too am slipping away with a withers, a hum,
with each heft & sink,

grooving its ruin into my palm: Contagion, empty me

to a riffling breeze, a tail that twitches, & lifts,
to each horse-apple as it strikes, in darkness, the ground,

& smolder me awake.

& when the stallion within steps forth to breathe, I sing:
both of us threaded together through our tearducts,

Why do you tear me, child, with the memory of *your* breathing?
With that morning when the breath passed from horse to horse,

& they suddenly woke with a scream,
a dozen starlings exiting a chimney

to a sudden, earful hush, & broke, *that I am dead,*
& stretch my darkling seams?

The Lesson

Afterwards, they kept the horse
in the back pasture, far enough away
from the house that the dead girl's mother
needed to drive to the edge of the field
and walk, hatless, jacket open, face
into the wind, until she reached the fence
where she would stand, for hours at a time,
staring at the animal she'd trusted
with her firstborn child. What could she
have been thinking? A child is
a child. A horse, a horse.
Some days, she'd swear
the gelding could read her mind.
Ears flattened, nostrils flared,
he'd charge, rear and kick,
his eyes wild with fury
or fear, or some combination of both.
Wisely, she stayed well back.
Other days, he'd turn and turn
in ever smaller circles, pawing
the dry ground with his sharp hooves,
raising dense clouds of dust
that eventually settled
on her shoulders and in her hair.
Finally, the woman told her husband
he could get his gun or call the vet,
she didn't care which. She'd learned
what she needed to know.

Moving the Moon

I'm not interested in the shaggy horse
(or is it a pony?) although it's white.
It's usually dirty, comes into my mind with steam
rising from thick fur.

I close the gate, improvise some
dark green and black, an undifferentiated
thickness above which I put a moon
for accent. Go 'way horse.   Shoo.

Stop chomping, stop blowing clouds of heat.
I stare away, increasing
the darkness, inventing an owl, also
white but perhaps oracular,

like the day the bird flew through the window,
the day I spoke in tongues,
          white fire
          white iron
          heat.
But heat brings back the horse, loaded

with things to trade, short, stocky,
not at all tired. So, this is an old landscape,
one I've hidden from myself
because it's stupid.

Dumb.
Doesn't speak, it insinuates a journey
and embarrassed I try to erase
the suddenly obvious owl before it drops a feather,

before a single symbolically meaningful feather
falls. But it's dangerous to imagine

owls, hard to blot them out,
even with chemicals,

scissors may fail, may leave another moon.
The horse lowers its head, eats.
Heat swells from the body and from
the bales of hay laid out

like giant erasers. Like desks
in a dark classroom. Still if I took drugs
this is where I'd go. I can't
banish the stupid white horse

but I can move the moon, divide it,
put it back together.
I can draw any face on it
I like. And the owl leaves the low tree

to sit at my feet (owl on the ground,
never meant to see that!)
More things catch moonlight, come
into being, distant silos,

small acorn crowns, each post moon-washed
and one-sided. It's warm enough here
to do without fire, but
that's it. No story. No arcane

wisdom or poignantly revealed momentous
event. I just like this quiet.
And the owl who opens his one
good eye. The horse

keeps his head in the hay making heat.
I prefer moonlight,
I like the green to be almost black.
I like a lot of space

with nothing going on.
A few white words
and the rim of the milk pail polished
and fine in my dark.

On the Possession of Horses

Their heads hunker forward when they canter
as if only one direction were possible
and they don't understand fire.
They gallop back to a burning barn.

Nothing about horses compels me now,
though once I wanted to be one.
What do horses have to do with love,
the quivering limbs of their bodies,
their hearts chiseled from stone,
and riders cling to them
as if just this holding on,
this staying on, could be everything?

Once an entire village banned horses.
You couldn't blame them after all the trouble.
One minute normal, and the next
the children were possessed,
leaving their comfortable beds at night,
cavorting with horses from all around
under the laden apple trees.
No one knows how they planned it.
They rode horses by moonlight,
bareback and bare-assed
even in thunderstorms.

When horses trot and canter,
their hooves clatter, their bones
chime like funeral bells, like clappers.
They ring against the earth, their heavy
hooves beat against the earth.

I Have Come to Witness the Sacred

Like conch shells washed ashore, the wild horses
of Corolla brought to Florida by Ponce De Leon

in 1526 are gifts to Outer Banks, to North Carolina.
I'm certain they'll be lean, sleeker than Indian ponies,

skim sand, kick foam to lace. No J. Alfred Prufrock,
wild horses will be sacred as mermaids, will sing to me,

Combing the white hair of the waves blown back.
It's only three hours north from here in Ocracoke

to Corolla's Currituck Lighthouse where I should find
them, free as cattle in New Delhi. No time for flight,

I bypass Nags Head, Kitty Hawk, 1900: hang gliders,
Dayton, Ohio bicycle builders, Wright brothers

bumping, stumbling, floating for seconds of glory. I do
stop at Duck to check in at the Sanderling. Its beaches

are glutted by mollusk, but there's no smell of chorine,
only Coppertone from children uncaged by their parents

who lounge like buffet silverware. Too much life is left
on these shores to thicken and clot like Jack Daniel's gravy

that is not stirred. I need the sacred, the wild horses
of Corolla, to be rinsed clean like Lewis and Clark portaging

dugout canoes at Great Falls in order to reach headwaters
of the Missouri River. No promontory like Cape Hatteras,

Currituck Lighthouse is surrounded by lawn of County Cork,
glowing but not green as bluegrass fencing Kentucky stallions

on Calumet Farms. My quest for the Holy Grail ends.
One head pokes out between white framed houses. Two,

five, finally six horses laze over the street. Short and portly,
with an air of salmon fed bankers, that last one must be

sleep walking. In conference about browsing, dumpy, trash
can clanging, shambling pests are the star I have followed.

No cherubim, thrones or dominions, just a line that echoes:
Heard melodies are sweet, but those unheard are sweeter.

Could Keats have transformed these horses to proud pagans,
carved them into Sanderling's black walnut mustangs?

I find nothing to worship at Corolla. In an old testament fury,
metaphoring gulls that hover into seraphim, I shred clouds

lacing blue sky into three pairs of wings. Eating sod to roots,
maybe these horses are endearing, but sacred, wild, never.

Ode to the Pa'u Rider

The florist, the tailor, the saddler know
your ten-thousand-dollar regalia secrets,
your who-rides-for-which-Island ways.
Seven Riders for Seven Islands, my Oahu the gold
of Ilima. Twelve yards of slung muslin
across your grade horse's barrel swirls,
his back sun-bleached copper to the shade
of a new Lincoln penny. Kuhio Street asphalt
hardly your challenge. Where are your creek beds,
your red mud running thick, your Hilo
through the jungle brush?

Your haku secrets, your headstall birds of paradise,
make me wonder if the *maile pilau* got caught
on the cheap-slung gowns that inspire this display.
The parade air drags against your satin
and in the air the missionary hush, everyone
thinking how you are astride under all those
modesty-giving gowns, how your culottes
grow thick with leathered sweat.

You on no errand and with no terrain
to transgress, go and keep your traditions hidden.
But let us pick them loose like the hala key,
let us parade-goers be the fruit seed core
fluffed open into a paintbrush, drawing you out.
Walk the ponies slower, let us get a look.
Nod with grace and do not answer.
Do not even wave back.

Judith Skillman

Horse Corridor

Such dirty leaves.
They fall from the apple-pear
to blacken the ground.

The sun's fallen too,
gone from its station in the sky
to leave the earth dark
in a poor age.

In their wooden cells
horse paw the ground.
When they breathe
steam comes from their nostrils.

Scent of girl's arm.
Lather and lather,
then they're gone, the metal combs and brushes,
soapy water
that could clean a sloppy animal.

In the southern quadrant
a gate leans into an arena.
The same trail circles the perimeter:
there she stopped and got on,

there her horse spooked
and reared.
In Lady's pen a room sways
under electric light.
I pass by, see the shovel smile,

hear the door bang shut.

Nervous starlings
pick at the ground
when I come home
these winter afternoons.

In rain-wet darkness
something grows,
but no one's certain whether
it's going to flower.

Bouquet

Flower of abundance, the sexual flower, flower of horses
galloping in a meadow, flower of criminal liability,
flower of neglect and eventual triumph, flower of the
archaic dream, the long-stemmed flower, flower of
perfumed neck, flower that sprouts between the legs,
the melting flower, flower of screaming in the night, the
thick-stemmed flower, flower with its head under the
pillow saying *no no no,* flower of girlhood, of leave-
taking, risk-taking, flower rocking in the evening breeze,
flower of walking alone under stars, moonflower, flower
of hummingbirds with jeweled throats, flower of car
crash, of motorcycle skidding along the highway, of
cancer opening like a hand, flower of midnight dog
howl and the click of nails, houndstooth, dog lily, the
flower of left lonely, flower of abandonment, flower of
the sad fathers, flower of cold fact, the flower of the
strummed guitar, toppled drumkit, flower of over-
whelmed mother, flower of mystery, the life-giving and
opulent flower, flower of walking hand in hand on the
breakwater, flower called girl on horseback, the loveliest
flower, for you, the flower called horse-fallen, the yellow
iris called horse-risen-to-gallop-again.

October Storm

1.

The green sky,
    the gray-green sky
    growling now,

the first stone-
    gray rain pellets
    starting down,

so he looped
    his leg over
    a fence-rail

to watch from
    the weed safety
    of the side

and I walked
    out—Carl wouldn't
    go—to fetch

the colt wild
    from a week at
    pasture alone.

What more? You'd
    gone to your chore.
    Knuckle of

stone to de-
    ice the trough, leaves
    in low whirls,

grist of dust.
    Thunder coming.
    His friend—

they liked the
word in knowing
company,

no longer
code for a covert
thing, but kitsch,

like a long
scar, healed enough
to amuse—

his friend was
at the barn door
watching you

work the black
water in the trough,
and turned.

Thunder com-
ing. And then
the colt was

2.

beside me,
pulling up snow-
eyed, slickened

with frenzy.
What more than to
raise my arm?

It tells him
I'm bigger. Easy.
All right.

But then I
turned my back,
the rain driving

mane after
mane flung full a-

cross the field,
the sky no
color I could
see—down-shove

of wind and
lightning all at
once. I saw

the shock of
a man's face as
teeth tore through

wet flannel
to my side,
the young horse,

teeth bared, fright-
ened by the
fury, as

in battle—.
I pulled him on,
to the barn,
where you were,
love. All of us,
stunned

at the nature
of the strike…
Storm, then calm.

Nothing else
but to heal. No-
thing to keep

from the watchers
at the gate,
ever more.

Strike

I had taken shelter under an overhang of sweet gum
as the rain noise began to crowd together through hanging
wave on wave of gray, like a rising smoke frozen in air.
Then I saw her coming along the high crest of the pasture's rise,

Redwood, our neighbor's mare, cantering with her neck
outstretched, head shaking off the rain. A great noise
broke above her, cleaving the drenched air down from the lowering

cumulonimbus, or it may have risen out of her:
the light was there and gone too fast to see. When I got to her,
the muscles of thigh, stifle, throatlatch, all her grand physique

had contracted, and she trembled as if the earth
under her trembled, her eye racked from its socket in terror
and outrage, and I touched her burning sides in the rain,
my own fear high up in me, my own eyes wide.

JOSEPH MILLAR

After Listening to a Lecture on Form

I'm afraid of the mountains
in this thin glacial air,
of going to sleep in their shadow,
that the granite inside them
and the threads of bright metal
may not hold once the night comes.

I'm afraid of so many people talking,
the cat smile of the poetry scholar,
his ridged skull.
When he spoke of measure
I could feel my wristwatch tighten,
remembered the payments coming due
on my daughter's tuition.

I went down by the horses.
Birds were walking in the hay
beside the Appaloosa.
He looked at me sideways
in the swaying dusk.
The wheels of his jawbones,
the great vein in his face.

Sometimes I can hardly breathe.

At Night

it is best
to focus your eyes
a little off to one side;
it is better to know things
drained of their color, to fathom
the black horses cropping
at winter grass,
their white jaws that move
in steady rotation, a sweet sound.

And when they file off to shelter
under the trees
you will find the pale circles of snow
pushed aside, earth opening
its single, steadfast gaze:
towards stars ticking by, one by one, overhead,
the given world flaming precisely out of its frame.

Midwinter Visitant

The boy has forgotten his socks again.
Cold settles in drifts
around his ankles,
the tongue-in-groove floors
bare but for a brief carpet of dust.
His father is not home.
His mother is in the attic retrieving a quilt.
Downstairs in the window seat, he is waiting
because he wants to see it again; there is just
one more chance before his mother says, *Now*
and bedtime begins, the hour or so
of brushing teeth and hearing
stories, the tucking in,
the soft singing.
He will be alone all night
and soon, a night too long to fill completely
with sleep, the cold so vivid beyond
the walls—the house banked by drifts of snow—
his blood will freeze, he is certain, in the small sack
of his body. He has fogotten his socks,
the thick pair his mother left at the foot
of his bed; his hair
is wet from the bath; the front window
faces the street, is smoked with frost.
He can hear his mother say
his name, say, *Where are you?*
and now she is coming down the stairs
as he watches and waits.
The streetlamp drops its light
into the snow; there are no cars, no people walking home.
His mother is on the landing, she can see
him now, can see he's forgotten

his socks, she is about
to say, *Now.*
He watches the street for it,
his forehead pressed against the glass—
he can hear the tick of snow settling
in the basement window wells,
the gentle hum
of the streetlamp.
Now, she says
as it rounds the corner, *Right now*
as it moves into a gallop, the piebald mare
that *Isn't there,* his father says,
There isn't a horse for miles,
though it runs past the house
through the falling light, the faint blur
of flurries just beginning,
the snow-dust that ages all that is motionless,
limns the cars and trash cans
in soft grays and vague whites, fills
the tire tracks and footprints,
the scalloped hollows of hooves,
until the trail of presence
is unprovable, just a whisper
stranded in a child's mouth.

Like Horses

Sometimes in winter just before dark
all the answers seem to be
right there, waiting
in the blue light of cold,
still and indifferent
as horses turned out in bare fields.

If I call softly, maybe one will come,
let me grasp the thick mane
and swing up on its back.
If I call, maybe one will let me ride.

But I stand silent, questions,
silver fish, fluttering
on my tongue, my whole life
water and worry. How could I hope
to bridle such resolute muscle and bone?

Steam smokes from their haunches.
They switch their blue tails,
shrug cold from withers to flanks,
and move off slowly,
looking back at me, their luminous eyes
inscrutable as deep water.

Horse

Among sixteen horses on the western slope
weathering the sleet and sunshine, reflecting field-lit
countours, one where I might bring my face to its cheek, feel

the eyelash of its thought, see myself reflected there, hand
extended—No, the horse had seen the early flash upon
a winter clarity, restaged on the iris of its companion,

and they whitened together in the comet's return. They bolted
at the man of Tarsus kept blind, who kept his name
staggering among the waiting husks, the sleepers beneath

patches of ice and tufts of bunchgrass. This horse watched
my mother as a girl passing in a train, fence posts
pulling to where the two-lane county road brought me

to the length of the animal's moment, which is always, skin
taut around the mouth, older than the skies that cured
the hide-locked region around its eye—avuncular, and at center

an eddy of weather and dust sifting the afternoons and roads,
the cave aperture where the stone holds its ground.
The animal did not move, I came no closer.

Near Winter

In the horse breath weather I remember...
—Carolyn Forche

This belongs to you alone.
It looks after my life and yours without
asking questions. It holds me in my own
eye country near winter, going about
with secrets you do not, could not, know.
Clabbered with floes, the millpond will jilt
and break the sky it holds. I know. I go
to lead the young horse out, her body built
with chill brown rain. A passing train
veils her neck arc with thunder, raising
sorrel hair from skin of grass and grain.
Our mouths, from which air leaves praising,
open. There is white breath between us,
between you and me, what we cannot discuss.

Nosing sisal ropes, the bay gelding waits
to be shod with the smith's winter cleats.
Already a late November wind opens gates
and scuds barn floors. The horse meets
his farrier with keen ears. The lean man's
shirt is woven with blue wood smoke.
A leather apron shines at his knees. Hands
hold shoe and hammer steady until one stroke
strikes nerve. Rearing, the horse scrapes
his high head, leaving blazed hide on
a loft joist. Swaying on his legs, he gapes
through blood, looking at me around his wound.
It's hard to feed such a face, more difficult

to bridle one without nail-sharp guilt.

Over the forge's fire, I melt
from white to clear the pan of pork fat
I rendered from the side bark, gut, suet
and skin. I smear the grease on the flat
raw face of the gelding. Blood still drains
from the blue horn of his quicked hoof.
I unsnap him from the tie post, lead his stains
across the planking and outside to the roof
cast shade on the barn's north side. Here
a drift of snow stays hidden safe from sun.
The hurt horse and I wade in to let his sore
hoof numb. Fretting the fence, the stallion
spins from the gimpy track, fearing the scent,
edgy and urgent in his flag of movement.

The exploded marrow of chicken bone
is the pupil of the gelding's eye opening.
He's listless from standing, blown
into walking on, his face salve glistening
like ice. When he offers, I let him wander.
Instead of riding, I spare his deadened foot
and walk beside him. He leads to a river
banked with the snarled pitch of cedar root
craning out of the ground for a better view.
Now he listens for the mare to lope the lane
toward us. Only the wind rouses to pursue
us over the tomb of ground. The horse's mane
stings into my face when he pauses, stands
and turns his head, breathing into my hands.

It begins to snow flakes heavy with waiting.
If we were in a fast car heading for home up
the road, they'd seem to be driven into colliding
with the windshield. But we walk and they drop.
Snow won't reflect us like the river does.

Bend and see: it shows us instead the ancient
plot of grey that relieves us of ourselves.

But snow can shine where our image isn't.
The horse wonders what I've stopped for.
He turns to me and I to him;
the salve of his face is a mirror
returning me to him as victim.
It's not what I should speak of—
I reach and push him away with my glove.

The flushed edge of horizon is the color
of harm. Over a year ago the vet knifed
the horse's hide open, tugged at the gore
of glands and sinews, freed parts to lift
from the scrotal pocket. The cords were thick
as writing sticks. A winching, gritty sound
cut them through. I buried the lymph slick
parts with lime in the pounded paddock ground
the gelding and I now cross toward the barn.
We pass the light pole marking the place.
Its beams poke my bedroom window to darn
my blanket by night and whiten my face.
In this horse breath weather I remember
the warm hurt scent, the slit skin color.

Night falls into the open afternoon
and I drag to the house through rising snow
that pushes dark back up to encircle its moon,
the nave of light and dark. The land's glow
blears my eyes with cold and tears and dream.
I see a sequence of women in the cured tamarack
of dock moorings. The sluggish grey stream
is dishwater waiting to be drained. Gazing back
the women stand in to their waists. Headbare
I enter my bright kitchen of the kill
where parings of potato scent the air

with dirt. I peel lemon, trim chilled bluegill
and count: two more fish heads, like gargoyles
glaring, will be nailed to the boathouse walls.

In sleep I see a horse with full nostrils
larger than my head. He's breathing the lake,
snorting my hair into stalks, stems and tendrils
of woodbine and ivy fresh red with dusk. Awake,
the lake rises from its bed, standing up sheer
as a museum of water moving with light. You walk
into it deep, past breathing, leaving me here.
Then the lake lowers, freezes, holds its ice back
from the river's clear mouth the way a yellow flame
doesn't touch upon its wick. The candle burns
in a kitchen window across the lake and lame
horses approach, scraping ice in root patterns.
I awake and feel the press of a damp mattress
breathing, breathing up against my breasts.

When the men rein in and dismount
their spur rowels startle the ground with silver.
The air is furred with the rasped count
of their lungs. They've cut through the river
and ice, like niter, crusts their stiff pants.
At dinner they sort out bones and salt russet
potatoes. At night I fit the day's sturdy remnants
into dream quilts. My breath goes out quiet
and invisible, the plainer poem, the one
like a woman who doesn't draw any notice to herself.
It's slight air going out, never to be frozen,
broken or lost, but traded for other life.
Come spring it will be in
the curled squirrel just born.

Feeding Horses During Snow

1

You must walk out to the horses. The pasture grass
glazed and the ice crunches underfoot; your arms
loaded with hay.
You know the horses are cold, their backs and manes
covered in white lace.
They quiver, stand and murmur at a far corner
beneath two elms that, leafless,
provide only comfortable presence, warm recollection.
Wind pushes, nudges, spurs.
You see how it is: the horses' heads bowed, bottom lips
pouting, their impatient hoof-stomp, neck-sway,
the nostril-steam.

2

Snow's haze makes small even the largest things: the barn
reduced, the trees.
The gray dissolving distance between you and
your neighbors,
lines of aspen, twists of raspberry, a progression of fence
rows—these all fade.
You know yourself as the cold which strides to
meet the horses
who, when wind began its cooling, danced and tossed
their heads, farted as they bolted, tails up,
feeling good. The geldings are now but spirits—you
must click your tongue to
stir them, you must summon their names aloud
and prayerfully: Bart, Jed, Rusty, Bob.

3

You know how it is with them. All that white weight
        like horse knowledge. When they turn their heads,
nickering and sighing, puffing steam,
        they don't see you. Do not hear your boots cutting
snow, breaking grass,
do not feel the layers that house the unfamiliar animal
stalking their way,
        do not see your face, not you who blankets,
saddles, cinches them,
bits them, rides them, but the hay that they want,
        the alfalfa heat, the green and necessary something.

Winter Scene at Evening Stables

Let's say, five o'clock in mid-December. You're down
at evening stables, your quilted Carhartt's on.
The bare brown hills roll pink with color
borrowed from tomorrow, and white's in every word
you mumble to the dogs. Your neighbor's barn's
a line of yellow squares, as yours must shine for her.
She's younger than you, has yet to get her horses in.

Each halter on its hook, water buckets full,
rakes and pitch-forks put away, you've had your whiff
of summer in the open bales of clover and alfalfa hay.
The horses have that look they get—thoughtful, far away—
chewing grain. Oh, sure, you think about Tahiti.
Or living life one wall away from other lives.
How it is to take your coffee back to bed
and read til nine. But then you'd have to lock the house.
And always pee inside. You'd weed and mow
for stranger's eyes. God knows what all.

Halfway up the hill, the dogs turn and wait.
Your neighbor leads two horses in
as yours stand deep in appetite. Their slopes of neck and rump
and counter-curving spines gleam under yellow light.
Another ordinary day. You flip the switch and shut the door.
Whatever ordinary means.

A Thousand Genuflections

Winter mornings when I call her,
out of falling snow she trots
into view, her tail and mane
made flame by movement, carrying,
as line and motion, back into air
her shape and substance—like fire
into heat into light, turns
the candle takes, burning.
And her head—her senses,
every one is a scout sent out
ahead of her, behind, beside:
her eye upon me, over the distance,
her ear, its million listeners,
delicate and vast her nose, her mouth,
her voice upon me, closing the distance.
I could just put the buckets down
and go, but I kneel to hold them
as she eats, as she drinks, to be
this close. For something of myself
lives here, stripped of the knowing
that is not knowing, a single thing
from the least webbed tissues
of the heart straight to the tips
of the guardhairs that shimmer off
beyond my sight into air, the grasses,
grain, the water, light.
I've come like this each day
for years across the hard winters,
seeing a figure for the thing itself,
divine—appetite and breath,
flesh and attention. This morning
her presence asks of me: And might
you be your body? Might we be
not the figure, but the thing itself?

Relativity in January

When the mare gallops
the sight of the valley
alive in her mane
is the only warmth drawn from morning,
from a desolate barn,
monastic pines, or a crescent moon
hung on blue. At ten above,
after yesterday's snow,
anything can noun its way
out of motion, so ignorance
and knowledge get a solid look
at each other, see what equals see.
Tending to water and hay,
I understand that old farmer
who recorded the name of every person
he ever met because those words alone
carried enough weight
to realize his life, a book
worth kissing as he put it.
Nosefirst, the mare stretches
for another apple and while she eats
I run my hands
through her thick winter coat,
edge my face down her neck
breathing the dark incense,
feeling for a minute those miles
of blood between here
and summer, a loneliness so welcome
it could take the shape
of nothing lonely. Deep snow
and clear sky seem to trade
cold around us. At this point
there's no sound
to catch how bodies
become one with themselves,
but there should be.

With the Horse in the Winter Pasture

Zero degrees, no wind, and barely
the January sun has begun to ripen.
You, who all day yesterday
brooked with your body
a brutal storm from the north,
now graze as amiably over the snow
and hay as if it were August.
Or more so: free of the flies, free
of the rider—bit, crop, and fetter.
What we endure need not turn us to stone,
insists the gray bird in the birch-on-blue,
who survives in her three least notes.
And so, today, I am victim
of nothing, nor am I mistress, just
hanging around the sun-catching corner
as if it were after school, a fool,
a woman carrying on like a girl.
I throw my arm over your withers
and bury my face in your neck:
white plush, pulse, smell
of woodsmoke. The child is alive
who prayed by her bed to die.

Afternoon

Wind is moving the pond's surface.
The light dims.
The leaves on the aspen stir.

Here is fresh manure, upturned black soil,
an open field of tall damp grass,
a human face pressed
into a horse's sun-warmed flank.

Welcome Dance

Weekends in Lincoln we camp out
at the tractor shed until the house is built
and walk the old dirt roads. Where the plow
has pushed the snow off Quaker Street
there's ice—I watch my step, plant boots with care.

Hoofprints dent white crust where deer
have pawed for apples beneath bare trees.
A neighbor's dog gives howl; she calls him in.
Is it the dog or neighbor's voice that sets
the horses off? The dark kicks high and snorts,

red bobs his head, white wheels around a pile
of hay, a full-speed sprint, hooves pounding hard.
I think of cowboy movies, where the mount
was spurred to gallop, mane straight out behind
as dried out prairie scrolled across the screen.

They've worked a sweat, these three, a gamy heat.
Against the fence, they halt and snort;
sides heave, the dark one shakes his head,
red twirls, then off on one more loop.
White slips on ice, too sharp around the turn,

regains control. The red one neighs;
the others answer suit. They eye the strangers,
take another lap. What got to them?
The slender beam of winter sun? Crisp wind?
No matter—praise be for such a welcome dance.

LOUELLA BRYANT

Cariña

In Havana once, you walked the seawall
in the wind. Bleeding fuchsia lined the way
and sun and salt spray clung to you.
"Cariña," you heard, and blushing,
turned. Your young body, a catchall of praise.
More gullible, you were, than vain,
so eager for the praise of men, sifting it out
even from an unknown language: cute, dear.

You've had to move that life aside
to make room for this one. Today,
you're here among chicory and confused grasses.
A bird calls, a sound like tinkling glass.
You see what you have longed to see,
so far absent from your life. A myth.
A miniature horse, but the horn grows

out of your imagination. *Cariña*
Dainty freak. The size of a sheep,
belly braced on short, tent-pole legs.
Mane, the mane is an emblem, a means
to swing up, on top of, away. The horn
you'd let nudge you to the end of the earth.

Cariña. It could be a cognate of
careening. Precarious. The way
a young woman might need to fight her way
out of a car or dark basement. For its size
you love the little horse. For the ground
it covers and doesn't want to leave.
The care it causes another creature to take
to step over or around, not trample it.

Conversion of Saint Paul

– Oil on canvas, 1601

Saul's body opens, arms wide & his legs
splayed like a woman welcoming her lover.

Why persecutest thou me? This plea the same
refrain I utter each night, my bed dark

as the oil out of which Caravaggio's figures
surface, spotlit. A skewbald's mane gleams

white, pale foreleg frozen over its rider's
thrown figure, the servant's bare toes. Faith

is a wrestling, like bridling an animal, metal
bit & headstall fitted tight. Not all is light.

The horse's rump & side, its patches brown
& wide, remind us where divinity resides:

an iron shoe, a man's naked leg, & the veins
that run like a rain-swollen river down

its length. The servant's fingers close on
the leather reins as he attends to the matter

at hand, unable to forget the long road
ahead. His forehead furrows its loose skin,

both eyes sunk in a chiaroscuro shadow.
He is the one I choose to acknowledge.

In him, the presence of the divine, tucked
into this scene's far corner—its equine power,

all bunched muscle & bone. Then his head,
inclined in prayer, having dared take hold.

The Lamed Mare

She's afraid of that horse, and she's right to be.
It's a mare, not young, but when the wind
Picks up and she scents distant prairie hay,
She lifts her tail, arches neck, and whinnies.
She doesn't even notice us much, women
Who walk her on frayed lead ropes, tie her
In the breezeway, examine her hooves' striped
Horn, one designed to lameness, a hole
In the sole where the farrier sliced away
What floored the soreness. An abscess gushed,
Making everyone sick and relieved at once,
Here's the problem, soon she'll be sound—
And nothing's worse when what you want is
Distance from hazard, anything but to mount
The living mare. The woman who paid cold cash
For this mare has only met me twice before.
I said, *they were my life, horses,* spun out
Stories of learning to ride, one day noticing
Something small about my mind or body,
I'd never be what I'd dreamed of becoming,
The rider whose touch speaks to calm the horse
That doesn't trust a word it's heard from humans.
Our minds, what we sell ourselves, something
To make up for lack of four legs, ought to be
Worth more than plain talk. I gave up horses.
Took up talk. But the past doesn't die. Doesn't
Even fade, not much, for all the paper
Stapled over memory, like those fly-specked
Bulletins hung in every bar, phone numbers
Of blacksmiths, Labrador puppies for sale.

Cross-tied, the mare's placid. Allows her hoof

To be soaked in a bucket, for whatever good
That does. It gives us humans hope we're
Solving problems, staving off the fear of riding
The talked-of lameness stands in to conceal,
Whatever measure of judgment and error is
Meant, moving through animal paces, pretense
Of joining, halting rhythms, marked stress:
In the diagrams I studied, dotted lines bisected
The rider's stance, closed angles at knee and ankle,
Wrong, right, left, right, oddly quicker to recall
Now it doesn't matter to me at all. We finish
Grooming, lead the mare to the metal-poled
Paddock to longe in halter. The way I learned was
Incorrect but I always did it anyway, panged
By remembered language. The mare flirts,
Calling the stolid nags turned out on pasture;
She'd rather be one of them, orders them to move
The way she would, uncoiling the springs
Of the shoulder just for how it feels. But they're
Beyond it. I'm sizing up the mare's gait. She's
Not really lame. If you wanted to ride her, you
Could, a little, for the leather and horsehair
Between your legs. Teen-aged, I never thought
It sexual. It was. But not arousing. Not between
The legs, at least, somewhere else, paragraphs
Read in texts on horsemanship, revised in talk
At horse shows: *He's going terrible today.*
Doesn't like the crowd. Kids with umbrellas,
The trailer ride, look how he's shortened
His stride... The woman longes the lively mare,
Never lets on, hopes it's been so long for me
I've forgotten fear, for body or the whole sweet
Self, exists. But I'll never forget the falls and
Blows I took in silence so no one would know.
I almost wept with terror before the ribbons
Were called and I had to stop pretending I
Hadn't looked as clumsy as I felt, posting the trot,
Sitting, willing my stiff spine would melt.

We invented horses to bring us back to earth.

Touching the mare, Arab, I felt something
I'd said was lost. Said it in sleep, dreams of stabled
Horses starved to death, as, I must've thought
In waking consciousness, my body had broken
From earth's body, like stars plunging away
From the sun, tails streaming the way kept horses'
Never do, wrapped in bags to shut out dirt that loses
Showmanship and halter classes. Different
Names for the same idea? I don't remember.
That kind of competition lost its charm after
I'd accepted other people could do it better.
I know what I was after then. What a horse
Wants is luck of another color. Call it dappled,
Same as the gelding I taught to shake hands.
I loved him, loved showing off, saw us in the eyes
Of the man in visored cap standing with clipboard
In ring's center. Shaking hands. That's what
Men do when they meet. They mean nothing
By it, though I've read the gesture was invented
To prove peaceful intentions. Some business
To be accomplished besides dying. I wanted
My horse to say, even an animal could see
What I was, a worthy girl, who knew the rules,
Calling "whoa" and "can-ter." We used to say
"Ho" when we wanted to stop. That was years ago.
The word means something worse now, everyone
Knows it does. I heard the woman shout WOE
When she wearied of watching the warped circle
The mare tramped out of moistened clay. WOE.

What remains when we're so human we only live
In mind and talk. I touched the mare's smooth
Dusty flank, I sat on a tack trunk and stared.
And woe called above me like swallows that twitter
At sundown, swimming the dusky sky like bats,
You know them by their scorn for silence.
It doesn't matter what fools we look when
Horses throw us down. If we survive, we rise
Again, shouting *woe, woe,* scrambling for dropped
Reins before real trouble sets in, loss of horses

Worse than the pun we forget has other meaning
When we've said it so often to mean, *just stop.*
We do. We all do. Sometimes too soon. Telling
Ourselves we had our reasons. Waking from
Dreams that insisted we didn't know, couldn't
Admit, our harsh sorrows. Sharply human woes.

The Horses Before They Start

All night   I curry the horses
                             Steaming and panting
Breathing fire in my body
          Stroke   quiet   rest…

Of course it is better to travel

Letting the day hit up against your life
                                        Pretending eternity is not
Above your head

Wanting more love than you
Can use.

Where do the horses go when

You forget them?
This is where you will
                             Go too.

The horses are in a tall barn

With shiny steel bars. Inside

Each is a heart moving. Now

The open field
          They run against a V shaped
          Sky through the
Spontaneous world
          Brushing away their footprints in the dust. How
          Much movement is allowed…

Sunflowers ahead drying on the stalk
Trampled now

Full throated birds urge them on,
Through Sycamores
Lining   brown   bark

They move forward away
Then   one foot in front of the other

Now streaming past.

Harvest

When you're young and out at night
searching for your lost pony
the black sky leans on your shoulders
like a rucksack full of sins.

Under invisible stars
you carry the burdens: gates left unlatched;
temper-tantrums that sent the pony
bucking away in his field

and all those times
you laughed at the farmer,
a dour man who watched the sky
as harvest approached—

watched the corn ripen while you
and your pony cut the corners
of those brittle fields, flattening
his bread and butter.

When you're young and out at night
calling for your black pony
through field after field of grain
an owl flings itself down from an oak

and you make vows.
If only you could find the pony
but remember too the vows
you make and remake on a dark night, searching.

Zaraf's Star

Walking changes as dusk starts to gather.
We're not able or sure anymore.
We don't know the path— and if we did know it,

we wouldn't go on. We're afraid of the dark
lowering its heavy, long familiarity
down on the grass. We're afraid of the night,

moonless, desert, California,
making us stumble. We shouldn't be lost,
out here like demons just at the border

that touches us solid, as if we were gone.
She's leading me on a path as narrow
as sisters can share. We pound back down the mesa.

Each of our feet finds its own way, delving
into the gulley whose trees never answer
until, with steps slapping soft as bandits,

I slow on the path, imagining horses.

Stretching necks right out of the stones,
out of the dusk where dark has achieved our
bodies, drawn by the strides that my sister

takes like a rider, Zaraf's Star,
Fashad, Kashmir, Arabian horses
raise her up with motionless shadow

so she can ride (like a rider, she walks),
cantering, encompassing the pace of the mountain.

Out in a landscape to curl or be curled in,

hunched like riders or curling like rides,
under the fairy-tale oaks of the mesa
that hide sleeping children or horses inside,

we talk about horses like hers who run carefully,
with thinner ankles, and mustangs who, fast,
wild grown, wild on the path to blackness,

hunger like stars reaching down for dark leaves.

Sonnets to Orpheus I:11

RAINER MARIA RILKE

Sieh den Himmel. Heißt kein Sternbild "Reiter"?
Denn dies ist uns seltsam eingeprägt:
Dieser Stolz aus Erde. Und ein zweiter,
der ihn treibt und hält und den er trägt.

Ist nicht so, gejagt und dann gebändigt,
diese sehnige Natur des Seins?
Weg und Wendung. Doch ein Druck verständigt.
Neue Weite. Und die zwei sind eins.

Aber sind sie's? Oder meinen beide
nicht den Weg, den sie zusammen tun?
Namenlos schon trennt sie Tisch und Weide.

Auch die sternische Verbindung trügt.
Doch uns freue eine Weile nun
der Figur zu glauben. Das genügt.

~

Scan the heavens. Where's the constellation
that's called "horseman"? Strangely we're imprinted
with this pride of earth. And there's another,
urging, checking it, and carried by it.

Isn't our own nature's sinewy being
just like this—first whipped, and then reined in?
Trail and turning. Pressure does the guiding.
New expanses. And the two are one.

Are they really, though? Are they committed
to the road they're traveling together?
Table, pasture—gulfs apart already.

Star connections also prove deceptive.
Let us only for awhile enjoy
our belief in them. That is enough.

Above Beaver Creek, Colorado

I

Nine years ago, as I was crossing a break
in timberline above Beaver Creek with a brisk

wind singing its wistful tune through
those woods, the snowy slopes of hills filled

with the gold of sunset opening before me.
Suddenly, one horse, thinner than any I had

ever seen, stood still and dark on a nearby
ridge just dimming in the developing veil

of dusk. Its spine caved, the rib cage
drooped as if for too long it had hauled

an unendurable weight. That apparition's
long legs appeared trapped in their own

tracks and seemed as stiff as the season's
brittle branches. Head bowed, slow clouds

of breath floated in the cold air. Steam
rose from its throat and shoulders as if even

the heat of that body had finally abandoned
all hope. In the false warmth of that last light,

every flinch, each involuntary and shivering
motion of relaxed or tensed muscle, showed

beneath its now inadequate hide. Although
I could not say how long ago this loner

may have strayed away from its herd,
I had no doubt about how late the hour.

II

And as I watched, I was reminded how little
time yet remained before the black hand

of sky held us both. Finally, as though
I had barely cared to notice, I lost sight

of that specter when it vanished back
into the trees and the tight cover of night

closed over that canyon. Sometimes
in late winter, when the sun settles again

beyond a distant hillside and evening
fades to gray haze quickly thickening

over everything, I will think of the cold,
of a stark far-off Colorado landscape,

and of how that horse's hoof prints
disappeared into the darkness. Once more,

in another desperate attempt at preservation,
I will imagine that frail animal—touched

by twilight, engaged in a dance for balance,
its fragile shadow loping along a white

incline, shaggy mane blowing in a mountain
downdraft, its ragged tail still trailing across

the deep snow—as if giving life in such
a manner were possible. Tonight, here

where I lie before sleep, listening to wind slip
through cedars, I'd like to believe I'm right.

Cuyama Valley, California

With special thanks to Shyboy and Monty Roberts

Moths draw nectar from
Yucca blooms
So white that the moon
Lights them, candles
Sprung up from granite, quartz, feldspar.

The sun pushes across the horizon,
burnt orange and cream.
Its light strikes sycamores
that line riverbeds.
Bees set out for sages.
Lark sparrows come alive.

Through sagebrush, wild mustangs lope,
against the lilac backdrop
Of the Calientes.
Over stretches of lush green,
grasses the color of honey,
Against strands of ocher,
The pigeon white sky,
They backup up dust.

One mustang leads the herd.
The sun lights up his rust coat,
black mane,
the white sock on his left hind leg,
feathers on his fetlocks.

Muscles swell his neck and shoulders,
Forelocks wild between his eyes.
He picks up speed,
His neck arched,

His tail erect,
long and full,
A black veil
Over haunches
And hocks.

This horse, powerful enough
To shift the vast plates
Of the San Andreas Fault,
Takes the breath out of me.

Oh, God, don't let me die yet,
Even if my sojourn here
Is no more than a day,
A sliver of blue,
between two nights.

Meeting the Horse

For Steve T. and Tex

I'm half afraid to be standing here
holding onto his lead rope
which he sways against like a ship,
twelve hundred pounds of dun-colored
strength leaning to reach the red clover,
chinked muscle bunching over one eye
as he chews and my friend pares
thin rinds of horn from his feet.

I'm not sure where we're going,
my body tells him, off balance, pitched
too far back in the stirrups, hands uncertain,
slack on the reins, but he is the soul
of courtesy as we walk to the water tank,
then to the gate, working his delicate
black dappled lips around
both sides of the snaffle.

The spirited ways of his ancestors
whisper across an ocean of sage
like the spellbound deer grazing near him
at night, their wild world flaring his nostrils:
rock dust, obsidian, juniper husk,
black mountain, hacked blue outcrop of shale
held in the dark trance of his iris
under the alkali moon.

Coffin Bone

It is
one thing not
to ride. But
not to end
afternoons
scooping grain,
not run
a hand
neck-flank-rump,
as he turns in
his stall,
not once
a day,
smell horse.

A Set of Hoofprints

A horse left this track as he walked.
Here a fore hoof made its print,
obscured as if by superscript
when hind came down where fore had been.
He turns toward home, extends his walk
till hind far overreaches fore
and every hoofprint is distinct.
You stand remembering how it felt
to sit those homeward-swinging strides,
to draw up by the darkening barn
and let your own feet touch the ground.

Living Without Horses

I believe in the gift of the horse which is magic
—Maxine Kumin

Living without horses
is like breathing into the lungs
but never further:
never deep into the great cavity below
where horses of emerald and blue
fill the void with their squeals,
their thudding feet,
their waltzes into deep space.

To live without horses
is to slow down on the Sunset Highway
at a glimpse of chestnut rump
or a pair of pricked ears
above a bay face with a kind eye
that gazes toward the forests
draped like shawls over the Coast Range
where bluejays and woodpeckers ring out false alarms

and to breathe in the sweat and dust
of the police horse found unexpectedly
tethered to your parking meter after lunch—
then, at night, to rewind the videotape over
and over as the Budweiser commercial
sends you flying with the royal herd,
manes and tails like curtains of water,
nostrils more finely flared than the shelled human ear,

their elephantine feet
pounding the doors of a shuddering underworld
in the slowest waltz you've ever heard—
until, suddenly
you're hearing it in your abdomen
and it spills over into arteries and bones

pulsing through all your crevices
like blood from the heart's pump.

To live without horses is to carry them with you always:
the one who lifted you over the tiger trap,
the one who kicked you when you deserved it,
and the dappled grey one who lay down under you
and died as you ran away
unable to stay with him on that path
beside the golf course, breathing in
what you would search and search for in the years to come.

Kissing a Horse

Of the two spoiled, barn-sour geldings
we owned that year, it was Red—
skittish and prone to explode
even at fourteen years—who'd let me
hold to my face his own: the massive labyrinthine
caverns of the nostrils, the broad plain
up the head to the eyes. He'd let me stroke
his coarse chin whiskers and take
his soft meaty underlip
in my hands, press my man's carnivorous
kiss to his grass-nipping upper half of one, just
so that I could smell
the long way his breath had come from the rain
and the sun, the lungs and the heart,
from a world that meant no harm.

In My Bones

I know I'm home
In these moonchilled woods.

I've seen the white coast of the Gulf, bleached
so bright it hurt my eyes. There's nowhere to go

Once you get there. So here I'll stay, at least
'Til the bluegill play out in Payne's Creek.

A cloak of foxgrape covers the barbed wire
Down by the cattlegap gate.

Untethered,
My old horse grazes.

Wild Green Grass

Oh man I just saw an old
scabby-coated
chocolate brown
bony-hipped
horse
sway-backed
and at least twenty years old
standing with all his hooves bunched together
and his tail tucked between the cheeks of his ass
stretching his long neck
way out
over the top strand of a barbed-wire fence
and down to the ground
on the other side
to chomp
with his big teeth
on some long strands
of wild green grass

Gas

Wouldn't it be nice, I think, when the blue-haired lady in the doctor's
waiting room bends over the magazine table
and farts, just a little, and violently blushes, wouldn't it be nice if
intestinal gas came embodied in visible clouds
so she could see that her really quite inoffensive pophad only barely
grazed my face before it drifted away?

Besides, for this to have happened now is a nice coincidence because
not an hour ago, while we were on our walk,
my dog was startled by a backfire and jumped straight up like a horse
bucking and that brought back to me
the stable I worked on weekends when I was twelve and a splendid
piebald stallion who whenever he was mounted

would buck just like that, though more hugely, of course, enormous,
gleaming, resplendent, and the woman,
her face abashedly buried in her *Ellenow,* reminded me I'd forgotten
that not the least part of my awe
consisted of the fact that with every jump he took the horse would
powerfully fart, fwap, fwap, fwap,

something never mentioned in the dozens of books about horses and
their riders I devoured in those days.
All that savage grandeur, the steely glinting hooves, the eruptions
driven from the creature's mighty innards:
breath stopped, heart stopped, nostrils madly flared, I didn't know if
I wanted to break him or be him.

Slant of Light

When the day's push of west wind
gasps, then cyclones around,
this big bronc sets to spinning
between north and south and north,
and if my failing sight stretched
from the heights of this perch
I could swing the loop of my eye
a hundred miles to either interstate,
those running slabs, volcanic flow
smoothed and channeled to carry
a heavy world of steel the closest distance
between point and pointless.

And if this bronc and wind don't settle
soon I'll leave this saddle,
this tanned skin of cow stretched
over rawhide, rawhide stretched
and shrunk over a tree
of what all trees are, and land
on earth that gives and gives
but won't give much more than concrete
to the falling timber of this brittle body.

These loess hills hold no rocks
to crack a skull nor scratch a pictograph
to record this or any history,
nor rare earths for trolls to scrabble
out from beneath a grassroot hide,
nor press of the long dead into oil or coal,
and if we melt down here
and are not found we will be
survived only by buttons

and a half-dozen brass conchos.

But if these chaps flap, the wind
turns and the bronc blows even harder,
I might fly away and save my skin
since skin is what I care for,
my own, and the second skin
that I cover with my skin
when I get lucky,
and the grass of earth cattle skin off
each time the earth loops around
the sun the way I'm spinning
from west to east to west
so that in the long light breaking
beneath the skyline clouds
I spin from sundown to sunrise
to sundown, each quick day an aging,
until I grow long in tooth
and the straight line of my spine
curves like a question within a cloud
of fine hoof-raised dust.

Rising day and falling night,
the bronc and I cut and re-cut
the turning light
in our three-dimensional shapes
this way and that and back,
tie hard and fast to the wind
long as we blow. No matter
our other sins, I know
that pounding hoof nor falling man
will leave no worse than they have lived—
light on the land.

Jumping Jack is a Mexican Horse

Jumping Jack is a Mexican horse.
And though he was born in America,
The soft roll of Spanish tongue still
Perks his ears. Miles Homer,
At 90 years old, says he goes to Mexico
For the warm air every winter.

He says Rocky Mountain winters
Crush across his joints like a wild horse
Stampede. He prefers Mexico,
Says it feels more like the America
From his youth. After Miles Homer
Returned from the war, he still

Longed to fish the Alpine still
Waters of the high country. When winter
Broke from the mountains, Miles Homer,
Every year, would saddle up his horse
To hunt spring wildflowers in America
Along the Sierra Nevada and into Mexico

Along the San Pedro Mártir. Mexico,
Washboard roads and unmarked trails, still
Hasn't changed much. While in America,
Someone's lighter or faster, and winter
Doesn't keep people out. Horses
Aren't even used. But Miles Homer,

He says he's seen enough. Miles Homer
Hangs his head like fitweed. From Mexico,
With a two-hundred dollar pregnant horse
He hauled across the border, it is still

There—that longing for a winter
That doesn't come, and an America,

A map-less, trail-less, old-growth America
He can't seem to let go of. Miles Homer
Pulls his flower press, at the end of winter,
From his pack-saddle purchased from Mexico.
Inside, Colter's Lupine, dried, the still
Flowers presented on the page. Horse

Hair strands tangle to the still pressed winter
Leaves gathered in Mexico. Miles Homer
Slowly feeds each delicate stem to his horse.

Wild Horses, Placitas

This old village is known for its horses, wild herds
that consider these foothills their home. They are said
to have run here for centuries, since they were left
by the conquistadores. You rarely will catch
any glimpse—only traces, the dust cloud kicked up
or the high-pitched calls traveling far in the cold
morning air. Very soon after moving out West,
I encountered them, first those mysterious calls
at the break of a dawn, re-inventing my ear
and my eye and the day and the trail with a still
unexplainable peace, like a long desert rain

but then, suddenly breaking, the radio's news
like a murder.

Why is it, again and again,
we will know of such beauty just as it is lost,
one herd harvested, auctioned—the lead stallion's neck
snapped, as he tried to resist. On a morning like this,
I can't help but want one, at least one mystery
to remain—I want something that large and that fast
and that—costly—to still be out there running free
to have even the tiniest possibility
on an average morning, on waking, or heading
off to work in the city, our sprawling Albuquerque
to hear their hoofbeats in the valley—echoing.

Jack

How pleasant the yellow butter
melting on white kernels, the meniscus
of red wine that coats the insides of our goblets

where we sit with sturdy friends as old as we are
after shucking the garden's last Silver Queen
and setting husks and stalks aside for the horses

the last two of our lives, still noble to look upon:
our first foal, now a bossy mare of 28
which calibrates to 84 in people years

and my chestnut gelding, not exactly a youngster
at 22. Every year, the end of summer
lazy and golden, invites grief and regret:

suddenly it's 1980, winter batters us,
winds strike like cruelty out of Dickens. Somehow
we have seven horses for six stalls. One of them,

a big-nosed roan gelding, calm as a president's portrait
lives in the rectangle that leads to the stalls. We call it
the motel lobby. Wise old campaigner, he dunks his

hay in the water bucket to soften it, then visits the others
who hang their heads over their Dutch doors. Sometimes
he sprawls out flat to nap in his commodious quarters.

That spring, in the bustle of grooming
and riding and shoeing, I remember I let him go
to a neighbor I thought was a friend, and the following

fall she sold him down the river. I meant to
but never did go looking for him, to buy him back
and now my old guilt is flooding this twilit table

my guilt is ghosting the candles that pale us to skeletons
the ones we must all become in an as yet unspecified order.
Oh Jack, tethered in what rough stall alone

did you remember that one good winter?

Stories Are Made of Mistakes

I.

Even the pole bean tendrils sought out and gripped their
frames within six hours of my setting them.
One of the things
that is breaking my heart is that I can't trust language to
express any thanks.
My pole beans, my honeybees, my coyotes,
my dog, all my good horses.

2.

The black mare I shouldn't have bought and bought, and once
I had, should have shipped, bucked me, too, the first time
I got up.
But God she was a beauty.
I thought if I just rode her
I could ride her down.
Her name was Sara and we kept it at that.
All she wanted to do was run.
Ears back, flat out, nose pushed
into the next life.
I wanted her to learn to walk.

3.

After about a year of chop I turned her uphill on a good gravel
road and said, "OK, you bitch, you want to run?"
I let go
her head and gave her the steel.
I'd never been on a horse so
fast.
I've never been on one since.
So fast you couldn't

count the beats in the rhythm of her gait.
Suicidal.
But when,
after some miles, she started to flag, I said, “I thought you
wanted to run,” and dug her out again.

4.

The pole bean tendrils sought their frames within six hours
of my setting them.
They broke my heart.
They gripped.

5.

A patch of sunlight mottled the shade.
Whether she never
saw the root that snaked through the shadow or was just too
far in front of herself, I’ll never know.
She stumbled
and fell.
First on her knees then over.
We rasped together
down the gravel road, black mare on top of me.
We rasped
to a halt.
She jumped to her feet.
She stared at me.
I
could see the bone in both her knees.
Ribbons of hide hanging.
Blood like volunteer firemen beginning to rise to the occasion.

6.

Ten years later, today, I’m riding her.
I keep her reined
in most of the time.
She tosses her head, snaps tie-downs.
She dances and whirls, doubles under and rears incessantly.

She makes me the butt of ridicule:
"So, uh, Jim, how old
is that mare?"
"She must be twenty now."
"Don't you think
it's time she was broke?"
Every once in a while I let her
run and break my heart.
Anyone watching stops breathing.

7.

If I ever get to heaven and know who I am, I'd like to over-
hear my daughter tell a story to her children.
"Sometimes
my dad used to ride this black mare..."

Peggy

The name of the horse of my friend's friend,
a farmer's son whose place we'd pass
when we rode out that way I remember,
not his name, just his mare's, Peggy,
a gleaming, well-built gray; surprising,
considering her one-stall plank shed.

I even recall where they lived,
Half-Acre Road—it sounds like Frost,
and looked it: unpaved, silos and barns.
I went back not long ago;
it's built up, with rows on both sides
of bloated tract mansions.

One lot was still empty,
so I stopped and went through and found
that behind the wall of garages and hydrants
the woods had stayed somehow intact,
and wild, wilder; the paths overgrown,
the derelict pond a sink of weeds.

We'd gallop by there, up a hill,
our horses' flanks foaming with sweat,
then we'd skirt Peggy's fields
and cross to more woods, then a meadow,
the scent of which once, mown hay,
was so sweet I taste it still.

But now, the false-mullioned windows,
the developer's scrawny maples, the lawns—
I didn't know what to do with it all,
it just ached, like forgetting someone
you love is dead, and wanting to call them,
and then you remember, and they're dead again.

Four Horse Songs

1. White One

the white horse
from the north clouds
sings from a dakota night
it is a pint of cheap vodka
that keeps him warm
as he dances
two feet off the ground
swaying from bar to bar
drinking his way south
he is the desperate one
who laughs too loud
at his own fate
2. Red One

the red horse
from the eastern sunrise
cannot see the next day
as he chases his life
across the streets of Gallup
he knows only
his red shameful eyes
in the morning
and it becomes
the same day always

3. Gray One

this horse stayed south
too near the railroad tracks
his bones are gray
in the dry sunlight
he wanted to go home

but the tracks always led
to the same place

4. Yellow One

yellow horse
gallops home near Tsaile
the sun is low and almost gone
but he has faith
in its returning

Dressage, or the Attempt at Training the Course of Illness

The numbness migrates,
charts the slowest route from left foot to my ribcage
along the thigh grown accustomed
to gripping a horse's abdomen, squeezing cues of forward,
reverse, *passage, side-pass* right. This numbness presses in, might be
a cue to *me* (*cue* so close to *cure*) to move
or lie down, lord knows which. Maybe this pressure,
both over and under
sensation, could become the thin bristles
—needles and pins is such an inadequate phrase—
of sorrel hair against the skin, soft, yet
irritating, a muscular wall of motion in the space
where nothing touches at all.
Further north, the journey traces
paths along my waist, midsection, settles there, the manifestation
this disease takes as it pleases, imprinting my body by stripping
away sensation and offering something else.
Or perhaps I am the horse,
this numbness squeezing my waist like a leather three-buckle girth,
like legs. Or—I can make it better: a lover's hands there
and there
on my body, holding me so that when I graze
my own hand across my stomach I see him feelingly, the subdued
sensation of someone else's skin pressed against my own,
the feeling of someone else there, but not there.
Look, on my stomach,
Look, if you can, at the invisible colonists finding home in my
neurons.
How they tear myelin, how they eat of my flesh,
invite me to make metaphors for this disease, to comfort, but
I'm sick of it. This is when I pull the reins.

Method

It's exactly the fact that you could die
that let's you forget that you will die.

Unridden colts are ideal
for assuring focus.

As separate now from the muck
of the everyday as you are from the ground,
even the mortgage, your son's
calculus grade, or your husband's mother
ebbing away in her hospital bed

replaced by instinct,
rhythm and sinew,
by unpredictability
and the quickness beneath you.

This suspension
in danger and pleasure is bodily,
pure
and compellingly whole.

The Flying Change

1

The canter has two stride patterns, one on the right lead and one on the left, each a mirror image of the other. The leading foreleg is the last to touch the ground before the moment of suspension in the air. On cantered curves, the horse tends to lead with the inside leg. Turning at liberty, he can change leads without effort during the moment of suspension, but a rider's weight makes this more difficult. The aim of teaching a horse to move beneath you is to remind him how he moved when he was free.

2

A single leaf turns sideways in the wind
in time to save a remnant of the day;
I am lifted like a whipcrack to the moves
I studied on that barbered stretch of ground,
before I schooled myself to drift away

from skills I still possess, but must outlive.
Sometimes when I cup water in my hands
and watch it slip away and disappear,
I see that age will make my hands a sieve;
but for a moment the shifting world suspends

its flight and leans toward the sun once more,
as if to interrupt its mindless plunge
through works and days that will not come again.
I hold myself immobile in bright air,
sustained in time astride the flying change.

Matins

Dawn comes on hard and the peaks take one step back.
Planetary residue eddies in the angling light.
A horse stomps in the yard.
What's it to you?

To apprehend perfection is
To presuppose intention, and we do.
The poem is richer for the writer since
It's my horse.

And it's my neighbor, Frank, in the hospital this time.
Death makes us possessive, I guess.
Its expressiveness depends on imperfection,
Which in turn depends on notions of perfection

Sufficiently out of reach
To prove illusive: *I've known him all my life.*
Roger drives out to bring the cows down for winter
Since Frank is in the hospital.

I see Roger coming ten miles away, pulling horses,
Raising a horsetail of dust at least a mile long
That sizzles down the road
Like a burning fuse.

JAMES GALVIN

Yet Another Life

What else could you do
having been ridden by love
for so long? We should have

expected you to rise up
on hind legs, to kick the stall's
gate in grief, spit out the bit

and bound recklessly into lust's
illusory race. Even so, it hurt
to see one who had run so well

stumbling—as if he wished
for the bullet, an end to what
was broken. Legs no longer

able to carry the weight; stone
laid heavy over her with no
hope for a return to things

as they should have been.
Despite this, the hand held
back, gun again upon the rack.

Today we see you near the river,
tall grass soft on belly, water
cool against flanks, your head

moving up and down to counter
flies. The recognition that scars
bear more than flesh uncut.

For Donald Hall

Paso Fino

What I remember most

is not the fall itself:
the slow inevitable slide
over your shoulder

the tug of hackamore
twisting arm and shoulder
the white rush of fear

not the bone-breaking crack
the grotesque arc
of limb falling forward
the sight of bones through skin

No. What I see is
the mincing return:
nostrils flaring
at blood scent

the sudden shudder of witherskin
and ripple of chestnut muscle
the largo beat of hooves
as you float away

Karin Tells Me Her Dreams of Horses

Ah, she says, her head
angled on the pillow,
eyes closed, the concentrator
across the room thumping
rhythmically, fizzing breath
to the cannula resting
lightly in her nose,
he was so beautiful.
A big bay, brown ears
and nose. But dark, so dark.
And his hair was early
winter growth. You know,
soft but not yet thick.
I brushed him and
brushed him, getting
him ready to saddle.
There were people all
around. They were touching
me, skimming by and there
were horses moving
around. Other horses.

I pull the crocheted throw,
one that must have been
made by a grandmother
or an old aunt, the stitches
perfect, the knots perfect,
up around her shoulders.
Did you ride him, I ask.

No, I didn't. But I dreamed
of mares and foals.

Those sunny Haflingers
running across fields
of alfalfa. I was standing
in the fields surrounded
by their bright bodies,
the bright bodies of
the mothers and their babies.
She opens her eyes
and sees me, my chair pulled
close, grazing on her face.
It's good, I say, that you
remember the details so well.

Bucked

Balanced for that instant
in mid-air, I watched
his rump, in white slow-motion
rise—heart-cleft, perfect—
to deliver the awesome blow.

How beautiful the muscles
of the world in their uses!
Great limbs of trees, waves
scaling seawalls, the moon's
dreadful flex on everything,

heart valves and minute
vessels, the spiraled cues
for weakness that I pass on
to my children: of which
might one ask to be spared?

Pour Vivienne

C'est l'heure, little wren,
little shadow on horseback,
wing of black hair,
little Vivienne.
C'est ton pere—
like a bell being rung:
C'est ton pere, c'est ton pere.
Il est mort, Vivienne.
What must your mother
have said meaning
gone and *forever,*
your father, your prince?
How must the news have struck
when she woke you to tell you:
son coeur
s'est arrete' —?
In which language
can such words be spoken
and not break the spell
of the sleeping child?
Leur princesse,
sur son cheval cheri.
And how will you run again,
small vivid one?
Long-legged,
smelling of grass,
pony and miracle,
wild rush of sun—
as he dreamed of you,
dreamed of you once,
as he dreams now
flying over the field.

Unheimiliche II

Nadie vuelve en forma de caballo,
no hay tal forma, ni en el sueño, más bien la muerte expandió
tus costillas
y dejó que tus ojos se centren en lo oscuro, que anochezcan.
No sé si morir fue una hazaña o tú último ademán, un alzar
las cejas
cuando me ves entrar y todo lo sospechado toma peso. Las
yeguas
de la noche que se paseaban cerca de la espuma fueron un
recordatorio
de ese sueño. Afuera en el patio oigo sus cascos
y avanzo en el núcleo de esa sombra. Eres completamente tú
no tú en coceando, sino por fin tú, anocheciendo.

La carta es el verdadero peso de tu cuerpo. Crin, crin, crin
espesura en un tacto agotado de tocar.

Cuando ibas a morir me enseñaste lo errores en una canción
de cuna.
Cuando ibas a morir comías sopa de habas.
Cuando ibas a morir, las horas en curva,

la carta se derrapo en lo oscuro. Me levanta, la electricidad
de la luna
sobre tu lomo. Reconocerte es leer. Reconocerte,

en el pasmo de que no hay más caballos. Sólo tú y los potros.
Los cascos en la duela
la resonancia de una libertad insospechada. Viajas por el
patio
como un tigre en su jaula. Sin ferocidad. Sin garras. Sólo en
círculo

aludiendo a un sol que conocí brevemente. Oigo tus cascos.
Ahí
el sonido
es la sombra de los vivos. Su melancolía. En un mundo sin
fotografías
ni ceniza, estás tú sin hambre, sin canciones, tu crin, tu crin
en salud
y lo único reconocible son tus ojos que se eclipsan. Todo se
calla
hasta el silencio con su insoportable murmullo. Ahí te
ensanchas,
tus costillas
tus patas ahora sin sarcoma y reconocerte es temblar sin
moverme,
es leer, en la electricidad de la luna que se trata de ti
convertido por fin en ti.

Al amanecer llueve en los establos y los surcos
se inundan. Las yeguas de anoche pisan la ceniza,
el hambre empieza
y los murmullos, la melancolía.

Unheimiliche II

translation by FORREST GANDER

Nobody comes back as a horse,
there's no such thing, not even in dream, it's more likely death
inflated
your ribs
and let your eyes center themselves in the blackness,
darkening.
I don't know if dying was a feat or your last gesture, that arch
in your eyebrows
when you see me come in, when every suspicion takes on
weight. The night's
mares, trotting beside the surf, were a remembrance
of that dream. Outside on the patio I hear their hooves
and I move deeper into the pit of that shadow. You are
completely yourself,

not your upstart self, but you finally, darkening.

The letter is the true weight of your body. Mane, mane, mane
impossibly thick to a touch exhausted from touching.

When you were going to die you taught me the errors in a
cradle song.
When you were going to die you were eating bean soup.
When you were going to die, the hours veered,

the letter skidded in the dark. I get up, the electric moon
at your back. To recognize you is to read. To recognize you,

in the astonishment of no more horses. Only you and the colts.
The dueling hooves,
the resonance of an unforeseen liberty. You walk the patio
like a tiger in its cage. Without malice. Without claws.
Only by circumlocution
alluding to the sun I briefly knew. I hear your hooves. Out
there, the sound
is the shadow of the living. Their melancholy. In a world
with neither photographs
nor ash, there are your hooves, you without hunger, without
songs, your mane, your healthy
mane,
but all I recognize are your eyes in eclipse. Everything hushes
into silence with its unbearable whisper. And so you expand,
your ribs,
your feet now without sarcoma, and to recognize you is to
tremble
without moving,
is to read, under the electric moon that would turn you,
finally,
into yourself.

At dawn it rains in the stables and the ditches
flood. Last night's mares stamp the dust,
the hunger begins
and the murmurs, the melancholy.

Legend with Sea Breeze

When you died I wanted at least to ring
some bells, but there were only clocks
in my town and one emblematic clapper
mounted in a pseudo-park for veterans.
If there had been bells I would have
rung them, the way they used to sound
school bells in the country so children
in my mother's time seemed lit
from the other side with desire
as they ran in from the fields
with schoolbooks over their shoulders.
Once more a yellow infusion of bells

empties like a vat of canaries into
the heart so it is over-full and
the air stumbles above rooftops, and death
in its quicksilver-echo shakes
our marrow with a yellow, trilling
silence. I would have given you that,
though these nightshift workers,
these drinkers in childless taverns, these mothers
of daughters seduced at fourteen — what
can the language of bells say to them
they haven't known first as swallows
blunting the breastbone? No, better

to lead my black horse into that grove
of hemlock and stand awhile. Better
to follow it up Blue Mountain Road
and spend the day with sword ferns,
with the secret agitations of creaturely
forest-loneliness. Or to forage

like a heat-stunned bear
raking the brambles for berries and thinking
only winter, winter, and of crawling
in daylight into the beautiful excess of earth
to meet an equal excess of sleep.
Oh my black horse, what's

the hurry? Stop awhile. I want to carve
his initials into this living tree.
I'm not quite empty enough to believe he's gone,
and that's why the smell of the sea
refreshes these silent boughs, and why
some breath of him is added if I mar the ritual,
if I put utter blackness to use
so a tremor reaches him as hoofbeats, as
my climbing up onto his velvet shoulders
with only love, thunderous sea-starved love,
so in the little town where they lived
they won't exaggerate when they say
in their stone-colored voices

that a horse and a woman flew down
from the mountain, and their eyes looked out
the same, like the petals of black pansies
schoolchildren press into the hollow
at the base of their throats as a sign
of their secret, wordless invincibility.
Whatever you do, don't let them ring any bells.
I'm tired of schooling, of legends, of
those ancient sacrificial bodies dragged to death
by chariots. I just want to ride my black horse,
to see where he goes.

On Learning of a Friend's Illness

For James Wright

The morning is so gray that the grass is gray and the side of the white horse grazing
is as gray and hard as the harsh, insistent wind gnawing the iron surface of the river,
while far off on the other shore, the eruptions from the city seem for once more docile and benign
than the cover of nearly indistinguishable clouds they unfurl to insinuate themselves among.

It's a long while since the issues of mortality have taken me this way. Shivering,
I tramp the thin, bitten track to the first rise, the first descent, and, toiling up again,
I startle out of their brushy hollow the whole herd of wild-eyed, shaggy, unkempt mares,
their necks, rumps, withers, even faces begrimed with patches of the gluey, alluvial mud.

All of them at once, their nostrils flared, their tails flung up over their backs like flags,
are suddenly in flight, plunging and shoving along the narrow furrow of the flood ditch,
bursting from its mouth, charging headlong towards the wires at the pasture's end,
banking finally like one great, graceful wing to scatter down the hillside out of sight.

Only the oldest of them all stays with me, and she, sway-backed, over at the knees,
blind, most likely deaf, still, when I approach her, swings her meager backside to me,
her ears flattening, the imperturbable opals of her eyes gazing resolutely over the bare,

scruffy fields, the scattered pines and stands of third-growth
oak I called a forest once.

I slip up on her, hook her narrow neck, haul her to me,
hold her for a moment, let her go.
I hardly can remember anymore what there ever was out
here that keeps me coming back
to watch the land be amputated by freeways and
developments, and the mares, in their
    sanctuary,
thinning out, reverting, becoming less and less approachable,
more and more the symbols of
    themselves.

How cold it is. The hoofprints in the hardened muck are
frozen lakes, their rims atilt,
their glazed opacities skewered with straw, muddled with
the ancient, ubiquitous manure.
I pick a morsel of it up: scentless, harmless, cool, as
desiccated as an empty hive,
it crumbles in my hand, its weightless, wingless filaments
taken from me by the wind and
    strewn

in a long, surprising arc that wavers once then seems to
burst into a rain of dust.
No comfort here, nothing to say, to try to say, nothing
for anyone. I start the long trek back,
the horses nowhere to be seen, the old one plodding
wearily away to join them,
the river, bitter to look at, and the passionless earth, and
the grasses rushing ceaselessly in
    place.

Even With No Hand To Hold It

after Picasso's Caballo Corneado

The horse holds frozen, her neck-stretched
gullet,   her head back-thrust as if to yowl
no sound she or we could bear,

we bear   a word
gyred to that wail for
warring so that God's our dirty word.   Bear

the horse, her knees wide-splayed to a blade-point
at her breast bone, the un-owned knife, like child-blood,
readying.

Bear the horse and the blade and no hand holding it,
no rider,   it's the horse, her utter quiet arc,   her
neck-stretched throat thrown backward as if to croon

no word that she or we can bear,   we bear that blade-
point keening up from soil that hosts it,   blade below
her lowered half-eviscerated roiled content of the living

body,   her forelegs' folded bones, her stiffened pose
of silence of   —crying higher and a higher
quiet, it's the soundless point : up-thrust from no hate or
hand that she or we see.

Done,   its martyred
now—   has done.   Her breast so
near it will fall for it. Will give it what it wants.
Will fall for wolves   in God's clothing.

The Paper It's Written On

At the millisecond of death, Custer is still on his horse.
A bullet has severed his brain-stem, & he is dead,
but in this instant even he does not know this.
The last strobe of consciousness is passing out of him.
Dead in the saddle, his dead body still on auto
before he disassembles, his horse unaware of his limbo,
he is the treaty imposed & signed with smoke & x's.

On the Fenestra Ovalis

Who has not mistaken the pulse of blood
from behind the ears as footsteps? The trot

of a horse with a burr in its tail? And who has not heard
the hand saw, then seen the cloth to cover the face

of the dead, dragged on the ground for washing?
To hear the grate. To hear the dog's nails

on the steps and the blossom in a sister's hand,
her sandals sliding into the room—the butcher paper

she removes from a velvet box.
To hear a pair of blue insects with diaphanous wings

emerge from the velour, rubbing their glass rattles
against each other.
Always the variable key—

in the distance, the horse drawn cart comes to take
the dead, the weight of the hooves

shake windows of the houses lining the street.
Always the latch and the scratched code of stone tablets

and the sounds that come from those who survive, their lips
looking for an ear. The living, they are not my name

or named in the Latin tongue of the body. They cannot be found
in the voice of the buried who have no hoof,

no blossom, no chord for a dog.

After the Funeral

What I want is a drink,
a long cold slug of dry white wine
drunk like water, hitting bottom with
a warm and spreading jolt, but what I do is
buy a shedding blade to brush the pony

and after she has her grain
and I put ointment in her half-blind eyes,
beginning at her neck, I stroke and stroke
the metal teeth until she stands in
a tan puddle of herself and I am covered too.

No one's picture of a pony — large-headed,
rheumy eyes — but a goer in her day,
she pony-raced and hunted, taught
Victor Borge's grand-kids to ride
Her neck fits underneath my arm.

And after I comb her mane's tangles
and brush her burr-clogged tail to flowing,
I turn her out on evening grass
and think again about the cold white wine.

Brood Mare

Late December under eighteen hours of lights
and she begins to come apart.

Or do I take her apart?
First her pretty red fur
peeling off in clumps.
Then the mournful eyes one at a time,
bright buttons
posing on the ground.

This is sewing.
Snip-snip.
This is the ripper
poking and unraveling
some seam or other.

So she's crazed already
when the wind begins to carry off leaves,
pieces of the pattern,
bit parts.

Just suppose hysteria works this way:
A sliver of glass finds its way in
and can't get back out.

I love her sensitive triangles,
the little frogs coated in mud.
The stony tone of detail work
that never lets go.

And God
how early in the day it is,
to be so tired.

Tamara Stands in Straw

and dreams her long-necked, sweet-grass reveries,
and shifts her weight in the patient way
of horses in the cold.
She will be a long time in this stall,
through the entire season of grass
she will have alfalfa, timothy,
an eight-foot, spare enclosure keeping her dry
on hooves held closed with polymer and wire.
This tall barn covers her strangely,
a mare who's never been kept in;
a worn-out structure roofed with tin,
it magnifies the rain.
I am to stay with her for several hours,
to keep her on her feet till the plastic sets.
The stable-owner sends a thermos of tea
and I drink slowly,
taking in its heat
in the faint warmth of the barn;
while the mare dreams and wakes and drinks
and returns to her hay and then her dreaming,
while darkness tightens to the single shape of horse
and night sounds of iron scud against concrete
through all the layered softnesses of straw.

Cleaning the Sheath

I feel my way beneath the horse's belly
to that swag of cock, a dull clapper
in the midsummer heat, in the thick
of an afternoon. I watch his back
hollow, tail fretting in the sodden air,
while my fingers, nails primly pared,
probe the fleshy pouch, and fumble
the quicksilver fish in its silky retreat,
an eclipse of flesh as easily caught
as a receding wave.

This is a task that begs apology.
This blind intrusion into the heated pocket
of himself, to where this dark harvest—
the thimble-sized berries—release
the darkly fruited heart-smell of private places.

Smegma. They call it smegma.
As if the laval core of the horse, the thing
that quivers his lips, sets his teeth snapping
at the flanks of ripening mares even these
seven castrated years, retains its molten pitch
in this humble essence. I lift it to the light,
the blackened sediment, an oily lubricant
waxing my fingers.

I talk to him, say easy and good boy
even as I'm contemplating what
it must feel like to have this clever implement

of hand rooting about, the impertinent
tug on the retreating shaft,
the alligator feel of old skin falling
away. The minutes grow long and overhead
the sun hums, while around my feet the grit
pelts the dirt in a dry rain.

The horse sighs, shifts his weight against my shoulder
and I understand the nature of his complaint,
the flesh tender, already plumped with mild
edema. I pluck the folds clear to ease
a cool-water sponge into the radiant
flesh and feel him soften, slump
into my hands,

understanding in whatever ways he must,
that there are few ministrations as tender
as these, so that he, this thousand-and-more
pound horse, abides this intrusion, this inexplicable
incursion into the dark of his belly,
even stabled as he is, just shy
of the widening sky,
the high navigation of clouds.

The Gift

When I offer the pear
and he takes it
with first
whiskered lips and then teeth
and soon it is no longer
fruit but goes into
betweenness and vanishment,
turning to pastern
and tail and good wall of the hoof
and small tithing of gold
for the pasture or fire roads—
for always where
there is offering, there is return;
when this happens
and when he is careful even in greed,
even in the undignity
of his foolish—no, it must be
named true—his entirely goofy adoration
and long-tongued worship of pears;
when he knows what is pear,
what is hand, when he looks
in my face as he chews and the crush
slobbers out and foams bright as spent happiness
onto my foot, onto my sleeve,
as I bend then to lift him a wedge he has dropped;
when the heron holds steady in
contemplation not a few feet away,
its eyes once again closed like two stones
that have rested an hour in the sun
and gone back into leaning and dimness,
a little heat kept in them still;
when the late cars sweep by without pause,

without seeing, yet store in the
blue-shadowed beakers their own mild exchanges
of hidden, unwordable sweetness—
then the world is that actress from a Sanskrit poem
whose greatness was showing two feelings at once:
The mercies are boundless. Every country is death's.

Horses

keep hearing them
along the river

making the leaves crack
making the coins spin

in the streets
of the city of horses

where it is always
raining or grieving

Mark Time

Sequence of horses—negatives of actual geldings

foundering near the aqueduct. Clinical, and pastoral.
Sick horses swim out for China

but it's a performance. And it always fails. They're opposed,
the geldings, to cowboys.

Secret gelding speech—something far inside them
beckoning to deer for comfort.

The horses are pristine, with no end. Stallions cake-walk
with other stallions

to choose which. The foamiest horses let
their riders off. Just let everyone be.

Let anyone bring
their lines to the lake and the horses don't swim past.

Instead they disguise, literally disguise
each other because the runners know that comparison

is violent. Then
buckers will watch the geyser become a conceit.

Pupil Dilated

The horse is black.
Like a grackle: bronze-
green flash
when the neck
bends its long face toward me.

Or the horse is a grackle:
yellow-eyed,
short hops forward.
It flies up
like a horse's neck stretching

as it would stretch toward me,
so the muzzle may lip
oats from a flattened palm.
The bird in flight
keeps stretching

upward, hooves cutting
air or running over water,
skidding—there's an oil
skim—purple-green weeps
out and it's down,

down and sliding, as on slick
pavement, and the hide—
The horse's beautiful hide—
It's torn, torn down to red mash,
down to bone and yellow eye.

The air bends down
under the wing.

The air beats down. The wing
beats the air down.
Look down.

Don't look at the bird.
Don't see a horse.

The Torturer's Stallion

Speaking in a voice of moderation
The torturer's stallion outlines the
Reasons he will not be slaughtered.
His tongue blue and red, he
Leans against the fence and pushes
Into the night, bypassing the
Honeysuckle, sure only of mountain air,
Doubting he will make it to the hills,
Feeling the hills talking to his bones.

Sentence

The body of a starving horse cannot forget the size it was born to.

12

In the drought no one speaks of,
the paddocks are nothing but sand
and dung piles cooked hard in the relentless
sun.
What is the point of making the horses
run; they cringe when you try to
communicate through our special
differences
as if the sad chanting of the earth
were a louder thing than the
mutual redness of blood.

Horses and the Human Soul

Undercover investigators in Tallahassee, Florida watched two men break a thoroughbred's right rear leg with a crowbar at 10:10 p.m. The men were part of a nationwide ring that injured horses to collect on insurance policies.

—*The Oregonian*

1

The bay mare lifts her head and listens.
There is darkness, the new moon barely revealing
trunks of scrub oak beside her meadow.

A car door has slammed.
The mare shifts her hoofs in the wet grass,
her belly round with the sweet spring growth.

Frogs are merely a backdrop of sound—
as much part of her world
as the post and rail fence against which

she scratches her rump
or the stamp stamp of Bess and William in the afternoon
when the sun is up and the flies biting.

A figure steps from the oaks, metal scoop in his hand.
He holds it out, jiggles it
till the mare hears the familiar sound of sifting oats.

2

They say when you dream a horse
that horse is your spirit.

Once the horse I dreamed
looked out of a trailer pulled by an old Volvo,

the driver a woman who one day
would teach me something about the spirit.

She drove carefully.
The horse was safe.

When you dream a horse it had better be safe
or we are all in trouble.

Did the investigators hide behind those same scrub oaks? Did they wear grey suits and carry notebooks as they pushed their way through the lush undergrowth? Did their ballpoint pens carry the name of their company? Did they smoke as they waited for the sound of the car or did they talk about money or football or the girls in the office? Did it occur to them then, as the man led the mare back to his friend with the crowbar, that they could stop this before it happened? Did the new moon shed enough light for them to see as the crowbar hit the right rear leg just below the hock, the blood spurted, the rich brown hair mixed with splintered bone, and the mare screamed, or did they have to note which leg it was later, after the arrest? And what happened to their souls? What happened to them? I want to know that.

Contraries and Opposites (Requestrian)

for Enja

When they blew up the building it went down in slow motion—
more like a ton of feathers than the bricks it was.
When
you put down a horse she falls so hard no ton of bricks
could compare.
But if the horse is down, unable to rise,
like the brood mare who, with a two-month foal at her side,
breaks her leg above the hock because the cut-bank caved
and there was a root, the bullet sends her striving straight
into the air, failing to stand one last time.
Then, without
dread or hint of bitterness, the foal noses her mother's
muzzle as more blood than you'd think was in a horse
gushes from the nostrils and the sandy earth accepts it all.
The
filly, because this is no stranger than anything else she's
seen, as the last of the blood and the last of the breath
begin to froth and bubble, serenely sniffs.
That's when
the muzzle of the rifle, its right work done, turns away.

But forget about that.
After the life drains and before
death grins through the mare (no absence but presence, I
swear) there is the sickening moment of nothing in
between.

That space of nothing, not the rifle's report, makes the
filly bolt.

She comes back to sniff and snort when death is
safely in place.
She turns to look at you as if to say what's
next?

The Eyes of a Dark Horse

on the Tantramar Marshes
a dark horse gallops
headlong into the
eye of an oncoming
train
        it is dusk, and
the steel rails glisten

of this much
& no more we
are certain:

they will meet   no brake
will check that heavy mass
of speeding metal   the horse
will not veer from her flight
the essential space lies
between them where

nothing can intervene

ears flattened, haunches
bunching, hooves caught
at that precise moment
when they make no contact
with the ground

she carries the whole of her
world with her plunging
like a planet in the grip
of its sun

it is the eyes of the horse
that Colville has withheld:

what do they see?
it is all we can
wonder about and
it is everything

drawn from a painting by Alex Colville, "Horse and Train"

Death at the Derby

The horse with the broken ankle
bowed, after dust settled, to all who
stood before it, as it always had
having been bred to obedience.
It lowered its head, as if glad
to see the man bringing
the gun, while it waited to feel
the bullet that would calm it beyond
all those days it was cornered
as a colt and raised to race.
With glazed half-dollar eyes, it snorted
only once then it gazed at its owner
who couldn't seem to set his mind
on anything else, but the money
this dying horse might have made,
had it not tripped
while rounding the track,
its mane windy as an angel's;
its fetlocks made for flight.

#41

When he was greasing, Pa was, the jay-pit
Went all along the ridge, and when logs broke
Fellas would yell, "Jay! Jay! Jay!" and all them
Cleared the track. Even the horses they knew
What *jay* meant, 'cause when logs went running
You got the hell off the skid road or you weren't
Never getting off. Well Pa heard 'em yelling
And looked up and saw the logs coming down,
And there was an old mare kindly standing
Slow in the pit.

Well she didn't jay fast enough, and Pa
Says when those logs hit, they hit hard enough
To knock the shoes off her, but they bucked
Her legs beneath her just like a tree, and it
Was a miracle it ain't cut her in two,
Or three if you reckon the back legs would
Be in pieces, but it didn't. It just mowed
Her down, and with no way to get her up
No more, they left her on the ground, not really
Dead but dying.

Practice

I.
We watched the horse die.
It was after I found him down.
After I got him up.
After you called the vet.
After we felt bad about getting her out on a Sunday morning.
After the horse went down again.
After the vet whacked him on the forehead.
After he got back on his feet again.
After he bled.
After the vet said, "I didn't expect that!"
and "We have a dying horse here."
After half the fatal dose.
After he fell and sprang to his feet again.
After he fell and got up again.
After he fell—fighting death with pain.
After the second dose.
After his eyes stared past us.

II.
Two weeks before,
it was Ben and his back hoe,
hands and levers like mating birds.
We had an appointment to watch this horse die.
He stood patiently and took his medicine.
Swayed in the haze of it.
Welcomed the fatal dose, sighed, knelt and lay.
And exhaled.
Left his eyes.

III.
The day after the second horse died,
you hoped God would give you a break
and spare your cousin Tessa.
But he was just giving us practice.

Whist

A horse is put down in
relief, in cat grass and dog tails,

cold rain rubbed, glistening it falls.
How close is safe?

Blood and flesh-warmed water,
no boundary, a loosening about the feet;

in this one, the animals themselves speak.
About what?

A broken chain—the death of a King
they know, and howl

feasting on calm, pushing up
against unfurled stones,

serving notice beside the defect
in long bone, of last wills:

Bury me above ground.
Bury me in sight of you.

The child rider hears breath
forming a new geography

as a headstone, sleeping into
the forgiven, ghostly flesh:

Climb inside my belly, he hears,
brush these flies from my face.

The Trouble with Horses

When our friend's horse died of colic
we took the barn door off,
but the big chestnut was rigid
and slippery to boot. More than once
the ropes gave way, and Ben laid there,
gold hairs igniting the hay.

Finally, we gave up and removed him
piece by piece—hacked the curved neck
from the head, muddy forelegs
from the unshod hooves, cut the good
fly-chaser tail from the muscled rump.

That night I dreamed the earth
was precisely severed. My thoughts
were of my children: how to make
of our scattered lives a family again?
When I woke, I recalled Ben's body
carefully approximated under the mud
we'd shoveled in, trying to hide
what we'd made of him.

Standing by the grave, we'd joked
about worn-out ideologies, our first
broken hearts, and the awful
silence of failed love—then went on naming
all things awkward as a dead horse
and that difficult to put to rest.

The Knacker

The knacker's the one you call
after your horse has died.
He's the one that disposes
of the remains. He says
"If you cain't be there,
stick the check in its ear."

His ear. His ear that once
moved and twitched and
scooped up sound. You look
down at your horse on his side
in the spring grass. Still nostril,
still ear, clouded eye and you
whisper "I'll wait. I'll be here."

The truck turns down the lane,
chains rattling, stained side boards
shifting, the knacker sitting always
solitary behind the wheel.

He wraps sturdy chain around
the hind fetlocks then stoops
to check the tail. This knacker
always checks the tail. He looks
for the clump of scissored hair
that tells him a memento has been
taken to be coiled and pressed
everlasting into a diary.

He studies the tail and finds
the sign, The knacker straightens
his burdened back and strokes
the cold haunch with his crusted
hand. "Well, now," he says
as he tucks soft rags under the
biting chain and turns the winch slowly.

Silk

For almost thirty years David has been talking to Fawn
and now he and I walk out to the meadow
where she stands motionless on three legs.
"Come on girl," David says,
slipping a halter over her head
and leading her to a shady area beneath the pines.

He slings an arm around her neck;
the two stand side by side
her ears point towards David.
"This old Tennessee mare," he tells me,
"smooth as silk.
I could read a book
while she carried me
all the way up Prosper Ridge
to Strawberry Rock,
her head nodding along with her gait."
David removes the halter
and clicks a bullet into place.
"Fawn, old girl," he says
aiming the rifle at her forehead.
Her head swivels following his voice;
there is a dull pop-gun sound.
Fawn falls and David squats beside her
smoothing her shoulder,
still talking.

I sometimes picture David and me
digging the packed soil,
dragging Fawn into the hole,
her shoulder poking up through the earth.
We tuck her feet against her belly,

PETER A. NASH

shovel dirt, then stand around the stain
looking at the sky.
But it wasn't like that.
David had arranged with Pete Cook
to come with his yellow excavator.
It takes Pete just a few minutes to dig the hole
and dump Fawn in with the scoop.
Two months later the dirt is covered
with winter grass. Over there.
That's where she's buried.

Apostrophe

–from a screened porch

Here is the pony, dead, in the grass
on the slope of a Smoky Mountain.

If I could, I'd say what came to pass
that left it so, in a light rain,

hooves heavenward, a new moss
beginning now to stain

the white rump, and the glass eyes
clouded with sky. Look how the mane

holds in its frill the wash
of hillside soil, brought down

another spring. Oh, pale horse
on a blue pole broken

from its swing set place,
are we reborn? In this ravine

you'll rot a thousand years, riderless,
who knew the embrace of children.

Horse

The architecture of these bones
Rises from green waves
Like a city long under,
Mythic, something old
And unspoken in us, a world
The horse has left behind
That cast shadows in moonlight.
Late summer wildflowers
Sway in the curve of her ribs;
Thunder across the sky
Is the sound of ghost herds.
From a distance her white gleams
Like the surprise of snow
In a mountain meadow;
Closer, the yellow age of ivory
Is more true to the story
Of her ruin.

We stand and measure loss here, think
About the flesh that tethers us.
We stand for a time in silence,
Knowing no prayer, only
What is wild and runs hard
And free across the open plains
Of the heart.

Appaloosa in Field of Camas, Supine

At first he thought the horse was resting most
unhorselike, flopped on its side, afloat
on a sea of grass like some old codger,
pale belly puffed, retired and coasting along
what's left of his life. Then he saw the bloat,

the sick white bulge of it, and thought
of those Brady photos from the Civil War,
dead stomachs stretched against gray
a few days after Pickett's charge,
or dark grainy blue at Cold Harbor.

He pictured himself like all of those sad
captains knocking on the door
of the shabby ranch house to announce
that death, but of course he chickened out,
he told himself, the way most folks would do,

leaving the rancher's kids to learn whatever
hard lessons their parents wished upon them.
Instead, he headed down the gravel road a few
hundred yards and about two hundred years
to the marker commemorating how

starving Lewis and Clark stumbled on a couple
of terrified Nez Perce kids who led them
to their village on a slight rise just behind him
where the modest ranch house squats,
and after some debate the old chief fed them.

Of course he'd expected to see more:
buffalo-skin tepees, perhaps, a cold campfire,
arrowheads, scattered bones. The marker
said it changed the lives of those Nez Perce
forever, but it did not say how.

March 17, 1876: The Ponies

A cavalry detachment attacked a Sioux village,
but had to withdraw through lingering winter,
ignominously. Accurate Indians had shot
too many horses out from under them,

& they'd been forced for the first time
to abandon a comrade to certain torture,
but they'd captured several hundred ponies
whose throats they slashed during retreat

southward. Lieutenant Bourke recalled,
"It was pathetic to hear the dismal trumpeting
of the dying creatures as the breath of life
rushed through several windpipes at once."

Following in the hills, the Sioux heard their ponies
calling out to them while dying.
Even unto now, sleepless in their village, they tell
of the pitiful deaths of the ponies.

The Eye

On this day that Crazy Horse rides out
into the rain, his paints wash down from him
onto his pony. The pony's fur blossoms
in these earthcolors, berrycolors, colors

of pumice & bone powders. Horse & rider
do not have a mirror except the rider's eye
in his loins that squints & seems
to laugh with him. Another good day to die.

WILLIAM HEYEN

Leaves of Horse

In 1877, the year Crazy Horse was murdered,
passenger pigeons still nested in great flocks
in the valley of the Ohio. In Brooklyn,
vendors served chestnuts from steaming carts.

That warrior is dead. The last passenger pigeon
died in a zoo in Cincy in 1913.
Chestnut trees were about wiped out by the '30s,
but here, among these leaves, a horse dances crazy.

Companions

After Crazy Horse was murdered,
his favorite pony, a pinto,
was gashed in the sides & legs.
Loved ones who saw the blood
answered in kind on their own bodies,
& sounds of grief flew up
into the pony's ears all night
from circles of mourners around it.
The pinto wondered whether
its master were near
& would ride him far away
from the keening & weeping—
at least it smelled such images
in its mind for the rest of its life,
& grew relentlessly lonely
for that rider & that journey.

Dream of Valverde Field

Devil rider,
hooves grating
whiskey shards,
uniform scraps,
men's bones.

Holding the foot
of the Mesa de
la Contadera.

Desert night,
diablo, I
will not keep,
will not pass,
will not try again.

Damnificado

Powder of a drowned horse
at my feet. As if he had cut the walls
of this canyon with the sure

color of his hooves, running
as the new river chases,
slams into him with its noise.

He drifts and then dries
into an outline of ribs and an ear
beneath the slow field of the sky.

Bone colored rain carved this riverbed.
Above us are the tatters of harvest.
And dirt on hot air

like the movements of tired people—
and the crowns of trees—
twitching, and then still.

Down the floodplain
is the arc of a young
man's swing. Neck bent, breaking

open ground like wind through
the stretch and hiss of wet clouds,
toward clean water.

His cattle surround the hole and he
is working on a name for the few
more hours left in the day.

Ghost Horses

On a morning thick with fog
I pass an olive grove in winter rest.
Among the dripping branches,
dark shapes loom. Fading in and out
through gray banners of mist
the large heads of quarterhorses
crop rye grass under the trees.
No doubt the farmer pictures
in his pragmatic way
short grass and free manure
for the coming spring. But I see
ghost horses floating among
ghost trees.

The Round Barn

I wonder if the horses balked
at the curvature, anticipating
clean, indigenous right angles.
They must have paced the perimeter
like their Chinese forbears, circling
the shafts that powered the mills
in the Han dynasty.
And did the farmer mourn the end
of linear thinking, did he pause
to consider the rectangles
of daily life? Haystacks, windows,
narrow rows of corn
in their righteous beds.

Good farmer, when you broke
with your neighbors and led
your livestock into the center
of the cosmos, were you only
following a hunch: that the wind
would sweep around
the progressive curves,
that revolution would harbor you?
Perhaps you saw in the repetitions
of history the wandering Mongolian
sleeping naked in his yurt,
who knew the world was a simple sphere
with an opening at the top for God.

Elegy

The ponies that aren't there anymore
where the two country highways met,
that bobbed their heads and flicked their tails
and kicked up their hooves with glee,
have said all they had to say,

and when the two new super highways growl
and spit and thunder and moan they race
away across the pasture that isn't there
and clear the fence that is
and disappear into the blue December air.

Biljana D. Obradovic

Where Does One Body End, the Other Begin?

for Meta Adamic

The sky is all colors, shapes.
Silent, like the painters in the studio;
the horses behave, keep still in their poses.
Everyone paints, or walks around barefoot,
checking what others have done with their canvases.
My friend remembers the hooved horses outside,
she saw them in a show, racing; she paints them still,
but moving in oil colors, Cerulean Blue, mixed with green.
The teacher couldn't bring her a model today;
my friend doesn't know
where a leg is to come out, where a head, a tail.
Her brush strokes over parts of bodies,
covering them, reincarnating them elsewhere.
Changing colors, poses, space — they enter each other's
bodies, reproducing themselves over and over.
Maybe in the end she will see just grass,
and horses floating among the clouds.

You Good Horse, You

Bones, by now.
Some skin.
A bit of mane and tail.
Your mound has hardened with sun and settling
and creeping green. Stones have scattered
where I wrote your name.

But still to see a certain kind of white-faced horse —
the startle of it,
and the sudden, glancing blow.

The Roan

The roan horse is dead.
He has left us a gift:

a finch's nest
woven of horsehair,

black, white, and red,
lodged in a hawthorn bush.

My Horse

The Chinese horse, glazed brown and green and gold,
  arches its neck,
though three centuries since it was only pale clay, watered
  in a potter's hands,
and three centuries hence will be lifted from a pit, shards
  slowly reassembled.

Handed up from a tomb, one horse from thousands sent
  as gifts to the gods,
it slept against a corpse dissolving to dust, this horse in
  elaborate trappings
waiting for the day, when, fragments on a table like pieces
  of a puzzle,

brown, green, gold—he'd teach the archeologist her trade,
  how to love a culture
strange as his, a new mystery replacing the old, a new life
  after death,
and then, bit by bit, the four legs will unfurl and the proud
  neck arch again.

A Poem from the Edge of America

There are ways of finding things, like stumbling on them.
Or knowing what you're looking for.
A miss is as good as a mile.
There are ways to put the mind at ease, like dying,
But first you have to find a place to lie down.

Once, in another life, I was a boy in Wyoming.
I called freedom home.
I had walked a long time into a high valley.
A river cut through it. It was late,
And I was looking for a place to lie down,

Which didn't keep me from stumbling
On something, believe me, I never wanted to find.
It was only the skeleton of someone's horse,
Saddled and bridled and tied to a tree.
When I woke in the morning it was next to me.

The rider must have wandered off, got turned around
And lost. It must have been winter.
The horse starved by the tree.
When we say, what a shame, whose shame do we mean?
In earnest of stability water often rages,

But rivers find their banks again, in earnest of the sea.
This ocean I live on can't hold still.
I want to go home to Wyoming and lie down
Like that river I remember with a valley to flow in,
The ocean half a continent away.

The horse I spoke of isn't a reason,
Although it might be why.

[Queen Anne's Lace crowds the air]

Queen Anne's Lace crowds the air; cicadas call from beyond the stream. Monkey flowers rouge the hill below a pasture where six horses crop sage; and beside the road, between riprap at the river mouth, down gullies and the wasted ravines, thistles are showing us their hearts again.

•

My son wakes screaming. His dreams are real; he's riding a horse, and the horse falls down. He's so young, I don't know how to tell him all our joy is wrung from that terror. Did you like it, I ask him. Fall down, he cries, fall down. Did you like riding the horse? And he looks at me, stops sobbing, and says, yes.

•

My mother wouldn't ride, but when the horses had been turned out to pasture, she'd pour salt on our cabin floor, and dance all night for the cowboys. One summer she missed a turn driving into town, and rolled her car into a ditch. She was so happy to be hurt, to be an event. In the hospital she introduced me to a girl who'd spent two days pulling slivers of glass from her teased and bloody hair. My mother asked, did you miss me? But before I could answer, she turned to the girl and said, we have had such a time.

•

Because a world may be called into being, or talked

away, the voice inside never quits. I once shamed a boy, called him bed-wetter in front of his friends, and the voice kept me up all night, repeating the bitter word. Later, the voice said, cancer, and she's dead. She's dead. You have cancer. This morning the air is sweet with bunch grass and the smell of horses milling in the corral. It's my birthday. I'm forty-one, and the voice says, you're in Wyoming. I am so happy, and I hear it again, you're in Wyoming.

Litany

When his absence blows over,
these hills will blush blue again,
and his bay mare's mane will go brown
in the sun. I will be able to take
out the trash, to light the pilot light,
without weeping. I will sleep
in my own scent. Rain will be rain,
not hot stones or sorrow, and crows
will wing down the mountain
with no message between their dark toes.
Soon the moon will sink
into the purple trees and heal herself,
and I will learn to braid my own hair
again. I will continue
to hum to the bay mare,
and bring her peppermint sticks,
until she gives up listening for
his step. Then one day
when I heft his saddle, she will whicker at me,
not at the emptiness over my shoulder;
I will stroke her neck, tie the girth knot,
and we will turn our heads
towards sun-washed fields.

The Last 400 Miles of a 3,000-Mile Trek

This gravel road rests its tip
on the horizon. A distant hill
hosts a gliding patch of shade.
Trees list to the east, trained by the wind
on this high Colorado plain.

We ride our five horses past footings
of farmsteads where in spring, iris
poke their heads above the grass
as if standing on their hind legs.

A flattened rattler marks every quarter mile.
At night, oil wells pop their single
piston engines like diesel tom-toms.

A coyote runs across the road
with a chicken in its mouth.
Not a car all day, and five bicycles
burst from behind like a covey of quail
and flush the pack string off the road.

Seven months in the saddle:
When I dream, I am always astride;
I am never in a car.

A black train slides eastward
half a section away, ribs
of perfectly laid coal in every car.
This KT & A railroad follows us
to Missouri like a seagull
behind a combine. One week
behind us is an ice storm,
like an omen.

In central Kansas, our horses dip
their heads to tracks in the road,
lift their feet too high, and snort.
We step onto 54 Highway
on horseshoes slick as snot
from hardfacing we've welded
on to make them last.

Semi's pass so fast the horses
squint in their backwash.
A motor home travels
cocked on its frame
and catty-corner to the wind.

Here's a curve in the road,
the first in 200 miles.

In eastern Kansas, we dismount
to wrap bath towels around our chests
and tie each other's collar over our faces.

This is some big sky,
fringed and uppity, and just now
I feel bits of ice on my cheek.

Here is Gas, Kansas,
and we arrive in a rain
to beat the blossoms off—
down Main in my poncho,
I can't feel my hands, but see their little
lit windows, them sitting in dry
living rooms, so clean,
in a café, in a car, on the way
to a game. I won't get near,
my lips won't move, neither my jaw;
we are lost trick-or-treaters.

Nevada, Missouri, 11 miles.
We pose beneath a mileage sign in Deerfield.
The last afternoon, our horses prick
their ears and quicken their steps.

We circle our hometown square.
Friends look out their windows.
Don Wood steps from his store.
Patty leaves her law office
to look at me. I am a wet dog
trying to hug her. In minutes,
they return to work.

Why do it?
Why open the blinds in the morning?
Why let the sun rise? Why wash
the car? Why learn to speak;
why pay the bills;
why nurse the child?

Why, when I squat and he stands to pee,
do the horses gather and stretch and grunt?
Together, we return to the seven states
what we took: a golden mist of minerals,
of protein, the run-off we sucked down,
the six-percent beer, the water
from a plastic canteen, the boiled coffee,
the summer squall.

Why swim up the river
at all?

On the last night, I lie awake
in the house of my father- and mother-in-law,
no horses chewing outside my tent,
no drum of rain or rising vaporous breath,
no tissue in my pocket to wipe with
today and again tomorrow.

Only—the white bulb of a water tower
set against a teary horizon
and under it, a Miller sign in a bar
that may expect us in six hours,
and I am thirsty now.

Horse Turning

Foreshortened horse,
foreshortened horse turning away,
the haunch close coupled,
the shoulder a smaller perspective,
the heavy haunch on the half-turn,
the heavy haunch when the horse leaves,
head dimming and distant
between the narrowing trees,
would be unbearable,
would presage such graveness,
without the hoist of his tail,
the white flax falling
one second to hang on the rush of twilight.

Without a Word

Go back
to that lateness
in the fall
when a crack
of light
between barnboards
makes another white
hair in the earth's
ragged beard,
then walk down
to the mare's grave,
still raw,
damp rocky soil
whose temper runs
in the family
of solitude,
and think about
owning living things.
Best let the whole place
disappear for now
like a choice
made right
by not being made,
until it's good
to see silence
burn so deep
in a heart
nothing is justified.
And finally
as truth begins,
left alone
without a word,
plant that heart
under the pasture,
joining every direction
it will keep.

[Here in the valley, sunrise first lights the sky]

Here in the valley, sunrise first lights the sky overhead, then the granite and pines on the western ridge. When the sun finally lifts above the mesa to the east, light moves quickly across the valley floor. The shadows travel in starts down the western slope, across the sage and bunch grass in the pastures, and up the orange cliffs to the east when the sun at last is high overhead. The light here is blinding, severe, a threat. The horses stand with bowed heads under the cottonwoods to escape it, and my own eyes rest on a small dark spot the shape of a swallow that passes over feldspar, sandstone, the beige adobe wall.

•

Two black geldings have joined the buckskin mare and her colt. They have grazed all afternoon in shade by the stream, but now they gallop and prance from one side of the canyon to the other. When they run full speed across the stream, it sounds like church bells muffled by rain. The colt comes up to me and prances and kicks, then the geldings, snorting and shaking their heads, race toward me and skid to a stop. All four of them jump, run, kick and gallop in circles in the pasture where I'm standing. I laugh, and shout, "Who are you trying to impress?" And suddenly I realize, it's me, they're doing this for me.

•

I have never experienced such a fracturing of the visual and the verbal in myself. I have been writing in a fever, twelve and fourteen hours a day for the past ten days, and the few times I have tried to draw, my hand felt insensible, like a deaf man who wakes with amnesia and can no longer sign. Last night at dusk I went into the pasture to make etchings of the horses. I could feel an imbalance in my head as I tried to stop thinking, and this was manifested in clumsy, self-conscious plates. But the horses, first fearful and threatening, then cautious but indifferent, began to offer me their forms, and the forms flowed through me, and guided the scribe. I could feel a physical shift as I started thinking, not with my head, but with my hands. I was caught up, and forgot what I was doing. When it was finally too dark to see, I went inside and discovered that my two best efforts had been done on the same plate; when one image was completed, I must have simply turned the plate around in my hand

•

This morning a pair of flickers bounced and shrieked on a limb of the dead cottonwood outside my window. A little mask of red glistened around the face of the one closest to me. I took my coffee out into the pasture like I've done every morning, and the cows and their calves stood in a cluster at the barbed wire fence and stared at me. An enormous bull stood behind them and held my gaze. One cow walked slowly around the side of the house, caught my eye, then as if embarrassed, turned sideways but still cocked her head to keep me in sight. The four horses walked across the stream and came up to me. First the colt and then its mother bent their heads and nuzzled my arm. I have wanted to touch these horses for weeks. I don't want to believe they know I am leaving; this is just a coincidence, but I'm part of it. This place has been like a world within a world. I am not returning to my life, but to the rest of it.

The Horses

In the savanna
we ran together

In the primal times
we were the Sagittarian
beast

Horse and Man
connected
on that journey
from predation

In the passing of
millenniums
what was given
in survival
—that mystery of communion—
—that journey with the beast—
is still a debt of honor
in the beat and breath
of memory
in the beat and breath
of deed

Even Now

There have been times when the blood within
has ached with the thunder of horses,
has been like the din of a thousand horses' hooves—

and still I can hear them pounding,
even now, when my mind is calm, the hooves of horses,
still filling my ears with their sound—

and the long rippling flanks are like pistons,
the rhythm of speed and of sweat—
always the hunger of horses,

always the clamor and roar,
of my death I want only horses—
in my memory, nothing before.

The Agnostic Speaks to Her Horse's Hoof

Come, frog, reveal yourself.
Surface out of the poultice
the muck and manure pack.
Make your miraculous V to stand up.
Show me as well the tickle place
that cleft between.

The Good Book says a man's life
Is as grass the wind passes over
And is gone.
According to the *National Geographic*
The oceans will lie down dead
As cesspools in sixty years.

Let us ripen in our own way—
I with my back to the trunk
of a butternut that has caught
the fatal red canker
and on my knee
this skillet of your old foot.

The hoofpick is God's instrument
as much as I know of Him.

In my hands let it raise
your moon, Amanda, your nerve bone.
Let us come to the apocalypse complete
Without splinter or stone.
Let us ride out
on four iron feet.

The Horse, Susan Said

The horse, Susan said, because it is the blankest of slates, or because our success—our genes' successes—are linked, has been written on extensively by our needs. Dumb giants pawing the ground, father, mother, escape, sexuality glistening and rippling, forelock and fetlock, footloose and fearless, or the pleasures of the fearful—fleeing the sudden gesture, careening through the green meadow at some imagined threat—shadow or shadow of a shadow, mirror glint—a world made meaningful by the creature's vulnerability, all the seams of that world, all the shifting angles. In here the cargo of a self; out there the quick and predatory gods inhabiting cliff top and meadow edge, lurking in arroyo and sink hole, slinking along the rooftop. The world's mouth, ready to rend the flesh, to devour us. And sometimes, the pain in the fetlock seems to be coming from outside and the horse tries to outrun it. Isn't this the lesson the Buddha tries to teach us? We in our horse natures, galloping on, Susan said, galloping on.

Up From the River

There is a naked man
awake in the early morning.

He knows it is Monday
because he is pacing
through the house

searching
for something
that keeps receding
like August current
from low, sandy banks.

At some point
he will be able
to stop and sit
but his hands
will keep moving

his eyes flying
around the room
as if he can sense
someone or something
coming after him
with a fleet of canoes

while his mind runs on
across rocky ground

praying for a small
muscular horse
with sure feet, good

eyesight and willing
to run until bone
and muscle
are ready to erupt
through its skin
and then to keep running
and running.

Gerard Manley Horses

GLORY be to Horses for dappled manes—
For eyes of couple-colour as a brinded cow;
For rose-mares all in stipple upon fetlocks that swim;
Fresh-firecoal chestnut-tails; haunches' wings;
Paddock plotted and pieced—foal, fallow, and plough;
And áll studs, their gear and tackle and trim.

All geldings counter, original, spare, strange;
Whatever is fickle, freckled (who knows how?)
With swift, slow; sweet, sour; adazzle, dim;
They nicker-forth whose beauty is past change:
Praise them.

Nighthorse

Horses of earth
Horses of water
Great horses of grey cloud
–Robert Dana

Horse of the dark.
Horse of broken ground.
Horse of last resort.

Horse with breath
like muffled wings
descending in cold air,
delicate, wise step,
light as a dragonfly
landing for the night,
eyes the color of banked fire,
eyes of the single bright precept.

Horse of silence.
Horse of the hardest mile.
Horse of the closed way.

Genius of ridgeline,
waterline, grinder of stone,
master of deadfall, detail, drop-off,
deceiver of shadow,
slipping like fog
into sunset, disappearing
along driplines, rootlines, faultlines.

Horse of oak.
Horse of flint.
Horse of blued steel.

Nighthorse,
get me there.
Level the ground beneath me.
Carry me up
to the edge of the trees
where the road curves by
in moonlight and rising sun
and lay your ears back and run
and run and run.

Contributer Notes

David Baker's books include *Midwest Eclogue* (poems, W. W. Norton, 2005) and *Radiant Lyre: Essays on Lyric Poetry* (Graywolf, 2007). He is poetry editor of *The Kenyon Review* and teaches at Denison University and in the MFA program for writers at Warren Wilson College. He crossed the Continental Divide in southern Colorado on a horse named Sandy.

Judith Barrington is a poet and memoirist who has published three collections of poetry, a prize-winning memoir, and a text on writing literary memoir which is used all across the United States and in Australia and Europe. Her most recent poetry book is *Horses and the Human Soul.* Her memoir, *Lifesaving,* won the Lambda Book Award and was a finalist for the PEN/Martha Albrand Award for the Art of the Memoir. She grew up in England and lives now in Portland, Oregon.

Robin Becker's sixth collection of poems, *Domain of Perfect Affection,* appeared in 2006 with the University of Pittsburgh Press. Among her awards and honors are fellowships from the Bunting Institute, The Massachusetts Cultural Council, and the NEA. In addition to writing a column on poetry called "Field Notes" for *The Women's Review of Books,* Becker serves as Poetry and Contributing Editor. Her book reviews appear frequently in *The American Poetry Review.* She is professor of English and Women's Studies at the Pennsylvania State University.

Margo Berdeshevsky lives in Paris. Her first poetry collection is *But a Passage in Wilderness* (The Sheep Meadow Press, 2007), with a foreword by Marie Ponsot. Her honors include the Robert H. Winner Award from the Poetry Society of America, The Chelsea Poetry Award, Kalliope's Sue Saniel Elkind Award, places in the Pablo Neruda and Ann Stanford Awards, and Border's Books / *Honolulu Magazine* Grand Prize for Fiction. Her writing has appeared in *The Southern Review, The Kenyon Review, Agni, New Letters, Poetry International, Margie, Pool, Siècle 21, Europe, Nimrod, Rattapallax, ACM, Women's Studies Quarterly,* and elsewhere. Her *Tsunami Notebook* of poems and photographs followed a journey to Sumatra in 2005, to work in a survivors' clinic in Aceh. A novel, *Vagrant,* and an illustrated short story collection, *Beautiful Soon Enough,* wait at the starting gate. A "visual poem" series, *Les Ombres de Versailles,* may be seen on the Parisian gallery site http://www.galeriebenchaieb.com/flash_fr.html.

Steve Black's work has appeared in or is forthcoming from *Number One, Eagle Eye, The Mindfulness Bell,* and *The Magazine.* He holds an MA from the University of Memphis and currently teaches in the Writing and Linguistics Department at Georgia Southern University.

Jonathan Blake lives and writes in Fitchburg, MA. Currently he is a member of the Languages and Literature Department at Worcester State College. Recent poems have appeared in *Poetry East, Blueline,* and *Amoskeag.* His essay "King of the Wood" can be found in the current *Worcester Review* commemorating Stanley Kunitz' one-hundredth birthday.

Linda Blaskey began riding as a little girl, bareback on her grandfather's farm horses in the Ozark Mountains of Arkansas. Her poems and short stories have appeared in numerous online and print journals and in several anthologies. One of her short stories was dramatically presented by InterAct Theatre in Philadelphia. She was the recipient of a poetry fellowship from the Delaware Division of the Arts, and she is on the editorial advisory board of *The Broadkill Review.* She teaches dressage in southern Delaware.

Barbara Bloom grew up in California and British Columbia. She earned a bachelor's degree in literature from UC Santa Cruz, a master's degree in English and creative writing from San Francisco State, and has taught composition and creative writing at Cabrillo College for over twenty years. She has a grown daughter and two grandsons and lives with her musician husband and their dog in the countryside south of Santa Cruz. Her first full-length collection of poems, *On the Water Meridian,* was published by Hummingbird Press in May 2007.

Deborah Bogen's *Landscape With Silos* won the 2005 XJ Kennedy Poetry Prize. Her poems and reviews appear widely. She can be reached through her website: www.DeborahBogen.net.

Don Bogen is the author of three books of poetry: *After the Splendid Display* (1986), *The Known World* (1997), and *Luster* (2003), all from Wesleyan. His awards include The Writer/Emily Dickinson Award of the Poetry Society of America, a Discovery/The Nation Award, a Fulbright Senior Lectureship in Spain, and fellowships from the Camargo Foundation and the NEA. He teaches at the University of Cincinnati and serves as Poetry Editor of *The Cincinnati Review.* He is the visiting Poet in Residence at the University of California, Irvine.

Kevin Boyle grew up in Philadelphia, where he created Big Jim, and he now lives in North Carolina with his wife and two daughters. His first book, *A Home for Wayward Girls* (2005), won the New Issues Poetry Prize. His poems have appeared in a number of magazines, including *Alaska Quarterly, Colorado Review, Denver Quarterly, The Michigan Quarterly Review, North American Review, Northwest Review, Poetry East*, and *Virginia Quarterly Review.* He teaches at Elon University.

Allen Braden has received fellowships from the NEA and Artist Trust of Washington State. Selected by Mary Oliver as one of the top ten finalists for the Walt Whitman Award, his book is forthcoming in the VQR Poetry Series.

Michael Dennis Browne's *Selected Poems 1965-1995,* published by Carnegie Mellon University Press, won the Minnesota Book Award for poetry in 1998. His previous book, *You Won't Remember This,* won a Minnesota Book Award in 1993. He has taught at Iowa, Columbia, Bennington, and, since 1971, the University of Minnesota, where he is Distinguished Teaching Professor of English. As a librettist, he has written numerous texts for music, working principally with composers Stephen Paulus and John Foley S.J. His poems have been published in many magazines and anthologies, and his awards include fellowships from the NEA, the Bush Foundation, the Jerome Foundation, and the McKnight Foundation.

J. V. Brummels' poems have been widely published in journals and magazines and have been recognized with a number of awards, including a Literature Fellowship from the NEA and the Mildred Bennett Award for contributions to the state's literature from the Nebraska Center for the Book. A new collection, his fourth, *A Book of Grass* is due out in 2007. For the last twelve years he's been the publisher of *Logan House,* which specializes in contemporary American poetry and short fiction. In 2006 he was named editor of the newly created WSC Press. Raised first on a farm and later on a ranch, he was educated at the University of Nebraska. After college, he went east to Syracuse University to pursue a graduate degree in creative writing. In 1984 he and his wife Lin fulfilled a lifelong dream and began a horseback cattle ranch, which they still operate.

Louella Bryant has won numerous awards for her short stories and poems, which have appeared in the magazines *Hunger Mountain, Fine Print, Carve, The Teacher's Voice,* and *Mobius,* and the anthologies *High Horse* (Fleur de Lis Press) and *Tartts 2—Incisive Fiction from Emerging Writers* (Livingston Press). Her essays are included in the anthology *Far From Home* 5

Tom Christopher teaches at UNC Greensboro and is one of the co-founders of the *Backwards City Review* (www.backwardscity.net). His work has appeared in numerous journals, including *DIAGRAM, Hayden's Ferry Review, The Iowa Review, the Mississippi Review, the Mid-American Review,* and *RHINO,* as well as *Best American Poetry 2006.*

Jeanne E. Clark's first collection of poems, *Ohio Blue Tips,* won the Akron Poetry Prize and was published by the University of Akron Press (2000). She is an associate professor in the English Department at California State University, Chico

Brad Comann is a lecturer in English at the University of California, Santa Barbara. His poetry has appeared in *Threepenny Review, Georgia Review, California Quarterly,* and elsewhere. A work of his literary non-fiction is forthcoming in *Fourth Genre.*

Star Coulbrooke is responsible for the popular open-mic/featured-readers series, Helicon West; has published a few dozen poems in lit-mags across the country; and, with the late Ken Brewer, former Poet Laureate of Utah, is co-author of *Logan Canyon Blend,* a chapbook of beasts and feet, published by Blue Scarab Press. Star also teaches poetry writing at Utah State University.

Darla Crist (formerly Darla Beasley) is the result of the school of life as well as an MA in English with a specialization in creative writing. Her work has appeared in various publications, including *The Mississippi Review, Quarter After Eight, Leviathan, Diagram, The Peralta Press* and *Earth's Daughters.* Awards for her fiction include the Andre Dubus Award for the Novella and the El Andar Prize for Literary Excellence. Her poetry has received the Joy Bale Boone Prize, and she has been the recipient of poetry awards from the Academy of American Poets in conjunction with Indiana State University.

Mary Crow, Poet Laureate of Colorado, is the author of nine books, five of her own poetry and four of translation. Her books of poetry include the full-length collections, *I Have Tasted the Apple* (1996) and *Borders* (1989) and the chapbooks, *The High Cost of Living* (2002), *The Business of Literature* (1981), and *Going Home* (1979). She is currently circulating *How Many Rivers,* a poetry manuscript that was a finalist for the May Swenson Poetry Prize.

Claire Davis' first novel, *Winter Range,* was listed among the best books of 2000 by the *Washington Post, Chicago Sun Times, Denver Post, Seattle Post, The Oregonian,* and *The Christian Science Monitor* and was the first book to receive both the PNBA and MPBA awards for best fiction. Her second novel *Season of the Snake* and her short story collection *Labors of the Heart* were both released to wide critical acclaim. She is co-editor of the anthology *Kiss Tomorrow Hello: Notes from the Midlife Underground by Twenty-five Women over Forty.* Her stories and essays have appeared in numerous literary magazines such as: *The Gettysburg Review, Shenandoah, Southern Review, The Pushcart Prize Anthology,* and *Best American Short Stories.* She lives in Lewiston, Idaho where she teaches creative writing at Lewis-Clark State College.

Cortney Davis is the author of three poetry collections, most recently *Leopold's Maneuvers,* winner of the Prairie Schooner Poetry Prize. An avid horse lover from an early age, she wanted to be a vet but ended up as a nurse practitioner. A memoir about her work in women's health, *I Knew a Woman,* was published by Random House in 2001. Her poems and prose are widely published and anthologized. www.cortneydavis.com.

Jon Davis has published five collections of poetry, including *Scrimmage of Appetite,* for which he was awarded a 1998 Lannan Literary Award in Poetry. He recently finished three new books of poetry, *The Immortals, Hetronymy: An Anthology,* and *Autohagiography: The Poems of Chuck Calabreze.* In addition to the Lannan, he has received a number of awards for his poetry, including two NEA Fellowships, the G.E. Younger Writers Award, the Lavan Younger Poets Prize from the Academy of American Poets, and a fellowship to The Fine Arts Work Center in Provincetown. He teaches at the Institute of American Indian Arts in Santa Fe, New Mexico.

Todd Davis teaches creative writing, environmental studies, and American literature at Penn State University—Altoona. His poems have been nominated for the Pushcart Prize and have appeared or are forthcoming in such journals and magazines as *The North American Review, The Iowa Review, West Branch, River Styx, Arts & Letters, Indiana Review, Quarterly West, Green Mountains Review, Poetry East,* and *Image: A Journal of the Arts and Religion.* He is the author of two books of poems, *Ripe* (Bottom Dog Press, 2002) and *Some Heaven* (Michigan State University Press, 2007). Poems from *Some Heaven* have been featured on Garrison Keillor's The Writer's Almanac and in Ted Kooser's American Life in Poetry.

Oliver de la Paz was born in Manila, Philippines. He is a co-founder and a board member of Kundiman, a not-for-profit organization committed to the discovery and cultivation of emerging Asian-American poets. A recipient of a New York Foundation for the Arts Fellowship, his work has appeared in journals such as *Quarterly*

West, Cream City Review, Third Coast, North American Review, and elsewhere. *Names Above Houses,* a book of his prose and verse, was a winner of the 2000 Crab Orchard Award Series and was published by Southern Illinois University Press in 2001. *Furious Lullaby,* his second book, will be published by Southern Illinois University Press in September 2007.

Mark DeFoe is professor of English at West Virginia Wesleyan College, where he has taught literature and writing for over 30 years. His chapbooks are *Bringing Home Breakfast* (Black Willow, 1983), *Palmate* (Pringle Tree Press, 1988), *AIR* (Green Tower Press, 1998), *Aviary* (Pringle Tree Press, 2001), *The Green Chair* (Pringle Tree Press 2003), *Mark DeFoe's Greatest Hits*(Pudding House 2004), and *The Rock and the Pebble* (Pringle Tree Press 2006). DeFoe's poetry has appeared in *Poetry, Paris Review, Christian Science Monitor, The Kenyon Review, Sewanee Review, Denver Quarterly, The Yale Review, The North American Review, Poetry Ireland Review, Poetry Salzburg, The Southern Humanities Review, Michigan Quarterly Review, Poetry International, The Literary Review, Mississippi Review,* and many others, and has been recognized for excellence by numerous magazines. He was twice a recipient of a West Virginia Commission on the Arts Fellowships in Literature. DeFoe lives with his wife Jeanne, a pianist, in Buckhannon, West Virginia.

Gregory Djanikian was born in Alexandria, Egypt in 1949 of Armenian parentage and came to the United States when he was eight years old. He has published five collections of poetry all with Carnegie Mellon, *The Man in the Middle, Falling Deeply in America, About Distance, Years Later,* and most recently, *So I Will Till the Ground.* His poems have appeared in numerous journals including *The American Poetry Review, Boulevard, The Georgia Review, Iowa Review, Poetry,* and in many anthologies including *Unsettling America* (Penguin), *The Bedford Introduction to Literature* (St. Martins), *Best American Poetry of 2000* (Scribners), *180 More* (Random House) and *Good Poems for Hard Times* (Viking). His awards include an NEA Fellowship and the Anahid Literary Award from the Armenian Center of Columbia University. He directs the creative writing program at the University of Pennsylvania in Philadelphia.

Sharon Doubiago has written two dozen books of poetry and prose, most notably the epic poem *Hard Country* (West End Press), the book length poem *South America Mi Hija* (University of Pittsburgh) which was nominated twice for the National Book Award, and the stories *The Book of Seeing With One's Own Eyes* (Graywolf) which in 2005 was selected to the Oregon Culture Heritage list, Literary Oregon, 100 Books, 1800-2000. She holds three Pushcart Prizes for poetry and fiction and the Oregon Book Award for Poetry for *Psyche Drives the Coast.* In 2008, *Love on the Streets, Selected and New Poems* will be published by the University of Pittsburgh as well as Volume One of her memoir, *My Father's Love/Portrait of the Poet as a Girl.* She's an online mentor in creative writing for the University of Minnesota and a board member of PENOakland.

Sean Thomas Dougherty is the author of eight full length books of poems and prose including the forthcoming experimental novella *The Blue City* (2008 Marick Press Wayne State U), *Broken Hallelujahs* (BOA Editions 2007), and *Nightshift Belonging to Lorca* (2004 Mammoth Books)—a finalist for the 2004 Paterson Poetry Prize. He is the editor of the critical collection *Maria Mazziotti Gillan* and the anthology *Along the Lake: Contemporary Writing from Erie PA.* His awards include a 2004 and 2006 PA Council for the Arts Fellowship in Poetry. He teaches in the BFA Program for Creative Writing at Penn State Erie.

Barbara Drake was born in Abilene, Kansas, moved to Oregon with her parents as a small child, and grew up in the coastal lumber town of Coos Bay. She earned her BA and MFA degrees from the University of Oregon, subsequently lived in Michigan for sixteen years and taught at MSU before returning to Oregon in 1983 to teach at Linfield College where she is a full professor. She and her husband live on a small farm in Yamhill County. They raise sheep and wine grapes and enjoy introducing their grandchildren to country life. Her books include *Peace at Heart: an Oregon Country Life,* a collection of personal essays; *Writing Poetry,* a college creative writing textbook; and several collections of poetry including *What We Say to Strangers, Love at the Egyptian Theatre,* and others. Her newest poetry collection is *Small Favors,* published by Traprock Press.

Chris Drangle is an undergraduate at Tulane University in New Orleans, where he is majoring in English with an emphasis in creative writing. He has presented poetry at the Sigma Tau Delta international conference, and published fiction in the *River Walk Journal.* His home is in Little Rock, Arkansas.

George Drew was born in Mississippi and raised there and in New York State, where he currently lives. *Toads in a Poisoned Tank,* his first book, was published in 1986, and a chapbook, *So Many Bones* (Poems of Russia), in 1997 by a Russian press, in a bilingual edition. A second collection, *The Horse's Name Was Physics,* appeared in 2006 from Word Tech Communications, under their Turning Point imprint. Drew has published widely, with poems upcoming in *Atlanta Review, The Sow's Ear Poetry Review, The Teacher's Voice,*

FutureCycle Poetry, and *Louisiana Literature.* He was the winner of the 2003 Paumanok Poetry Award, and the 2007 Stephen Dunn Poetry Award. Drew also is a runner-up this year in the Louisiana Literature Poetry Prize competition, and the Fugue Poetry Contest.

Felicia DuBois is originally from Virginia and currently lives in Santa Fe, New Mexico. Her poems have appeared in *Manzanita Quarterly, Tar River Poetry, American Letters & Commentary, PMS (poemmemoirstory),* and *So To Speak: A Feminist Journal of Language and Art.*

Denise Duhamel's most recent books are *Two and Two* (University of Pittsburgh Press, 2005), *Mille et un sentiments* (Firewheel Editions, 2005), and *Queen for a Day: Selected and New Poems* (University of Pittsburgh Press, 2001). She teaches creative writing at Florida International University in Miami.

Rebecca Dunham's first collection, *The Miniature Room,* won the 2006 T.S. Eliot Prize and was published by Truman State University Press. She was awarded a 2007 NEA Fellowship and is an assistant professor at the University of Wisconsin-Milwaukee.

Susan Elbe is the author of *Eden in the Rearview Mirror* (Word Press) and *Light Made from Nothing* (Parallel Press). Her poems appear or are forthcoming in many journals, including *After Hours, Ascent, Blackbird, Calyx, MARGIE, Nimrod, The North American Review, Passages North,* and *Salt Hill.* Her work also appears in many anthologies, including *A Fierce Brightness: Twenty-five Years of Women's Poetry* (Calyx Books), *On Retirement: 75 Poems* (University of Iowa Press), and *Eating the Pure Light: Homage to Thomas McGrath* (Backwaters Press). She has received the Calyx Lois Cranston Memorial Poetry Prize, the 2006 Lorine Niedecker Award, and a Rowland Foundation residency to the Vermont Studio Center. Susan serves on the Council for Wisconsin Writers Board and the Wisconsin Poet Laureate Commission. She lives and works as a webmaster in Madison, Wisconsin.

Karl Elder is Poet in Residence at Lakeland College. His seven collections include *A Man in Pieces* (1994), *The Geocryptogrammatist's Pocket Compendium of the United States* (2001), *The Minimalist's How-to Handbook* (2005), and *Mead: Twenty-six Abecedariums* (2005). His work has also appeared in *The Best American Poetry 2000; A Fine Excess: Fifty Years of the Beloit Poetry Journal; September 11, 2001: American Writers Respond;* and several other anthologies, including *The Best American Poetry 2005.* Among his honors are a Pushcart Prize, the Chad Walsh Award, the Lorine Niedecker Award, the Lucien Stryk Award, grants from the Illinois Arts Council for poetry and fiction, Lakeland's Outstanding Teacher Award, and the Robert Schuricht Endowment. "Gilgamesh at the Bellagio," his 1,300-word mini-epic in acrostics, appears with an introduction by Beth Ann Fennelly in a recent issue of *Black Warrior Review.*

Margot Farrington's second collection is *Flares And Fathoms* (Bright Hill Press, 2005). Her poetry has appeared in other anthologies, most recently in *Other Land: Contemporary Poems On Wales And Welsh American Experience* (Parthian Press, 2007). Steeped in theater—her earliest love—she has also written and performed pieces combining poetry with other media.

Annie Finch's books of poetry are *Calendars* (Tupelo, 2003); *The Encyclopedia of Scotland* (Salt, 2004); and *Eve* (Story Line, 1997). Other works include a translation of the poems of Louise Labe, (University of Chicago Press, 2006) and an opera libretto based on the life of Marina Tsvetaeva (American Opera Projects, 2003). Her most recent of several anthologies and books on poetics is *The Body of Poetry: Essays on Women, Form, and the Poetic Self* (Michigan, 2005). She is professor of English and director of the Stonecoast Brief-Residency MFA in creative writing at the University of Southern Maine, and her website is www.anniefinch.com.

Deborah Fleming has published poems in such journals as *Hiram Poetry Review, Sucarnoche Review, Karamu, Cottonwood, Mid-American Poetry Review, The Journal, Interdisciplinary Studies in Literature and Environment, Blueline, Natural Bridge, Organization and Environment,* and others. A chapbook of her poetry, *Migrations,* was published in 2005 by Finishing Line Press of Georgetown, Kentucky. She has published nonfiction essays about nature and place and continues to write fiction and nonfiction as well as poetry. Her scholarship includes "'A man who does not exist'": The Irish Peasant in the Work of W. B. Yeats and J. M. Synge," published by the University of Michigan Press, and articles about Yeats, Robinson Jeffers, Eamon Greanna, Aldo Leopold, and George Orwell. She teaches literature and writing at Ashland University where she is professor of English and associate editor of the *Ashland Poetry Press.* She lives on a farm near Perrysville, Ohio, where she raises and rides horses.

CB Follett has been published in many journals and anthologies; received contest honors in several contests including Billee Murray Denny, New Letters, Ann Stanford, Glimmer Train Poetry Contest and several contests from Poetry Society of America. Five poems have been nominated for a Pushcart Poetry Prize plus a nomination as an individual poet. She has five collections of poetry, the most recent *Hold and Release,* 2007. She is the publisher/editor of ARCTOS

PRESS, including the anthology, *GRRRRR, A Collection of Poems About Bears;* she is publisher and co-editor of *RUNES, A Review of Poetry,* 2001-to present.

Alice Friman's new book is *The Book of the Rotten Daughter* (BkMk Press). Her previous recent books are *Zoo* (Arkansas, 1999), winner of the Ezra Pound Poetry Award from Truman State University and the Sheila Margaret Motton Prize from the New England Poetry Club, and *Inverted Fire* (BkMk, 1997). Her poems appear in *Poetry, The Georgia Review, Boulevard, The Southern Review, The Gettysburg Review,* and *Shenandoah,* which awarded Friman the 2002 James Boatwritght III Prize for Poetry. She has received fellowships from the Indiana Arts Commission and the Arts Council of Indianapolis and has been awarded residencies at many colonies including MacDowell and Yaddo. In 2003-04, she was named Writer in Residence at Bernheim Arboretum and Research Forest in Kentucky. She has won three prizes from the Poetry Society of America and in 2001-02 was named to the Georgia Poetry Circuit. Professor Emerita at the University of Indianapolis, Friman now lives in Milledgeville, Georgia, where she is Poet in Residence at Georgia College & State University.

Tess Gallagher is a poet, essayist, novelist, and playwright. Her honors include a fellowship from the Guggenheim Foundation, two NEA Awards, the Nancy Blankenship Pryor Award, the Maxine Cushing Gray Foundation Award, and the Elliston Award for "best book of poetry published by a small press" for the collection, *Instructions to the Double* (1976). In 1984, she published the collection, *Willingly,* which consists of poems written to and about her third husband, author Raymond Carver, who died in 1988. Other collections include *The Lover of Horses* (Graywolf, 1992), *Portable Kisses* (Capra Press, 1992), *At the Owl Woman Saloon* Simon & Schuster, 1999), *My Black Horse: New and Selected Poems* (Bloodaxe Books, 1995), *Owl-Spirit Dwelling* (Trask House Book, 1993), *Moon Crossing Bridge* (Graywolf, 1992), *Call If You Need Me* (Vintage, 2001), and *Dear Ghosts* (Graywolf, 2006). Gallagher holds an Honorary Doctorate in Humane Letters from Whitman College and has taught at St. Lawrence University; Kirkland College; University of Montana, Missoula; University of Arizona, Tucson; Syracuse University; and Willamette University.

James Galvin is the author of six books of poems, including *Lethal Frequencies, God's Mistress, Element, X:Poems, Imaginary Timber,* and *Resurrection Update* and two prose books, *The Meadow* and *Fencing the Sky.* He has some land and some horses in southern Wyoming, and he is a member of the permanent poetry faculty at the Iowa Writers' Workshop.

Christine Gelineau is the author of *Remorseless Loyalty,* (Ashland Poetry Press, 2006) winner of the Richard Snyder Memorial Prize. *Remorseless Loyalty* has been nominated for the Los Angeles Times Book Awards. She is also the author of two chapbooks from FootHills Publishing, *North American Song Line* (2001) and *In the Greenwood World* (2006). She is co-editor (with Jack Bedell) of *French Connections: A Gathering of Franco-American Poets* (2006). Gelineau's poetry, essays, and reviews have appeared in numerous journals and anthologies, including *Prairie Schooner, Connecticut Review, The Iron Horse Review, Green Mountains Review, Georgia Review, American Literary Review* and others. Her poems have twice been nominated for a Pushcart Prize, and her essay "Foal Watch" is cited as a Notable Essay in the *2004 Best American Essays.* Gelineau lives on a farm in upstate New York and is associate director of the Creative Writing Program and coordinator of the Readers' Series at Binghamton University. She also teaches poetry in the low-residency graduate writing program at Wilkes University.

Danielle Legros Georges is a writer, translator, and author of *Maroon,* a collection of poems (Curbstone Press, 2001). Her poems have appeared in anthologies including *Beyond the Frontier: African-American Poetry for the 21st Century* and *Role Call: A Generational Anthology of Social and Political Black Literature and Art* and in literary journals including *Agni, Callaloo,* and *The Caribbean Writer.* She has contributed biographical entries and translations to the *Encyclopedia Encarta Africana* and the book *Beyond Fire Walking on Fire: Haitian Women's Stories of Survival and Resistance*, respectively. She is an associate professor at Lesley University.

Rebecca Kaiser Gibson's work has been published in *Agni, Field, The Harvard Review, The Boston Phoenix, Mothering, The Antigonish Review, Northwest Review, Verse Daily, MARGIE,* and *Slate,* and is forthcoming in *The Greensboro Review.* She has two chapbooks, *Admit the Peacock* and *Inside the Exhibition.* A fellow at the MacDowell Colony and The Heinrich Böll Cottage, Ireland, Rebecca teaches poetry at Tufts University. She lives in Somerville MA and New Hampshire with her husband.

Benjamin Gotschall was born and raised on a cattle ranch in the Sandhills of Holt County, Nebraska. He obtained a degree in English from Nebraska Wesleyan University and an MFA in creative writing from the University of Idaho. His poetry has appeared in *Cimarron Review, Meridian, Poetry Southeast,* and *South Dakota Review.* He currently lives on Branched Oak Farm near Raymond, Nebraska.

N. Tzivia Gover is the author of *Mindful Moments for Stressful Days*

(Storey Books, 2002). Her poetry chapbook, *Dream House,* (a hand-bound limited edition) was published last year. Her poetry has appeared in numerous journals, magazines, and anthologies including *Lilith, Bark Magazine, The Berkshire Review, Sinister Wisdom,* and *Bridges,* among others. Her essays and articles have appeared in periodicals and anthologies including *The New York Times, The Christian Science Monitor, The Boston Globe,* and dozens more. She received her MFA in creative writing from Columbia University and currently teaches poetry to teen mothers who are studying for their GEDs in Holyoke, Massachusetts.

Alice Wirth Gray's poems have been in *Poetry, The American Scholar, The Atlantic* and many other magazines and journals. The Cleveland State University Poetry Center published her book, *What the Poor Eat,* in 1993. She also has about a dozen short stories published. She is married to a retired structural engineer and architect, has two adult daughters, two perfect grandchildren, and lives in a decaying house in Berkeley.

Coppie Green has worked throughout North Carolina as a teaching poet. Her poems have appeared in *Triquarterly, The Greensboro Review, Permafrost,* and numerous additional journals and anthologies. Her books include *Horse Turning* (Felix Press) and *The Southern Outcasts* (Moonlight Publications), and her songs as a lyricist in collaboration with composer Sean Egan have been performed at the NC Museum of Art. She bought her first horse with her own money at age eleven and has owned horses for most of her life. A former resident of interior Alaska, she once watched the sunset part the snow long enough to light up Denali and the white mane of the horse she was riding, whose name was Galaxy.

Gabriel Gudding is the author of two books, *A Defense of Poetry* (Pitt Poetry Series, 2002) and *Rhode Island Notebook* (Dalkey Archive Press, Nov 2007), a book he wrote in his car. His work appears in numerous periodicals and such anthologies as *Great American Prose Poems: From Poe to the Present* (Scribner) and as translator in such anthologies *The Oxford Anthology of Latin American Poetry, Poems for the Millennium,* and *The Whole Island: Six Decades of Cuban Poetry* (University of California Press). He teaches creative writing, literature, and poetics at Illinois State University.

Catherine Hardy is chair of the Academic Studies Department at the Art Academy of Cincinnati (Ohio), where she teaches writing, literature, and film studies. Her poetry has also appeared in *Georgia State University Review, The Journal, Quirk,* and *Yale Anglers Journal,* among others. She has never owned a horse, but her parents attended the Kentucky Derby on their honeymoon.

Joy Harjo is an internationally known poet, performer, writer, and musician. She has published seven books of poetry, including *She Had Some Horses, In Mad Love and War, The Woman Who Fell From the Sky*, and her most recent *How We Became Human, New and Selected Poems* from W.W. Norton. In Harjo's first music CD, *Letter from the End of the 20th Century* she is featured as poet and saxophone player. Her second CD of original songs is *Native Joy for Real.* She is currently in the studio working on her fourth musical release: *Wings of Night Sky, Wings of Morning Light.* She has been featured on Garrison Keillor's Literary Friendships show, and was recently profiled on the Jim Lehrer News Report. Her photographs were featured in the May 2007 art show "Looking Indian" at the Untitled ArtSpace Gallery in Oklahoma City. She writes a monthly column for her tribal newspaper: the *Muscogee Nation News.* She is currently the Joseph M. Russo endowed professor at UNM in creative writing where she will be in residence every fall through 2007. When not teaching and performing she lives in Honolulu, Hawaii.

James Harms has published four books of poetry, the most recent of which are *Freeways and Aqueducts* (2004) and *Quarters* (2001) from Carnegie Mellon University Press; a fifth collection, *After West,* will appear from Carnegie Mellon in 2008. Newer work is in recent issues of *The Gettysburg Review, Oxford American, The North American Review, Crazyhorse, Shenandoah, Quarterly West,* and others. A recipient of an NEA Fellowship and three Pushcart Prizes, he currently directs the creative writing program at West Virginia University.

Jana Harris's books include two Pulitzer Prize nominees: *Manhattan as a Second Language, Poems* (Harper & Row) and *Oh, How Can I Keep On Singing? Voices of Pioneer women, Poems* (Ontario Press, Princeton), which was a Washington State Governor's Writers Award winner and a PEN West Center Award finalist. Her seventh book of poems, *The Dust of Everyday Life* (Sasquatch) won the 1998 Andres Berger award, and her eighth collection, *We Never Speak of It, Idaho-Wyoming Poems* (Ontario) was nominated for the Kingsley Tufts Award. She won a Reader's Choice Award in poetry from *Prairie Schooner* in 2004. She is a poet, novelist, short story writer, and essayist who was born in San Francisco, raised in the Pacific Northwest, and now lives with her husband in the foothills of the Cascade Mountains where they raise horses. She teaches creative writing at the University of Washington where she is editor and founder of Switched-on Gutenberg (www.switched-ongutenberg.com).

Lola Haskins has published eight collections of poetry, most recently

Desire Lines, New and Selected Poems (BOA, 2004). Two prose books are forthcoming in 2007: an advice book called *Not Feathers Yet: A Beginner's Guide to the Poetic Life* from Backwaters Press, and a book of fables about women, with illustrations by Maggie Taylor, called *Solutions Beginning with A* from Modernbook. For more information, please see www.lolahaskins.com.

Wendell Hawken, a retired marketing executive and former foxhunter, lives on a farm in the northern Shenandoah Valley where she and her husband raise Hereford cattle. In 2005, thirty-nine years after receiving her BA, she earned her MFA from Warren Wilson College. Her first collection, *The Luck of Being* will be published in 2008 by Backwaters Press.

Julie Hensley grew up on a small farm in the Shenandoah Valley of Virginia, but now she makes her home with her husband, the writer R. Dean Johnson, in southwestern Oklahoma, where she directs the creative writing program at Cameron University. She holds an MA in fiction from Arizona State University. Recently, her work has appeared in *Redivider, Phoebe, Western Humanities Review, Blueline, Louisiana Literature, Briar Cliff Review, Crab Orchard Review,* and *Karamu.*

Sonya K. Hess lives in central Minnesota with her husband and two children. A graduate of the MFA Program for Writers at Warren Wilson College, her work has recently appeared in *St Anne's Review* and *Heliotrope.*

William Heyen was born in Brooklyn, New York, in 1940. He is Professor of English/Poet in Residence Emeritus at SUNY Brockport, his undergraduate alma mater. His MA and PhD degrees are from Ohio University. A former Senior Fulbright Lecturer in American Literature in Germany, he has won NEA, Guggenheim, American Academy & Institute of Arts & Letters, and other fellowships and awards. He is the editor of *American Poets in 1976, The Generation of 2000: Contemporary American Poets,* and *September 11, 2001: American Writers Respond.* His work has appeared in over 300 periodicals including *Poetry, American Poetry Review, New Yorker, Southern Review, Kenyon Review, Ontario Review,* and in 200 anthologies. His books include *Pterodactyl Rose: Poems of Ecology, The Host: Selected Poems, Erika: Poems of the Holocaust,* and *Ribbons: The Gulf War from Time Being Books; Pig Notes & Dumb Music: Prose on Poetry* and *Crazy Horse in Stillness,* winner of 1997's Small Press Book Award for Poetry, from BOA; *Shoah Train: Poems,* a Finalist for the 2004 National Book Award, from Etruscan Press; and *The Rope: Poems, The Hummingbird Corporation: Stories,* and *Home: Autobiographies, Etc.* from MAMMOTH Books. Carnegie-Mellon University Press recently released his first book, *Depth of Field* (LSU Press, 1970) in its Classic Contemporaries Series.

MICHAEL HICKS is the author of three books: *Mormonism and Music: A History* (1989), *Sixties Rock: Garage, Psychedelic, and Other Satisfactions* (1999), and *Henry Cowell, Bohemian* (2002), all published by University of Illinois Press. He has also authored historical and analytical articles that have appeared in many books and journals (including *American Music, Journal of Aesthetic Education, Journal of the American Musicological Society, Musical Quarterly,* and *Perspectives of New Music*). He has been a guest lecturer at Stanford and the University of California at Berkeley and has read papers at various conferences (including UCLA's multidisciplinary Conference on American Studies Connecting with Religion, 1991) and national meetings of the Society for American Music and the American Musicological Society. His Mormon-related articles and poetry have appeared in several books (including *Macmillan's Encyclopedia of Mormonism, 1995*) and in the journals *Dialogue, Sunstone, BYU Studies, Journal of Mormon History,* and *Utah Historical Quarterly.*

JANE HIRSHFIELD is the author of six collections of poetry, including *Of Gravity & Angels* (Wesleyan University Press, 1988), *The Lives of the Heart* (HarperCollins, 1997) and *After* (HarperCollins, 2006), as well as a book of essays and three books collecting the work of women poets from the past. Her honors include fellowships from the Guggenheim and Rockefeller foundations, the NEA, and the Academy of American Poets; the California Book Award in poetry; a Bill Moyers PBS television half-hour interview; and five appearances in *The Best American Poetry.* Her work appears in *The New Yorker, The Atlantic Monthly, Slate, Orion,* and many literary reviews. She lives in northern California.

ELIZABYTH A. HISCOX is a Poet in Residence at University of Durham's St. Chad's College in North East England. Winner of the Sonoran Prize in Poetry, and recipient of grants from the Arizona Commission on the Arts, she is also a Virginia G. Piper Center for Creative Writing International Fellow. Her verse has most recently appeared in *Gulf Coast* and *Foundation.* She enjoys instructing writing courses for Arizona State University in the monsoon, dust storm, and desert-bloom seasons.

PETER HUGGINS teaches in the English Department at Auburn University. His books of poems are *Necessary Acts* and *Blue Angels,* both from River City Publishing, and *Hard Facts,* Livingston Press; *South,* his next book of poems, is forthcoming from Louisiana Literature Press in 2008. In addition, he is the author of a picture book, *Trosclair and the Alligator,* Star Bright Books, New York, and a soon to be released novel for middle grade readers, *In the Company of Owls,* NewSouth Books. For 2006 he was awarded a literature fellowship from the Alabama State Council on the Arts.

Austin Hummell's books are *Poppy,* winner of the Del Sol Press Poetry Prize, and *The Fugitive Kind,* winner of the University of Georgia Press's Contemporary Poetry Series. He has recent work in *Poetry, Gettysburg Review, Gulf Coast, the Minnesota Review* and some anthologies, including *American Poetry: The Next Generation.* He teaches at Northern Michigan University and is poetry editor of *Passages North.*

Mark Irwin is the author of five collections of poetry, *The Halo of Desire* (1987), *Against the Meanwhile,* (Wesleyan University Press, 1989), *Quick, Now, Always,* (BOA, 1996), *White City,* (BOA, 2000), and *Bright Hunger,* (BOA, 2004); he has also translated two volumes of poetry, one from the French and one from the Romanian. Recognition for his work includes The Nation/Discovery Award, four Pushcart Prizes, NEA and Ohio Art Council Fellowships, two Colorado Council for the Arts Fellowships, two Colorado Book Awards, the James Wright Poetry Award, and fellowships from the Fulbright, Lilly, and Wurlitzer Foundations.

Suzan Jantz lives in the mountains of northern California with her partner, their dogs, cats, horses, and an abundance of wildlife. Her poetry has landed in *Calyx, Inkwell, Sinister Wisdom, The Rectangle, The Studium, The Suisun Valley Review,* and *Watershed.* In 2006, she was a finalist in *Inkwell's* 10th Annual Poetry Competition. She is the recipient of two California State University, Chico Research and Creativity Grants: in 2005 for work on a poetry chapbook, *The Heartache Season: Traveling the Lassen-Applegate Trail,* and in 2006 to establish Yarroway Mountain Press and to publish its inaugural anthology, *Cadence of Hooves.* As a teenager, Suzan's first horse was a twelve-year-old quarter horse mare that had been running free for nine years, and who swiftly and consistently launched her out of the saddle and left her on the trail to contemplate the errors of her ways.

Carrie Jerrell recieved an MA from the the Writing Seminars at Johns Hopkins University and is completing a PhD in English at Texas Tech University as a Chancellor's Fellow. Her work has appeared or is forthcoming in *32 Poems, Passages North, Painted Bride Quarterly,* and other publications.

William Johnson teaches at Lewis-Clark State College in Lewiston, Idaho. His critical study, *What Thoreau Said,* appeared in 1991

(University of Idaho Press), and Confluence Press has published two collections of his poetry, a chapbook, *At the Wilderness Boundary* (1996), and a full collection, *Out of the Ruins,* which won the Idaho Book Award for 2000. Johnson has received fellowships from Fishtrap, the Environmental Writing Institute, the Idaho Humanities Council, the Idaho Commission on the Arts, and the NEA. He served as Idaho Writer in Residence from 1998-2001.

Ilya Kaminsky is the author of *Dancing In Odessa* which won the Whiting Writer's Award, American Academy of Arts & Letters' Metcalf Award, the Dorset Prize, Poetry magazine's Ruth Lilly Fellowship, and was named the best poetry book of 2005 by *ForeWord* magazine. He teaches at San Diego State University.

Ellen Chavez Kelley is an award-winning poet whose work has appeared in magazines, anthologies, and literary journals. She has been a California Poet in the Schools and a lecturer in writing at the University of California, Santa Barbara. Currently she leads private poetry workshops and teaches community college classes in Santa Barbara, CA. Ellen also writes books for young readers, including *The Lucky Lizard* (Dutton/Penguin 2002), *Buckamoo Girls* (Abrams, 2006) and *My Life As A Chicken* (Harcourt, 2007). To learn more, visit Ellen at www.ellenakelley.com.

Robert Morris Kennedy is a native of Florida and lifelong journalist. He is night city editor in Tampa for the *St. Petersburg Times.* His poems and stories have appeared recently in *Freefall, The Tampa Review, Blue Collar Review, Avatar Review, Penwood Review, Muscadine Lines, Remark,* and *Hidden Oak.*

Willie James King writes and resides in Montgomery, AL. He holds an MFA from Queens University, Charlotte, NC. He has been nominated for four Pushcart prize awards. His books are: *At the Forest Edge, Wooden Windows*, and *The House in the Heart,* (Tebot Bach Press, 2007). His work has appeared in *America, Appalachian Heritage, Blue Unicorn, Confrontation, Crazyquilt Quaterly, Mudfish, Obsidian:ll & lll, Poem, Puerto del Sol, Rattle, The Southern Poetry Review, Wallace Stevens Journal, Willow Review,* and in many others. The poem included in this anthology was first published in *Pembroke,* where he is a regular contributor, and subsequently in *Peregrine;* also, it appears in *The House in the Heart.*

Kathryn Kirkpatrick is a Professor of English at Appalachian State University in North Carolina and has poems published or forthcoming in *Another Chicago Magazine, Calyx, Epoch, The Florida Review, Kalliope, The Laurel Review, Poem, Rattle, Room of One's*

Own, Shenandoah, Southern Poetry Review, Sycamore Review, South Carolina Review and other magazines. Her first book of poems, *The Body's Horizon,* won the Brockman-Campbell award, selected by Alicia Ostriker. Her second collection, *Beyond Reason* (Pecan Grove Press, 2004), received the North Carolina Literary and Historical Association's Roanoke-Chowan Poetry Award. Chapbooks include *Looking for Ceilidh* (Mill Springs Press, 2004) and *The Master's Wife* (March Street Press, 2004). Her third collection, *Out of the Garden,* is forthcoming from Mayapple Press.

John Kooistra is a commercial fisherman, carpenter, and former teacher living in Fairbanks, Alaska.

Jo Koster teaches medieval literature and writing at Winthrop University and says that most of her creative writing takes place in her checkbook. Recent work has appeared in the collections *Mountain Time* and *Home for the Holidays* (Old Mountain Press) and in the e-zine *More than Words*. Her most recent chapbook, *No Going Home,* was published by Devil's Millhopper Press. She and her cats live in comfortable chaos and in Rock Hill, SC.

Judith Krause is a Western Canadian poet, based in Saskatchewan, whose fourth collection, *Mongrel Love*, will be published by Hagios Press in 2008. Her poems have appeared in many Canadian journals including recent issues of *The Fiddlehead;* (she was co-winner of the 2006 Ralph Gustaphson Poetry Prize), *Grain, The Antigonish Review,* and *CVII.* She has studied writing in Canada and the U.S. and has participated in residency programs at The Atlantic Center for The Arts, Vermont Studio Center, and the Virginia Center for The Creative Arts.

Jeri Kroll was born in New York City and completed a BA at Smith College, a Masters at the University of Warwick, and a PhD at Columbia University. She taught in the U.S. and England before moving to Australia in 1978. Professor of English and program coordinator of creative writing at Flinders University in Adelaide, South Australia, she has published over twenty books for adults and young people, including poetry, picture books (two Children's Book Council Notable Awards) and novels. *Death as Mr Right* won second prize in the Anne Elder Award (best first poetry book in Australia). She has written three young adult novels with an equestrian focus (*Better Than Blue, Beyond Blue,* and *Riding the Blues*). *The Mother Workshops,* a mixed genre collection, was adapted for ABC Radio National's PoeticA in 2006. She is involved with her local pony club and still competes in one-day eventing.

Maxine Kumin's newest poetry collection is *Still To Mow,* (W.W. Norton). Norton also published *Jack and Other New Poems, Bringing Together, The Long Marriage* and earlier collections, including *Connecting the Dots* and *New and Selected Poems 1960-1990.* Kumin's new children's book, *Miles to Mastodons*, has recently been published by Houghton Mifflin. She is also the author of a memoir about a nearly fatal carriage-driving accident, *Inside the Halo and Beyond: Anatomy of a Recovery.* Her awards include the Pulitzer and Ruth Lilly Poetry Prizes and the Harvard Arts and Robert Frost Medals. She and her husband live on a farm in Warner, New Hampshire.

Laurie Clements Lambeth grew up in California. Her first collection of poetry, *Veil and Burn* (University of Illinois Press), was selected by Maxine Kumin for the 2006 National Poetry Series. A PhD and MFA graduate of the University of Houston, her poems and essays have appeared in *The Paris Review, Indiana Review, Mid-American Review, The Iowa Review,* and elsewhere.

Lance Larsen has published two poetry collections: *Erasable Walls* (1998) and *In All Their Animal Brilliance* (2005), the latter of which won the Tampa Review Prize. A third collection will appear in 2008, with University of Tampa Press. His poems have appeared in *New York Review of Books, Paris Review, Southern Review, Kenyon Review, Threepenny Review, TLS, The Pushcart Book of Poetry: the Best Poems from the First 30 Years,* and elsewhere. A professor at Brigham Young University, Larsen has received a number of literary awards, most recently a poetry fellowship from the NEA. He does not own any horses, but lives next door to the 2007 Little Buckaroo Rodeo Queen.

Dorianne Laux's fourth book of poems, a finalist for the National Book Critics Circle Award, *Facts about the Moon* (W.W. Norton), is the recipient of the Oregon Book Award. It was also short-listed for the 2006 Lenore Marshall Poetry Prize for the most outstanding book of poems published in the United States in the previous year and was chosen by the Kansas City Star as one of the ten best books of poetry published in 2005. Laux is also author of three collections of poetry from BOA Editions, *Awake* (1990) introduced by Philip Levine, soon to be reprinted by Eastern Washington University Press, *What We Carry* (1994), and *Smoke* (2000). Red Dragonfly Press will release *Superman: The Chapbook,* later this year.

Kerry Lawrynovicz' poetry has most recently been published in the *Electronic Literature Collection, Volume One,* and will be featured in N. Katherine Hayles' forthcoming book, *Electronic Literature: Teaching, Interpreting, Playing* (Notre Dame University Press, 2007).

Donna J. Gelagotis Lee's book, *On the Altar of Greece* (Gival Press, 2006), is the winner of the Gival Press Poetry Award. The collection received a 2007 Eric Hoffer Book Award: Notable for Art Category. *On the Altar of Greece* has been nominated for seven awards, including a *Los Angeles Times* Book Prize. Donna's poetry has appeared in numerous literary and scholarly journals, such as *Calyx: A Journal of Art and Literature by Women, Feminist Studies, The Massachusetts Review, The Midwest Quarterly, and Seattle Review.* Donna's manuscript "Deciding Not to Wear Glasses" was a finalist for the May Swenson Poetry Award. Her equine-themed manuscript is "Chaps." Donna earned a BA, cum laude, in English and creative writing from Sweet Briar College. She worked as a researcher for *CLASSIC: The Magazine About Horses & Sport.* Donna is a freelance editor in New Jersey.

Joseph Leff has an MFA in fiction writing from Columbia University and has been nominated for a Pushcart Prize for poetry. He is currently working on a long poem set in New York in the 1960s and a short novel set in Paris in the 1860s. He lives in Santa Monica, CA and works as a teacher.

Ken Letko is the author of three chapbooks of poetry and numerous poems published in anthologies and magazines nationwide, including the *North American Review,* which nominated "Mannequin with Teeth" for a Pushcart Prize in 2005. Recently he was named the recipient of the Frederick Morgan Poetry Prize, a first book competition sponsored by Story Line Press. His manuscript, tentatively titled *Shelter for Those Who Need It,* was chosen from a field of 800 applicants. He currently teaches at College of the Redwoods.

Larry Levis received a BA from CSU, Fresno in 1968, an MA from Syracuse University in 1970, and a PhD from the University of Iowa in 1974. His first book of poems, *Wrecking Crew* (1972), won the United States Award from the International Poetry Forum. *The Afterlife* (1976) was the Lamont Poetry Selection of The American Academy of Poets. *The Dollmaker's Ghost* (1981) was a winner of the Open Competition of the National Poetry Series. *Winter Stars* was published in 1985 in the Pitt Poetry series. Among his honors are a YM-YWHA Discovery Award, three fellowships in poetry from the NEA, a Fulbright Fellowship, and a Guggenheim Fellowship. He taught English at the University of Missouri from 1974-1980, was an associate professor and directed the creative writing program at the University of Utah from 1980-1992, and from 1992 until his death in 1996 was a professor of English at Virginia Commonwealth University. His last collection, *Elegy*, edited by Philip Levine was published posthumously in 1997.

Lisa Lewis is the author of *The Unbeliever* (University of Wisconsin Press, 1994, as a winner of the Brittingham Prize) and *Silent Treatment* (Penguin Books, 1998 and a 1998 National Poetry Series selection). She directs the creative writing program at Oklahoma State University and serves as poetry editor for the *Cimmaron Review.* Her recent work has appeared or is forthcoming in the *Crab Orchard Review, Michigan Quarterly Review, Florida Review, Sweeping Beauty: Contemporary Women Poets Do Housework, Smartish Pace, Under the Rock Umbrella: Contemporary American Poets 1951-1977, The Journal,* and *32 Poems.*

George Looney's third full-length collection of poetry, *The Precarious Rhetoric of Angels,* won the tenth annual White Pine Press Poetry Prize and was published by White Pine Press in 2005. His first collection, *Animals Housed in the Pleasure of Flesh,* won the 1995 Bluestem Award. Cleveland State University Press published his second collection, *Attendant Ghosts,* in 2000. He is chair of the BFA in Creative Writing program at Penn State Erie, where he is editor-in-chief of *Lake Effect,* and translation editor of *Mid-American Review.* He received a $10,000 fellowship in poetry from Pennsylvania for 2006.

Jacqueline M. Loring is an avid photographer and poet whose publications include the Scribner anthology *From Both Sides Now: Poetry from the Vietnam War and its Aftermath* and *A Sense of Place: An Anthology of Cape Women Writers.* She is the executive director of the Cape Cod Writer's Center. She has received grants from the Massachusetts Cultural Council, the Bourne Cultural Council and Arts Foundation of Cape Cod, and in 2005 she was granted an artist's residency at The Ragdale Foundation in Lake Forest, Illinois. She is a yearly judge of the Veterans for Peace Poetry Contest and has been a poetry judge for the Cape Cod Times' Prime Time Poetry Contest. She has written five scripts and two short plays. In 2006 she was included in the Cape Cod Life's top 100 Cape Codders. She and her husband are the parents of biological, adopted, and foster children and live on the west coast of Cape Cod.

Christiane Marks was born in Germany in 1938 and came to the U.S.A. in 1947 with her mother and sister to rejoin her father who had been detained here while on a visit just before the States entered World War II. She holds a BA in comparative literature (English, German, and French) and an MA in German. She is a member of the American Translators' Association and has translated numerous articles and two books on anthroposophical subjects. She has also translated poetry, including Rilke's ninth "Duino Elegy" and all fifty-five of his "Sonnets to Orpheus." Her translations of seven of the sonnets have been published in *The International Poetry Review* (Spring 2003) and one, along with her commentary, appeared in *The Potomac Review* (Fall 2000). Her original poems are taken from a cycle of fifty short poems and are being used by a Hospice counselor in his practice, and by another acquaintance in her "threshold work."

Beverly Matherne, director of the MFA program at Northern Michigan University, has published four books of bilingual poetry, including *La Grande Point/Grand Point and Le blues braillant/The Blues Cryin.* Her translation, with Nicole J. M. Kennedy, of *The Artist/l'Artiste,* by former U.S. Poet Laureate Stanley Kunitz, was released at the Fine Arts Work Center in Provincetown, MA, in 2006. She received the Hackney Literary Award for Poetry and has read at the United Nations and on Grace Cavalieri's radio show, "The Poet and the Poem." Currently on sabbatical, she is completing two books of prose poetry, one set in Cajun Country in Louisiana; the other, along the Garonne River in France. She received BA and MA degrees in English from the University of Louisiana at Lafayette, received a PhD in drama from Saint Louis University, and did extensive post-doctoral work in French literature and critical theory at the University of California at Berkeley.

Gail Mazur's new book, *Zeppo's First Wife: New & Selected Poems* (Chicago, 2005), is winner of the 2006 Massachusetts Book Award, a finalist for the 2005 *Los Angeles Times* Book Prize and for the 2006 Paterson Poetry Prize. She is author of four earlier books of poetry, *Nightfire, The Pose of Happiness, The Common,* and *They Can't Take That Away from Me* (University of Chicago Press), which was a finalist for the National Book Award in 2001. She is Writer in Residence at Emerson College and Founding Director of the Blacksmith House Poetry Series in Cambridge, a weekly poetry reading series she ran for twenty-nine years. Mazur was a fellow at the Bunting Institute of Radcliffe College, and the 2005 recipient of the St. Botolph Club Foundation's Distinguished Artist Award. An interview with Mazur about her work is online at *The Atlantic*. She and her husband, the artist Michael Mazur, live in Cambridge and Provincetown, Massachusetts, where she serves on the Writing Committee and Summer Program Committee of the Fine Arts Work Center.

Linda McCarriston says that until she was forty-three, her horses were dreams and wishes. Growing up in a tenement in Lynn, Massachusetts, and remaining in her hometown until she was nearly thirty, she was unable to pursue her dream until she settled in Vermont in 1979. She lives in Maine now with her half Arab mare, Moriah Jane, whom she bought (at eighteen months old) in 1986, brought with her in 1994 when she traveled to Alaska for work, and brought back home in September 2006. Both are well and young for their ages.

Pamela McClure lives in Columbia, Missouri with an assortment of animals, many of whom are equines. Her book, *Rock Dove,* is forthcoming from Red Dragonfly Press. She holds a PhD from the University of Missouri and teaches creative writing at Columbia College, Columbia, Missouri.

Ron McFarland teaches literature and creative writing at the University of Idaho. His new & selected poems, *Stranger in Town,* was published by Confluence Press in 2000; his most recent publications are chapbooks from Pudding House Press, *Ron McFarland's Greatest Hits, 1976-2002* (2003) and *At the Ballpark* (2006).

Valerie Mejer, poet, painter, and essayist, was born in 1966 in Mexico City. She has twice been the recipient of grants from FONCA (Jóvenes Creadores), and for her book *De Elefante a Elefante,* she was awarded the International Award "Gerardo Diego 1966" by the Spanish Government. She is also the author of the books of poetry *Esta Novela Azul,* (Editorial El Tucán de Virginia, México, 2004) and *Ante el Ojo del Cíclope (*Ed Tierra Adentro, México, 2000). Her poetry has appeared in the anthologies *El Corazón Prestado, Antología de Poesía de Tema Prehispánico* and *El Manatial Latente, Muestra de poesía mexicana desde el ahora: 1986-2002.* Her poems in English have appeared in England in *Poetry London* and in the United States in *Hunger Mountain Review* and in *Translations.* She has translated (in collaboration with E. M. Test) Charles Wright's *Apalaquia/ Apalachia,* Forrest Gander's *Torn Awake/Arrancado del Sueño,* and Pascal Petit's *The Zoo Father/ El Padre Zoológico* (all published by Tucan de Virginia Press). Recently she received a grant from Sistema Estatal de Creadores from the state of Guanajuato to translate the Australian poet Les Murray. She is the cover artist for *Cadence of Hooves: A Celebration of Horses.*

Ann E. Michael (www.annemichael.com) writes poems and essays from her home in Pennsylvania, where she lives with her husband and two children. Her work has been published in many journals, including *Poem, 9th Letter, The Writer's Chronicle, Natural Bridge, Runes,* and others. She is a past recipient of a Pennsylvania Council on the Arts Fellowship in Poetry. Her chapbooks include *More than Shelter, Small Things Rise & Go,* and *The Minor Fauna.*

Jen Michaels is currently a lecturer at the University of Michigan-Ann Arbor, where she was hired as a faculty member in the Sweetland Writing Center after graduating from their MFA program in April

2006. After work each day, she visits her horse Skyler, a chestnut Thoroughbred who is both her best student and her favorite teacher. Before pursuing her MFA, she studied as an undergraduate with Charles Wright and Rita Dove at the University of Virginia. Her work appeared in the Spring 2006 issue of the *Hiram Poetry Review.*

Joseph Millar's first collection, *Overtime* (EWU Press, 2001) was a finalist for the Oregon Book Award. Millar grew up in Pennsylvania and took an MA from Johns Hopkins in 1970. He spent the next 25 years in the San Francisco Bay area working at a variety of jobs, from telephone repairman to commercial fisherman. His work has won fellowships from the NEA and Oregon Literary Arts. Recent poems can be found in *Willow Springs, New Letters, River Styx* and on *Poetry Daily.* In 1997 he gave up his job as telephone installation foreman and moved to western Oregon where he now teaches in Pacific University's low residency MFA. His second book, *Fortune,* was recently published by Eastern Washington University Press.

Nathaniel Miles Millard received an MA in English from California State University, Chico and is currently a doctoral student at Utah State University in the Department of Environment and Society in the College of Natural Resources. A land-locked surfer, he spends his free time from school exploring the crags with his dog, Chico, trying to write a few good lines. He hasn't ridden a horse since he was bucked from a bareback ride he stole from an unknown mare in a field near his house at the age of six. It didn't get his goat, but the pigs were called, and he's been on the lam ever since.

Judith H. Montgomery's poems appear in *The Southern Review, The Bellingham Review, Gulf Coast,* and *Northwest Review,* among other journals, as well as in several anthologies. She's been awarded prizes from the National Writers Union, Americas Review, and Red Rock Review, and several nominations for Pushcart prizes. Her chapbook, *Passion,* received the 2000 Oregon Book Award for poetry. Her first full-length collection, *Red Jess,* appeared in February 2006. Her new chapbook, *Pulse & Constellation,* is just out from Finishing Line Press. She holds a PhD in American literature from Syracuse University.

Peter Nash is a semi-retired family physician who lives in a small rural community in northern California. He writes, helps his wife in the garden, boards horses, makes house calls in his pickup with his dog Henry, and participates in the Mattole Salmon Group whose goal is the restoration of the Mattole River. Much of his writing attempts to reflect his awe of the natural world. He has recently been published in *Snowy Egret, Tapestries, Camas, Off the Coast, Passager,* and *City*

Works. He received honorable mention in the 2005 Thomas Merton Poetry of the Sacred Contest.

Charles Nauman is a filmmaker, whose most recent film release: "Tarahumara: Festival of the Easter Moon," was honored in March 2006 at the International Festival of Ethnographic films, at The Museum of Man in Paris, France. His prose and poetry have been published in the *Iowa Review,* the *Lakota Journal, Prairie Winds* and others.

Sheila Nickerson has received two Pushcart Prizes for her poetry, which has appeared in numerous magazines, anthologies, and chapbooks. Her most recent nonfiction titles are *Disappearance: A Map* and *Midnight to the North: The Untold Story of the Inuit Woman Who Saved the Polaris Expedition.*

Biljana D. Obradovic, a Serbian-American, is associate professor of English at Xavier University of Louisiana, in New Orleans. Her collections of poems include *Frozen Embraces* (Belgrade, Center of Emigrants from Serbia, and Merrick, NY, Cross-Cultural Communications 1997), *Le Riche Monde* (Belgrade, Raška Škola, adn Merrrick, NY, Cross-Cultural Communications,1999). Her poems also appear in *Three Poets in New Orleans* (New Orleans, Xavier Review Press, 2000). In addition to her own poetry, other works include her Serbian translation of John Gery's *American Ghosts: Selected Poems* (Belgrade, Raška Škola, 1999) and *Fives: Fifty Poems by Serbian and American Poets, A Bilingual Anthology,* as editor and translator (Co-published by Belgrade, Contact Line and Merrick, NY, Cross-Cultural Communications, 2002). Forthcoming books include her translation of Stanley Kunitz into Serbian, *The Long Boat* (Co-published by Plato, Belgrade, Yugoslavia and Cross-Cultural Communications, Merrick, NY, expected 2007), and of Desanka Maksimovi and Bratislav Milanovi into English.

Carole Simmons Oles is the author of eight books of poems, most recently *Waking Stone: Inventions on the Life of Harriet Hosmer* from University of Arkansas Press. Among her awards are an NEA Grant in Poetry, the Virginia Prize, two Strousse Awards and the Virginia Faulkner Award from *Prairie Schooner,* a Pushcart Prize, and the Poetry Society of America's Gertrude B. Claytor Prize and Robert H. Winner and Ruth Lake Memorial Awards. Her work has appeared in *American Poetry Review, Field, Poetry, Prairie Schooner, The Women's Review of Books* and other magazines. Since 1992 she has been on the faculty at California State University in Chico, where she is Professor Emerita. For many summers, she was on the faculty at Bread Loaf

Artist/Scholar at American Academy in Rome.

Gregory Orr is the author of nine collections of poetry, including *Concerning The Book That Is The Body Of The Beloved* (Copper Canyon Press, 2005), *The Caged Owl: New and Selected Poems* (2002), *Orpheus and Eurydice* (2001), *City of Salt* (Finalist, *LA Times* Poetry Prize), *We Must Make a Kingdom of It, The Red House, Gathering the Bones Together,* and *Burning the Empty Nests.* He is the recipient of a Guggenheim Fellowship, two poetry fellowships from the NEA, the Award in Literature by the American Academy of Arts and Letters, and he has been a Rockefeller Fellow at the Institute for the Study of Culture and Violence. He is a professor of English at the University of Virginia, where he has taught since 1975 and was the founder and first director of its MFA Program in Writing. He served from 1978 to 2003 as poetry editor of the *Virginia Quarterly Review.* He lives with his wife, a painter, and his two daughters in Charlottesville, Virginia.

Sarah Pape is a writing teacher at California State University, Chico. Her poetry was selected by Kim Addonizio as a finalist for *The Southeast Review* 2006 Poetry Contest, and has been published in *Watershed.* She lives and writes in Chico, California with her daughter, Sylvia.

Joy Passanante is the associate director of creative writing at the University of Idaho. Her poems, essays, and stories have appeared in numerous magazines including *The Gettysburg Review, Short Story, The Georgia Review,* and *College English.* Her awards include two fellowships from the Idaho Commission on the Arts and a Research Fellowship from the Idaho Humanities Council. She has published a fine-press collection of poems, *Sinning in Italy*; a novel, *My Mother's Lovers*; and a collection of stories, *The Art of Absence.* Both her prose books were finalists for several awards, including the *ForeWord Magazine* Book of the Year Award and the Idaho Book of the Year Award.

Molly Peacock wrote "In a Long Line of Horses" after taking a few horseback riding lessons with the poet Phillis Levin in New York City, then going West and visiting Bryce Canyon. She is former president of the Poetry Society of America and one of the founders of Poetry in Motion on the nation's subways and buses. She is the author of six books of poetry, including *Cornucopia: New and Selected Poems* and, forthcoming, *The Second Blush,* from W.W. Norton and Company. Molly Peacock is a member of the graduate faculty of the Spalding University Brief Residency MFA Program.

Natalie Peeterse has an MFA from the University of Montana. Her poetry has appeared in *CutBank 30th Anniversary Edition, Blackbird,* and *Sonora Review,* among other journals. She has been a fellow with the Arizona Commission on the Arts.

C. E. Perry graduated from the Iowa Writers' Workshop in 1992 and Dartmouth Medical School in 1999. Her work has been published in *Southern Poetry Review, Pool, Southeast Review,* and *GSU Review.* She lives in San Francisco with her family.

Roger Pfingston is a retired teacher of English and photography. His poems and photographs have appeared recently in *Innisfree Poetry Journal, Poems Niederngasse, The Sun, The Ledge, Triplopia,* and *Diner.* He also has poems in two anthologies just out from Iowa Press: *Say This of Horses* and *75 Poems on Retirement.* His most recent chapbooks are *Earthbound* from Pudding House Publications and *Singing to the Garden* from Parallel Press.

Donald Platt is the author of *My Father Says Grace,* (University of Arkansas Press) and *Fresh Peaches, Fireworks, & Guns,* and *Cloud Atlas,* (Purdue University Press as winners of the Verna Emery Poetry Prize). A letterpress, limited edition of his poems, entitled *Leap Second at the Turn of the Millennium,* was published in 1999 as the winner of the Center for Book Arts' Poetry Chapbook Competition. He is a recipient of a fellowship from the NEA, of the Paumanok Poetry Prize, and of the Discovery/The Nation Prize. Over the years, his poems have appeared in numerous literary journals as well as in *The Best American Poetry 2000* and *2006* and in *The Pushcart Prize XXVII* and *XXIX* (the 2003 and 2005 editions). Currently he is an associate professor of English at Purdue University.

Ruth Porritt's work has appeared in *The Bedford Introduction to Literature, Writing Poems, Thirteen Ways of Looking for a Poem,* and *How Shall We Tell Each Other of the Poet?,* among others.

Marnie Prange is the author of *Dangerous Neighborhoods* (CSU Press), and she teaches poetry in the schools through the Missoula Writing Collaborative. She lives in the Bitterroot Valley of western Montana with her husband, poet Greg Pape, and their two sons. She owns a dressage horse. "Courting Terror" was written after she came back to horses after a twenty-five year hiatus.

Noah Raizman is a resident in orthopedic surgery in Washington, DC. He received his MFA from Columbia University and has published poems in *Barrow Street, Western Humanities Review,* and *Journal of the American Medical Association,* and he reviews in *The*

Lancet and elsewhere. He is at work on his first book of poems.

Tony Reevy is the associate director for advancement of the Institute for the Environment at the University of North Carolina at Chapel Hill and is a graduate of North Carolina State University, UNC-Chapel Hill and Miami University. He is a David P. Morgan Award winner (2006) and a Pushcart Prize nominee. His previous publications include poetry, non-fiction, and short fiction. His poems are anthologized in *Earth and Soul: An Anthology of North Carolina Poetry, Poets for Peace: A Collection,* and many others. His books/chapbooks are *Ghost Train!: American Railroad Ghost Legends, A Directory of North Carolina's Railroad Structures* (with Art Peterson and Sonny Dowdy), *Green Cove Stop,* and *Magdalena.* His poetry chapbook, *Lightning in Wartime,* is pending publication from Finishing Line Press. He resides in Durham, North Carolina with wife, Caroline Weaver, and children Lindley and Ian.

Bethany Reid's poems have recently appeared in *Calyx, Santa Clara Review, North Dakota Quarterly, Prairie Schooner, Cascade, Pontoon, Stringtown,* and *Crosscurrents.* Although she grew up on a farm (complete with horses), she now lives near Seattle with her husband and three daughters.

James Richardson's most recent books are *Interglacial: New and Selected Poems and Aphorisms,* which was a finalist for the 2005 National Book Critics Circle Award, and *Vectors: Aphorisms and Ten-Second Essays.* He teaches at Princeton University.

Alberto Álvaro Ríos, a recent finalist for the National Book Award, is the author of nine books and chapbooks of poetry, including most recently *The Theater of Night*—winner of the 2007 PEN/Beyond Margins Award—three collections of short stories, and a memoir about growing up on the border, *Capirotada.* Ríos is the recipient of the Western Literature Association Distinguished Achievement Award, the Arizona Governor's Arts Award, fellowships from the Guggenheim Foundation and the NEA, the Walt Whitman Award, the Western States Book Award for Fiction, six Pushcart Prizes in both poetry and fiction, and is included in *The Norton Anthology of Modern Poetry,* as well as over 200 other national and international literary anthologies. His work is regularly taught and translated, and has been adapted to dance and both classical and popular music. Ríos is a Regents' Professor and the Katharine C. Turner Chair in English at Arizona State University.

Anele Rubin's poems have appeared in *Great River Review, The Midwest Quarterly, River Styx, Rhino, Paterson Literary Review, O,* the

Oprah Magazine, and many other places. Her first book, *Trying to Speak,* won the Wick Poetry Prize and was published by Kent State University Press in 2005. She is the recipient of the Great Lakes Colleges Association's 2006 New Writers Award in Poetry.

Benjamin Russell is a recent graduate of the MFA Program at New England College in New Hampshire. His poetry has appeared most recently in *RE:AL* and *Ward 6 Review.* Poems are forthcoming in *5 AM* and *Blood Orange Review.* He was also co-director of the award-winning Mad Poets' Cafe program at the Warwick Museum of Art before its closure. He teaches high school English in Providence, where he is a lacrosse coach and the co-moderator of the student poetry union.

Alan Botsford Saitoh, born in Connecticut and educated at Wesleyan University, has published two books of poetry: *A Book of Shadows* (Katydid Books, 2003), and *mamaist: learning a new language* (Minato No Hito, 2002). He has been a Pushcart Prize nominee for poetry in 2001 and holds an MFA from Columbia University. He lives in Japan with his wife and son where he teaches at Kanto Gakuin University and co-edits Poetry Kanto (http://home.kanto-gakuin.ac.jp/~kg061001/). His website is http://home.kanto-gakuin.ac.jp/~alan.

Floyd Salas is an award-winning author of seven books, including the novels *Tattoo the Wicked Cross, What Now My Love, Lay My Body on the Line,* and *State of Emergency,* the memoir *Buffalo Nickel,* and two books of poetry, *Color of My Living Heart* and, most recently, *Love Bites: Poetry in Celebration of Dogs and Cats.* He was 2002-2003 Regent's Lecturer at University of California, Berkeley, staff writer for the NBC drama series, Kingpin, and the recipient of a California Arts Council Literary Fellowship, Rockefeller Foundation Fiction Scholarship, an NEA creative writing fellowship, the Joseph Henry Jackson Award, a Eugene F. Saxton Fellowship, and two outstanding teaching awards from the University of California, Berkeley. *Tattoo the Wicked Cross* and *Buffalo Nickel* are featured in *Masterpieces of Hispanic Literature* (HarperCollins 1994). His manuscripts and papers are archived in the Floyd Salas collection in the Bancroft Library, University of California, Berkeley.

Michael Salcman is a physician, brain scientist, and essayist on the visual arts. He was chairman of the Department of Neurosurgery at the University of Maryland and president of the Contemporary Museum in Baltimore. Recent poems have or will appear in such magazines as *Harvard Review, Raritan, River Styx, Southern Poetry Review, Notre Dame Review,* and *New York Quarterly.* His fourth chapbook is *Stones In Our Pockets* (Parallel Press, University of Wisconsin-Madison), and his first collection is *The Clock Made of Confetti* (Orchises, Washington, D.C.).

Mark Sanders is a professor of English at Lewis-Clark State College; he and his wife have six horses on their acreage in the Lewiston Orchards. His creative prose has appeared in such journals as *Shenandoah, River Teeth, South Dakota Review, North Dakota Quarterly,* and *Glimmer Train.* His most recent collection of poems is *Here in the Big Empty* (Backwaters Press, 2006); his other books are *The Suicide* (Cummington Press, 1988), *Before We Lost Our Ways* (Hurakan/College of the Mainland, 1996), and *A Dissimulation of Birds: Stories* (Crane Editions, 2002). A Nebraska native, he has a PhD in Modern Poetry from the University of Nebraska and is nearing completion of his second PhD in Higher Ed Administration at the University of Idaho.

Jeannine Savard has published three volumes of poetry, the most recent in 2005, *My Hand Upon Your Name* (Red Hen Press), and a republished first book, *Snow Water Cove* with Carnegie Mellon's Classic Contemporary Series in 2006. She is working on her next manuscript of poems, *Spring Advisory From A Book Of Changes.* She is the director of the undergraduate concentration in creative writing for English majors at Arizona State University.

Maggie Schwed is a former English teacher who lives in New York City and spends not enough time every year in Wyoming where she learned to ride bareback. Her work has appeared or is forthcoming in *Raritan, Nimrod, Rattapallax, Commonweal, Pleiades,* and other magazines, as well as in the Phil Miller and Gloria Vando anthology, *Chance of a Ghost.* On-line publications include NYCBigCityLit.com, RealPoetikBlog.com, and Blackbird. She was a semi-finalist in the 2006 Morton Marr Poetry Prize contest. She reviews poetry books for *Pleiades* and Greekworks.com. She is sending around her first manuscript of poems, called *Cricket and Thunder.*

Vivian Shipley is a Connecticut State University Distinguished Professor and Editor of *Connecticut Review* from Southern Connecticut State University. Shipley's seventh book, *Hardboot* (Southeastern Louisiana University Press, 2005), received the 2006 Paterson Prize for Sustained Literary Achievement. She was awarded Library of Congress's 2005 Connecticut Lifetime Achievement Award. *Gleanings* (Southeastern Louisiana University Press, 2003), nominated for the Pulitzer Prize, received the 2004 Paterson Prize. *When There Is No Shore* (Word Press Prize, 2002) won the Library of Congress 2003 Connecticut Book Award for Poetry. Raised in Kentucky with a PhD from Vanderbilt, she has also published five chapbooks. Her most recent prize is the 2007 Hackney Literary Award for Poetry from Birmingham-Southern University.

Sue Sinclair is a Canadian poet who has published three collections of poems. The latest of these, *The Drunken Lovely Bird,* won the American Independent Publishers Association's poetry award. A new collection of poems is forthcoming with Brick Books in 2008.

Anita Skeen is the author of four volumes of poetry, *Each Hand A Map; Portraits; Outside the Fold, Outside the Frame;* and *The Resurrection of the Animals,* and she has just co-authored a book of poems, *When We Say Shelter* with poet Jane Taylor. Her poetry, short fiction, and essays have appeared in numerous literary magazines and anthologies. She has completed a new volume of poetry, *Never the Whole Story,* begun while she was a Fellow at the Virginia Center for the Creative Arts and is working on a collection of short stories and a first novel. She is the director of the Creative Arts Festival at Ghost Ranch Conference Center in Abiquiu, New Mexico each August and the October Writing Festival there each fall. She is currently a professor in the Residential College in the Arts and Humanities at Michigan State where she is the arts coordinator and director of the Center for Poetry.

Judith Skillman's book *Heat Lightning: New and Selected Poems 1986-2006* was published in April, 2006 by Silverfish Review Press. Her tenth book, *The Coppelia, Certain Digressions* was released in October 2006 from David Robert Books. Skillman is the recipient of the Eric Mathieu King Fund Award from the Academy of American Poets for "Storm," (Blue Begonia Press, 1998). Her poems have appeared in *Poetry, FIELD, The Southern Review, Northwest Review, The Iowa Review, Prairie Schooner,* and other journals. She is a faculty member at University of Phoenix and the Richard Hugo House. Please see www.judithskillman.com for more information.

Hannah Stein's full-length collection of poetry, *Earthlight,* is published by La Questa Press. Her chapbooks include *Schools of Flying Fish* and *Greatest Hits of Hannah Stein, 1981-2004.* Recent and forthcoming poems, as well as essays on contemporary poetry, appear in numerous journals, including *Nimrod, Hunger Mountain, Calyx, Poetry Flash, Confrontation,* and *American Literary Review.* Her work has been featured online in Poetry Daily, Verse Daily, PoetryMagazine.com, and Perihelion. Prizes she's won include the National Poetry Competition, the Anna Davidson Rosenberg Award, the Americas Review prize, and the Betty Hall Cobb Memorial poetry contest, plus several Pushcart nominations. She lives in Davis, California.

Barry Sternlieb's work appears in *Poetry, The Southern Review, The Gettysburg Review, Virginia Quarterly Review, New England Review, Alaska Quarterly Review,* and others. He is the recipient of a 2004 Massachusetts Cultural Council Artist Grant in Poetry. In addition, he edits Mad River Press, specializing in handmade letterpress poetry prints and chapbooks since 1986.

Margo Stever's first full-length collection of poetry, *Frozen Spring* (2002), was the winner of the Mid-List Press First Series Award for Poetry. Her chapbook, *Reading the Night Sky,* won the 1996 Riverstone Poetry Chapbook Competition. Her articles and book reviews have appeared in the *Connecticut Review, Minnesota Review, Rain Taxi Review, Home Planet News, New Delta Review, Calyx,* and *Poets & Writers,* among other places. She has edited *Imperiled Landscapes, Endangered Legends* (Rizzoli International Publications, 1997) and *Voices from the River* (Slapering Hol Press, 1990). Her poems have appeared widely in literary magazines and in numerous anthologies including *Dire Elegies* (Foothills Press, 2006); *Chance of a Ghost* (Helicon Nine Publications, 2005); and *The Breath of Parted Lips, Volume II,* (KavanKerry Press, 2004). She is the founder and current board member of The Hudson Valley Writers' Center and the founding editor of the Slapering Hol Press.

Lisa Stewart is marketing director for Old World Spices & Seasonings in Kansas City, Mo. where she lives with her husband Robert Stewart and 15-year-old daughter Natalie Brown. She is also a weekend freelance magazine writer and poet. Stewart is working on a prose memoir about a 3,000-mile horseback trip she took in 1982, through the western United States.

Leon Stokesbury teaches in the graduate creative writing program at Georgia State University in Atlanta. His first book, *Often in Different Landscapes,* was a co-winner of the first AWP Poetry Competition in 1975. His latest book, *Autumn Rhythm: New & Selected Poems,* was awarded The Poets' Prize in 1998. He has also edited the largest and most comprehensive anthologies on the subjects of World War II and Contemporary Southern Poetry.

David R. Surette's first book of poetry is *Young Gentlemen's School* (Koenisha, 2004). Koenisha published David's second collection, *Easy to Keep, Hard to Keep In* in 2007. He also has three poems in *French Connections: A Gathering of Franco-American Poets* (Louisiana Literature Press 2007) and a poem in *Look! Up In The Sky!- An Anthology of Comic Book Poetry* (Sacred Fools Press 2007). He co-hosts Poetribe, a poetry series in southeastern Massachusetts.

Pablo Tanguay lives in Columbus, Ohio, with wife Sandy, dogs Gabriel and Sadie, and brand new baby Lola. He has never ridden a horse.

Stephen Tapscott has published five books of poems and has translated, recently, The *Selected Prose and Prose-poems of Gabriela Mistral.*

Henry Taylor is Professor Emeritus of Literature at American University, where he taught from 1971 until 2003. His books of poems are *The Horse Show at Midnight* (1966), *An Afternoon of Pocket Billiards* (1975), *The Flying Change* (1985; Pulitzer Prize), *Understanding Fiction: Poems 1986-1996* (1996), *Brief Candles:101 Clerihews* (2000), and *Crooked Run* (2006). He has received fellowships in creative writing from the NEA, awards from the American Academy and Institute of Arts and Letters, and the Aiken Taylor Award in Modern American Poetry.

Elaine Terranova was named a Pew Fellow in the Arts in poetry for 2006. Her most recent book is *NOT TO: New and Selected Poems.* She won the Walt Whitman Award of the Academy of American Poets for her first book, *The Cult of the Right Hand.* Her translation of Euripides' *Iphigenia at Aulis* is part of the Penn Greek Drama Series. She received an NEA fellowship and two Pennsylvania Council on the Arts grants for her poetry. She has been Banister Writer at Sweet Briar College and a winner of the Anna Davidson Rosenberg award. Her poems have been published in magazines and anthologies such as *The New Yorker, Prairie Schooner, The American Poetry Review, and Virginia Quarterly Review.*

Diane Thiel is the author of six books of poetry, nonfiction, and creative writing pedagogy: *Echolocations* (Nicholas Roerich Prize), *Writing Your Rhythm, The White Horse: A Columbian Journey, Resistance Fantasies, Crossroads: Creative Writing Exercises in Four Genres,* and *Open Roads: Exercises in Writing Poetry.* Her work appears in *Poetry, Best American Poetry 1999,* and is reprinted in over thirty major anthologies. A recent Fulbright Scholar, she is Associate Professor at the University of New Mexico.

Matthew Thorburn's first book is *Subject to Change* (New Issues, 2004). His poems have also appeared more recently in *Paris Review, Barrow Street,* and *Michigan Quarterly Review.* "Horse Poetica" is part of a new manuscript entitled *Like Luck.*

Georgia Tiffany is a native of Spokane, Washington, and now lives in Moscow, Idaho. Her work has appeared in such publications as

Agenda, The Xavier Review, Hampden-Sydney Poetry Review, Tar River Poetry, Flint Hills Review, Willow Springs, Mid-America Poetry Review, Rhino, Hubbub, Iris, South Dakota Review, Malahat Review, Poetry Ireland, Fugue, North Dakota Quarterly, and *American Forests.* She holds advanced degrees from Indiana University and the University of Idaho. Her chapbook *Cut From The Score* was published this year by Night Owl Press.

Annie Tobin is a poet, artist, and teacher who lives in San Jose, California with her partner Kate, their two dogs, and a cat. She'd have a horse, but the back yard is a little too small.

Daniel Tobin's poems have appeared in *The Times Literary Supplement, Poetry, Agenda, Stand, The American Scholar, The Paris Review, Shenandoah, DoubleTake, Yankee, The Dalhousie Review, Poetry Ireland Review, The Hudson Review, The Southern Review,* and elsewhere. His awards include The Discovery/The Nation Award from the NEA, the Robert Frost Fellowship from Bread Loaf, and The Robert Penn Warren Award, among others. His poems have been anthologized in *The Bread Loaf Anthology of New American Poets, Hammer and Blaze, The Norton Introduction to Poetry,* and elsewhere. He is the author of *Where the World is Made* (1998 Katherine Bakeless Nason Prize co-winner, University Press of New England, 1999), *Double Life* (Louisiana State University Press, 2004), *The Narrows* (Four Way Books), *Passage to the Center: Imagination and the Sacred in the Poetry of Seamus Heaney* (University of Kentucky Press, 1999). He is the editor of *The Book of Irish American Poetry from the Eighteenth Century to the Present* (Notre Dame, 2007), and is the chair of the Writing, Literature, and Publishing Department at Emerson College in Boston.

J. C. Todd was a finalist in the Poetry Society of America's 2005 Lucille Medwick contest. Her work has appeared in *Wild River Review 1:2, American Poetry Review, Paris Review,* and on Verse Daily. Pine Press has published two chapbooks, *Nightshade* (1995) and *Entering Pisces* (1985). *What Space This Body,* a full-length collection, will be released by Wind Publications in fall 2007. Awards include a fellowship in poetry from the Pennsylvania Council on the Arts and two Leeway Awards. An associate editor at *The Drunken Boat,* she teaches creative writing at Bryn Mawr College.

Alison Townsend is the author of three books of poetry, *The Blue Dress, And Still the Music,* and *What the Body Knows.* Her poetry and creative nonfiction appear widely in journals such as *Fourth Genre, Gulf Coast, MARGIE, Michigan Quarterly Review,* and *The Southern Review.* Recent work in anthologies includes *Best American Poetry*

2006, Flash Fiction Forward, Sweeping Beauty, and *Kiss Me Goodnight: Poems and Stories by Women Who Were Girls When Their Mothers Died.* She has received many awards, including the 2005 Lorine Niedecker prize in poetry from the Council of Wisconsin Writers, a 2006 residency at the Virginia Center for the Arts, and a 2007 Fellowship from the Wisconsin Arts Board. She teaches English and creative writing at the University of Wisconsin-Whitewater, and lives with her husband on four acres of restored prairie and oak savanna in the farm country outside Madison.

Robert Tremmel teaches at Iowa State University. He is the author of *Zen and the Practice of Teaching English.* His most recent collection of poems is *Crossing Crocker Township* from Timberline Press.

Eric Trethewey has published six books of poems, most recently *Songs and Lamentations* and *Heart's Hornbook.* His poems, stories, essays, and reviews have appeared in numerous magazines and anthologies in Canada, Britain, and the U.S., among them *The Atlantic Monthly, The American Scholar, Canadian Literature, Encounter, The Georgia Review, The Gettysburg Review, The Hudson Review, The Iowa Review, The Kenyon Review, Missouri Review, New Letters, The New Republic, North American Review, Parnassus, The Paris Review, Ploughshares, Poetry, The Sewanee Review, The Southern Review, Stand,* and *The Yale Review.* He lives in Catawba, Virginia and teaches at Hollins University.

Sarah Vap is the co-editor of poetry for the online journal 42opus. She grew up in Montana with horses. Her book *Dummy Fire* won the 2006 Saturnalia Poetry Prize, and her book *American Spikenard* won the 2006 Iowa Poetry Prize.

Rosalynde Vas Dias is originally from Pennsylvania and currently lives in Providence, Rhode Island. Her poems have appeared in *The New Delta Review, Main Street Rag, The Comstock Review,* and *Christianity and Literature.* Ms. Vas Dias holds an MFA in Poetry from Warren Wilson College's Low-Residency Program for Writers. She is still captivated by the wild ponies of Assateague Island, twenty-one years after first learning of them.

Miles Waggener's first collection of poems, *Phoenix Suites* (The Word Works 03), won the 2002 Washington Prize. Recent poems have appeared in *Beloit Poetry Journal, The Antioch Review, Seneca Review, Crazyhorse, Green Mountains Review,* and others. A recipient of the Richard Hugo Memorial Scholarship at the University of Montana, an Academy of American Poets Prize, and a creative writing fellowship from the Arizona Commission on the Arts, Waggener is a member of the creative writing faculty at The University of Nebraska at Omaha.

Scott Ward's books are *Crucial Beauty* (SCOP Publications 1991), and *Wayward Passages* (Black Bay Books, 2006). His poems have appeared in *Christian Century, Southern Humanities Review, Shenandoah,* and in other journals and anthologies. He lives in St. Petersburg, Florida with his wife Jana and sons Caleb and Garland. He teaches creative writing at Eckerd College.

Michael Waters teaches at Salisbury University in Maryland and in the New England College MFA Program. Recent books include *Darling Vulgarity* (2006) and *Parthenopi: New and Selected Poems* (2001) from BOA Editions, and the new edition of *Contemporary American Poetry* (2006) from Houghton Mifflin. His poems have appeared in *Poetry, The American Poetry Review, The Yale Review, The Kenyon Review, The Georgia Review, The Gettysburg Review,* and *Rolling Stone,* as well as in three Pushcart Prize anthologies. The recipient of a fellowship in creative writing from the NEA, he was a Fulbright Lecturer in American literature in Romania in 2007.

Ellen Waterston's essays, short stories, and poems have been widely published in numerous journals, anthologies, and reviews. Her memoir, *Then There Was No Mountain,* (Rowman and Littlefield), was selected by the *Oregonian* as one of the top ten books of 2003 and earned her an appearance on Good Morning America with Diane Sawyer. *I Am Madagascar* was awarded the WILLA Prize in Poetry in 2005. She is the 2007 Obsidian Prize winner in poetry. Waterston has received nine writing residency fellowships, including a 2004 Ucross residency and the two-month Fishtrap Writer-In-Residence in 2005 funded by the Wildhorse Foundation. In 2003, she was awarded the Special Literary Fellowship for Women Writers given by Oregon's Literary Arts, Inc. She is the founder of the Writing Ranch, and director of The Nature of Words. Waterston received her BA from Harvard University and MA from the University of Madagascar. For more information please visit www.ellenwaterston.com; www.writingranch.com; and www.thenatureofwords.org.

Don Welch is a native of the grasslands of Nebraska and has taught English and Philosophy at the University of Nebraska at Kearney for almost fifty years. Among his poetry prizes is the Neruda Prize for Poetry when judged by William Stafford.

Patricia Wellingham-Jones, a former psychology researcher and writer/editor, is a three-time Pushcart Prize nominee. Chapbooks include *Don't Turn Away: Poems About Breast Cancer* (PWJ Publishing) and *Hormone Stew* (Snark Publishing). She just won the Palabra Productions Chapbook Contest with *End-Cycle*, poems about care giving. Her website is www.wellinghamjones.com.

Maggie Wells grew up in the West but currently lives on the Eastern Seaboard in New York City. She is a recent Master of Fine Arts graduate from the New School University. Her latest projects include being co-founder of PressBody Press, and editor of *Choose the Right Anthology*, a collection of ex-Mormon art and writing. Forthcoming is *Emotion Road: Perspectives on Homoerotic Small Town American Synth-pop*. She is currently celebrating her recent publication in *The Best American Erotic Poetry: 1800 to the Present* by drinking champagne and kissing boys.

Laurie Anne Whitt's poems have appeared in various journals, including *The Spoon River Poetry Review, Puerto Del Sol, The Malahat Review, Wisconsin Review, Hawai'i Review, PRISM International, Cottonwood,* and *Poetry Canada Review.* Her most recent manuscript, *Interstices,* won the 2006 Holland Prize and was published by Logan House Press in May 2006. Two collections of her poetry were published in 2001. *Words For Relocation* (Will Hall Press), won the 2001 Norma O. Harrison Chapbook Competition, and *a long dream of difference* (Frith Press), placed second in the 2000 Open Poetry Chapbook Competition. Currently, she lives in the Wasatch Mountains near Spanish Fork, Utah and teaches philosophy and integrated studies at Utah Valley State.

L.E. Wilber has held reins or a pen in her hand as long as she can remember. She has worked as a polo groom, trainer, and riding instructor and is currently pursuing dressage with her favorite Andalusian mare. She has been previously published in the *Greyrock Review.* She shares a century-old home in Denver, Colorado with her two dogs and cat.

C. K. Williams' *Collected Poems* appeared in 2006. He has published nine other books of poetry, the most recent of which, *The Singing,* won the National Book Award for 2003. His previous book, *Repair*, was awarded the 2000 Pulitzer Prize, and his collection *Flesh and Blood* received the National Book Critics Circle Award. He has published translations of Sophocles' *Women of Trachis*, Euripides' *Bacchae*, and poems of Francis Ponge, among others. His book of essays, *Poetry and Consciousness*, appeared in 1998, and a memoir, *Misgivings*, in 2000. He is a member of the American Academy of Arts and Letters, and teaches in the Writing Program at Princeton University.

Sam Witt was born in Wimbledon, England, but spent most of his time growing up in North Carolina and Virginia. He graduated from the University of Virginia and Iowa Writers' Workshop and worked as a free-lance journalist in San Francisco for several years. His first book, *Everlasting Quail* (UPNE, 2001), won the Katherine Nason Bakeless First Book Prize in 2000. He received a Fulbright Fellowship to live and write in Saint Petersburg, Russia for a year. Witt has participated in poetry festivals at Druskininkai and Vilnius at the invitation of the Lithuanian government; he has been a resident at the Breadloaf Writers' Conference and at Yaddo. He has taught at the University of Iowa, Harvard University, and the University of Missouri Kansas-City. His second book *Sunflower Brother,* won the Cleveland State University Press Open Book competition for 2006.

Cecilia Woloch is the author of *Sacrifice*, a BookSense 76 selection in 2001; *Tsigan: The Gypsy Poem;* and *Late,* for which she was named Georgia Author of the Year in Poetry for 2004. Her newest collection, *Narcissus,* was awarded the Snowbound Prize from Tupelo Press in 2006 and will be published by Tupelo as a chapbook in 2007. A celebrated teacher, she serves on the faculty of the MFA Program in Writing at Western Connecticut State University as well as the BA Program in Creative Writing at the University of Southern California. She spends part of each year traveling and teaching in Europe.

Doog T. Wood was raised in Western North Carolina between Nantahala and Pisgah National Forests. He attended school in Massachusetts and Ireland before moving to Morocco. He still lives and teaches in Marrakech.

Deborah Woodard's poetry and translations have appeared in *Artful Dodge, Bellingham Review, Chelsea, Monkey Puzzle, Threepenny Review,* and elsewhere. She has published two chapbooks of poetry, *The Orphan Conducts the Dovehouse Orchestra* (Bear Star Press, 1999), and *The Book of Riddles* (Boxcar Press, 1998). Her full-length collection *Plato's Bad Horse,* was published in 2006, also by Bear Star Press. A translator from Italian, she is currently working on a selected poems of the distinguished modernist Italian poet Amelia Rosselli to be brought out by Chelsea Editions in 2007. Deborah teaches at The Richard Hugo House, a community writing center in Seattle.

Chad Woody lives in Springfield, Missouri, where he enjoys a wife, owns a house, coaxes an old car, fiddles at minor creations, battles weeds, entertains a weakness for toy robots, and has little to do with horses anymore. That's why he's gone almost thirty years without getting bucked off.

Gary Young's honors include grants from the National Endowment for the Humanities, the Vogelstein Foundation, the California Arts Council, and two fellowship grants from the NEA. He has received a Pushcart Prize, and his book of poems, *The Dream of a Moral Life*, won the James D. Phelan Award. He is the author of *Hands, Days, Braver Deeds* (Peregrine Smith Poetry Prize), *No Other Life* (William Carlos Williams Award of the Poetry Society of America), and most recently, *Pleasure.* He is the co-editor of *The Geography of Home: California's Poetry of Place,* and has produced a series of artist's books, most notably *Nine Days: New York, A Throw of the Dice,* and *My Place Here Below.* Since 1975 he has designed, illustrated, and printed limited edition books and broadsides at his Greenhouse Review Press. His print work is represented in numerous collections including the Museum of Modern Art, the Victoria and Albert Museum, The Getty Center for the Arts, and special collection libraries throughout the country. He lives in the mountains north of Santa Cruz, California with his wife and two sons.

Karen Zealand's collection, *X-Testaments,* was the 2003 winner of the Elixir Press Chapbook Competition. She's a 2007 recipient of a Maryland State Arts Council Individual Artist Award in Poetry. Her manuscript, *Friendly Fire,* was a 2003 runner-up for the Maryland Artscape Emerging Voices Award. Her poems are widely published in journals and anthologized in *The Carnegie Mellon Anthology of Poetry* and *Outerbridge's* retrospective anthology, among others.

Su Zi says that horses have figured in her drawing and prose since the years she hid from the world by working at stables and farms. Horses, she says, require unswerving dedication because the comfy bed must be left in the January gray morning to feed them their breakfast, and the exhausted soul must bring the grain, the hay in the evening long before thoughts of one's own food are satisfied. Su Zi says that many folks think of having a pretty horsie in the yard, but few think of how a horse can frame a day and fill it too.

Lisa Zimmerman received her MFA from Washington University in St. Louis. Her poetry and fiction have appeared in the *Colorado Review, Redbook, The Sun, River Styx, Atlanta Review, The Portland Review*, and *Indiana Review,* among other journals. Her poetry has been nominated twice for the Pushcart Prize and was a finalist for the Lois Cranston Memorial Prize in 2006. In 2004 her poetry collection *How the Garden Looks From Here* won the Violet Reed Haas Poetry Award. Her next collection is forthcoming from Anhinga Press in 2008. She teaches creative writing and composition at the University of Northern Colorado.

Index of Contributors

B

C

D

E

F

G

H

N

O

P

R

S

T

V

W

Y

Z

Index of First Lines

D

E

F

G

H

I

J

K

L

M

N

O

P

Q

R

S

T

U

W

Y

Z

Permission Credits

Grateful acknowledgment is made to the following for permission to reprint previously published material:

Avalon Books (Thunder's Mouth Press): "She Had Some Horses" from *She Had Some Horses* by Joy Harjo, copyright © 1985 by Joy Harjo. Reprinted by permission of Avalon Books.

Judith Barrington: "Black Beauty," "Harvest," "Horses and the Human Soul," "Living Without Horses," "Why Young Girls Like to Ride Bareback" from *Horses and the Human Soul* by Judith Barrington (Story Line Press, Ashland, OR), copyright © 2004 by Judith Barrington. Reprinted by permission of the author.

Margo Berdeshevsky: "Even With No Hand To Hold It," originally published in *Beauty/Truth: a journal of ekphrastic poetry* (Beauty/Truth Press, Spring/Summer 2007). Reprinted by permission of the author.

Jonathan Blake: "Two Horses," originally published in *Blueline*. Reprinted by permission of the author.

Barbara Bloom: "Omeline" from *On The Water Meridian* by Barbara Bloom (Hummingbird Press, 2007), copyright © 2007 by Barbara Bloom. Reprinted by permission of the author.

BOA Editions, Ltd.: "Horse" from *White City* by Mark Irwin, copyright © 2000 by Mark Irwin. Reprinted by permission of BOA Editions, Ltd., www.boaeditions.org; "Neon Horses" from *Smoke* by Dorianne Laux, copyright © 2000 by Dorianne Laux. Reprinted by permission of BOA Editions, Ltd., www.boaeditions.org; "Bareback Pantoum" and "Pour Vivienne" from *Late* by Cecilia Woloch, copyright © 2003 by Cecilia Woloch. Reprinted by permission of BOA Editions, Ltd., www.boaeditions.org; "Horse" from *Parthenopi: New and Selected Poems* by Michael Waters, copyright © 2001 by Michael Waters. Reprinted by permission of BOA Editions, Ltd., www.boaeditions.org; "Saturday Matinee" and "The Horses" from *I Have Tasted the Apple* by Mary Crow, copyright © 1996 by Mary Crow. Reprinted by permission of BOA Editions, Ltd., www.boaeditions.org.

Deborah Bogen: "Moving the Moon," originally published in *Iron*

Horse Literary Review, Vol.4, No. 2, Spring 2003, reprinted in *The Gettysburgh Review,* Vol. 19, No. 1, Spring 2006, and reprinted on Verse Daily. Reprinted by permission of the author.

Michael Dennis Browne: "Horses" from *Panthers* by Michael Dennis Browne (Indulgence Press, Minneapolis, 2007), copyright © 2007 by Michael Dennis Browne. Reprinted by permission of the author.

Elizabeth Wade Buckalew: "If caterpillars come out, the mares will drop their foals," originally published in *The Cream City Review,* Vol. 30.2, Fall 2006. Reprinted by permission of the author.

Grace Butcher: "Results of the Polo Game," originally published in *The Antioch Review,* XXVIII, No. 2, Summer 1968. Reprinted by permission of the author.

C & C Press: "[Here in the valley, sunlight first lights the sky]" forthcoming in *New Mexico Journal* by Gary Young, copyright © 2008 by Gary Young. Reprinted by permission of the author.

Carnegie Mellon University Press: "Midwinter Visitant" from *Freeways and Aqueducts* by James Harms, copyright © 2004 by James Harms. Reprinted by permission of Carnegie Mellon University Press; "Just Because" from *Years Later* by Gregory Djanikian, copyright © 2000 by Gregory Djanikian. Reprinted by permission of the author and Carnegie Mellon University Press; "Prehistoric Horses" from *The Book of Changes* by Stephen Tapscott, copyright © 2002 by Stephen Tapscott. Reprinted by permission of Carnegie Mellon University Press.

Cleveland State University Poetry Center: "Appaloosa" from *Another Body* by Stephen Tapscott, copyright © 1989 by Stephen Tapscott. Reprinted by permission of Cleveland State University Poetry Center.

Copper Canyon Press: "Stories Are Made of Mistakes," "A Poem from the Edge of America," "The Measure of the Year," "Matins," and "Contraries and Opposites (Requestrian)" from *Resurrection Update: Collected Poems 1975-1997* by James Galvin, copyright © 1997 by James Galvin. Reprinted by permission of Copper Canyon Press, www.coppercanyonpress.org; "Clemente's Red Horse," "Impossible Still Life," "Refugio's Hair," "Signal Right," and "What Happened to Me" from *The Smallest Muscle in the Human Body* by Alberto Ríos, copyright © 2002 by Alberto Ríos. Reprinted by permission of Copper Canyon Press, www.coppercanyonpress.org; "Horses" from

The Caged Owl: New and Selected Poems by Gregory Orr, copyright © 2002 by Gregory Orr. Reprinted by permission of Copper Canyon Press, www.coppercanyonpress.org.

Mary Crow: "The Horses" appeared as "Rain-in-the-Face" in *The Poetry of Horses,* William Cole, editor (Charles Scribner's Sons, 1979), and in *Pursuits,* Jane Christensen, editor (Scott, Foreman, and Co., 1983), copyright © 1979 and 1983 by Mary Crow. Reprinted by permission of the author; "After a Certain Number of Years, the Light Changes," originally published in *Ploughshares* and *Borders* (BOA Editions, Ltd, 1989). Reprinted by permission of the author.

Jon Davis: "Bouquet," originally published in *Calapooya,* "Loving Horses," originally published in *Ploughshares* and *Photographers, Writers, and the American Scene: Visions of Passage* (Arena Editions, 2001), and "The Horse, Susan Said," originally published in *Ontario Review.* Reprinted by permission of the author.

Sean Thomas Dougherty: "Alphabet of Ordinary Horses & Yellow Light," originally published in *Paper Street.* Reprinted by permission of the author.

Barbara Drake: "Wet Land," originally published in *Windfall,* Vol. 5, No. 1, Fall 2006. Reprinted by permission of the author.

George Drew: "Elegy," originally published in *Vermont Literary Review,* Vol. IX, No. 2, Winter/Spring. Reprinted by permission of the author. "Riding the Black Man Killer," originally published in *Cimarron Review,* Vol. 83, No. 2, April 1988. Reprinted by permission of the author.

Farrar, Straus And Giroux, LLC: "Gas," "On Learning of a Friend's Illness," "Peggy," and "Work" from *Collected Poems* by C. K. Williams, copyright © 2006 by C. K. Williams. Reprinted by permission of Farrar, Straus and Giroux, LLC.

Felicia DuBois: "At the Stables," originally published in *PMS,* No. 2, 2002. Reprinted by permission of the author. "White Lilies," originally published in *Manzanita Quarterly,* Vol. 6, No. 1, Fall 2003. Reprinted by permission of the author.

Finishing Line Press: "Horses of San Marco" from *Migrations* by Deborah Fleming, copyright © 2005 by Deborah Fleming. Reprinted by permission of the author.

Deborah Fleming: "Filly," originally published in *Interdisciplinary Studies in Literature and Environment,* and "The Roan," originally published in *Tucamcari Literary Review.* Reprinted by permission of the author.

Alice Friman: "The Rope," originally published in *Shenandoah.* Reprinted by permission of the author.

Tess Gallagher: "Legacy" from *Willingly* by Tess Gallagher, copyright © 1984 by Tess Gallagher. Reprinted by permission of the author.

Christine Gelineau: "A Short Poem about the Long Poem," originally published in *Remorseless Loyalty*, (Ashland Poetry Press), copyright © 2006 by Christine Gelineau. Reprinted by permission of the author.

Danielle Georges: "A Painting at the Met," originally published in *Artist and Influence,* Vol. 19, 2000. Reprinted by permission of the author.

Rebecca Kaiser Gibson: "Inside the Church," originally published in *Northwest Review* and reprinted on Verse Daily. Reprinted by permission of the author.

Graywolf Press: "Close To Me Now" and "Legend With Sea Breeze" from *Moon Crossing Bridge* by Tess Gallagher, copyright © 1992 by Tess Gallagher; "From Dread In The Eyes Of Horses" from *Amplitude: New and Selected Poems* by Tess Gallagher, copyright © 1988 by Tess Gallagher. Reprinted by permission of Graywolf Press, Saint Paul, Minnesota.

Coppie Green: "Horse Turning," originally published in *The Greensboro Review* and "Look," originally published in *Edge of Our World.* Reprinted by permission of the author.

Gabriel Gudding: "Gerard Manley Horses," originally published in *Lit,* No. 9, Fall 2004. Reprinted by permission of the author.

Catherine Hardy: "The Country for Which There Is No Map," originally published in *Mid-American Review,* Vol. 13, No. 2, Spring 1993. Reprinted by permission of the author.

Joy Harjo: "Four Horse Songs" from *What Moon Drove Me To This,* originally published by I. Reed Books, copyright © 1980 by Joy Harjo. Reprinted by permission of the author.

HarperCollins Publishers: "Sentence" from *After* by Jane Hirshfield, copyright © 2006 by Jane Hirshfield. Reprinted by permission of HarperCollins Publishers; "Studying WuWei, Muir Beach" from *The Lives Of The Heart* by Jane Hirshfield, copyright ©1997 by Jane Hirshfield. Reprinted by permission of HarperCollins Publishers.

Lola Haskins: "Ardor" from *Solutions Beginning with A* (Modernbook), copyright © 2007 by Lola Haskins. Reprinted by permission of the author.

Wendell Hawken: "You Good Horse, You," originally published in *Covertside,* the newsletter of The Masters of Foxhounds Association; "Winter Scene at Evening Stables, originally published in *Poet Lore.* Reprinted by permission of the author.

Heyday Books: "[Acrobats vanished behind a veil]" from *Pleasure* by Gary Young, copyright © 2006 by Gary Young, and "[Queen Anne's Lace crowds the air]" from *No Other Life* by Gary Young, copyright © 2005 by Gary Young. Reprinted by permission of Heyday Books.

William Heyen: "The Eye," "Leaves of Horse," "March 17, 1876: The Ponies," "The Paper It's Written On," and "Companions" from *Crazy Horse in Stillness* (BOA Editions), copyright © 1996 by William Heyen. Reprinted by permission of the author.

Austin Hummell: "Kaspar Hauser" from *Poppy* by Austin Hummell (Del Sol Press), copyright © 2004 by Austin Hummell, originally published in *Gulf Coast.* Reprinted by permission of the author.

Carrie Jerrell: "Phaethon," originally published in *Passages North,* Vol. 28:1. Reprinted by permission of the author.

Ilya Kaminsky: "My Mother's Tango" from *Dancing in Odessa* by Ilya Kaminsky (Tupelo Press), copyright © 2004 by Ilya Kaminsky. Reprinted by permission of the author.

Robert Morris Kennedy: "The Fire Sermon," originally published in *Willow Review,* Spring 2003 under the title "What the White Horse Sees," and "In My Bones," originally published in *Muscadine Lines,* Spring 2006. Reprinted by permission of the author.

Willie James King: "Death at the Derby" from *The House in the Heart* (Tebot Bach Press), copyright © 2007, originally published in *Pembroke Magazine* and *Peregrine.* Reprinted by permission of the author.

Kathryn Kirkpatrick: "On Human Maps" from *Out of the Garden* (Mayapple Press), copyright © 2007 by Kathryn Kirkpatrick. Reprinted by permission of the author.

Judith Krause: "The Lesson," originally published in *The Antigonish Review,* No. 145, Spring 2006. Reprinted by permission of the author.

Lance Larsen: "Neighing Horses Behind My Right Shoulder," originally published in *Runes, A Review of Poetry: Connection,* 2007. Reprinted by permission of the author.

Donna J. Gelagotis Lee: "The New Filly," originally published in *Women's Studies Quarterly: Women and Sports,* Vol. 33, No. 1 & 2, Spring/Summer 2005. Reprinted by permission of the author.

Louisiana State University Press: "A Little Respect" and "A Set of Hoofprints" from *Crooked Run* by Henry Taylor, copyright © 2006 by Henry Taylor. Reprinted by permission of Louisiana State University Press; "Riding Lesson," and "Riding a One-Eyed Horse" from *The Horse Show at Midnight* and *Afternoon of Pocket Billiards* by Henry Taylor, copyright © 1991 by Henry Taylor. Reprinted by permission of Louisiana State University Press; "The Flying Change" from *The Flying Change* by Henry Taylor, copyright © 1985 by Henry Taylor. Reprinted by permission of Louisiana State University Press.

Gail Mazur: "Queenie" from *Zeppo's First Wife* (The University of Chicago Press), copyright © 2005 by Gail Mazur. Reprinted by permission of the author.

Pamela McClure: "No Time for Virgil, No Time for the Horses," originally published in *Poem,* No. 73, May 1995. Reprinted by permission of the author.

Ann E. Michael: "Horsewomen," originally published in *One Trick Pony* and appeared on Verse Daily on September 11, 2005; "No White Horse," originally published in *Minimus,* Vol. 9, 2000. Reprinted by permission of the author.

Michigan State University Press: "Yet Another Life" from *Some Heaven* by Todd Davis, copyright © 2007 by Todd Davis. Reprinted by permission of Michigan State University Press.

Mid-List Press: "On the Possession of Horses" from *Frozen Spring* by Margo Stever, copyright © 2002 by Margo Stever. Reprinted by permission of Mid-List Press.

Judith Montgomery: "Gallop" from *Passion* (Defined Providence Press), copyright © 1999, originally published in *Red Rock Review,* 1999 and later in *Red Jess* (Cherry Grove Collections), 2006. Reprinted by permission of the author.

Peter A. Nash: "Windy and Fawn," originally published in *Passager,* 2006. Reprinted by permission of the author.

Northwestern University Press: "A Thousand Genuflections," "Bucked," "Le Coursier de Jeanne D'Arc," and "With the Horse in Winter Pasture" from *Little River: New and Selected Poems*, copyright © 2002 by Linda McCarriston. Reprinted by permission of TriQuarterly Books/Northwestern University Press.

Biljana D. Obradovic: "Where Does One Body End, The Other Begin?" from *Frozen Embraces* (Belgrade, Center of Emigrants from Serbia, 1996, and Merrick, NY, Cross-Cultural Communication, 2000), copyright © 1996 and 2000 by Biljana D. Obradovic. Reprinted by permission of the author.

Carole Simmons Oles: "At the Races with Jan" from *Sympathetic Systems,* (Lynx House Press), copyright 2000 by Carole Simmons Oles. Reprinted by permission of Lynx House Press and the author.

Joy Passanante: "Horses in the Cathedral" from *Sinning in Italy* (Limberlost Press), copyright © 1999 by Joy Passanante. Reprinted by permission of the author.

Penguin Group (USA) Inc.: "Kissing a Horse" from *Lives Of The Animals* by Robert Wrigley, copyright © 2003 by Robert Wrigley. Reprinted by permission of Penguin, a division of Penguin Group (USA) Inc.; "Girls Who Love Horses," "Field With No Horse In It," "The Lamed Mare," and "Coupled" from *Silent Treatment* by Lisa Lewis, copyright © 1998, Penguin Group. Reprinted by permission of Penguin Group, Inc.

Natalie Peterse: "Damnificado," originally published in *CutBank 30th Anniversary Edition,* Vol. 59, Spring 2003. Reprinted by permission of the author.

Roger Pfingston: "The Sorrel" from *Something Iridescent* by Roger Pfingston (Barnwood Press), copyright © 1987 by Roger Pfingston. Reprinted by permission of the author.

Ruth Porritt: "Near Winter," originally published in a different version in *Beloit Poetry Journal,* Vol. 33, No. 2, Winter 1982-83. Reprinted by permission of the author.

Noah Raizman: "Whist," originally published in *Barrow Street,* Summer 2005. Reprinted by permission of the author.

Tony Reevy: "Dream of Valverde Field," originally published in *Magdalena,* 2002. Reprinted by permission of the author.

James Richardson: "Out of School" from *As If* by James Richardson (Persea Books/National Poetry Series), copyright © 1992 by James Richardson. Reprinted by permission of the author.

Bethany Reid: "The Horse," originally published in *Prairie Schooner,* Fall 2002; "Then," originally published in *Crosscurrents,* 2006. Reprinted by permission of the author.

Mark E. Sanders: "On Horseback" from *The Big Empty* by Mark E. Sanders (Backwaters), copyright © 2006 by Mark E. Sanders, originally published in *Poetry East.* Reprinted by permission of the author.

Silverfish Review Press: "Brood Mare" and "Horse Corridor" from *Red Town* by Judith Skillman, copyright © 2001 by Silverfish Review Press. Reprinted by permission of Silverfish Review Press.

Sue Sinclair: "Surrender," originally published in *Malahat,* Winter 2006 and appeared on Verse Daily. Reprinted by permission of the author.

Southern Illinois University Press: "On the Fenestra Ovalis" from *Furious Lullaby* by Oliver de la Paz, copyright © 2007 by Oliver de la Paz. Reprinted by permission of Southern Illinois University Press.

Hannah Stein: "Woman and Horse on the Beach," originally published in *Prairie Schooner,* Vol. 68, No. 2, Summer 1994. Reprinted by permission of the author.

Barry Sternlieb: "Relativity in January," originally published in *Alaska Quarterly Review,* Vol. 10, No. 1 & 2, Fall & Winter 1991; "Without a Word," originally published in *North Dakota Quarterly,* Vol. 58, No. 4, Fall 1990. Reprinted by permission of the author.

Leon Stokesbury: "Even Now," originally published in *The Kenyon*

Review, Vol. XXI, No. 3-4, 1998. Reprinted by permission of the author.

Story Line Press: "Zaraf's Star" from *Eve* by Annie Finch, copyright © 1997 by Annie Finch. Reprinted by permission of the author.

David Surette: "Practice" from *Easy to Keep, Hard to Keep In* by David Surette (Koenisha), copyright © 2007 by David Surette, and "The Tryout" from *Young Gentlemens' School* by David Surette (Koenisha), copyright © 2004 by David Surette. Reprinted by permission of the author.

Matthew Thorburn: "Horse Poetica," originally published in *Passages North,* Vol. 27.1, Winter/Spring. Reprinted by permission of the author.

Daniel Tobin: "Wild Stallion, Point Reyes, 1977," originally published in *The Cumberland Review* and forthcoming in *Second Things* (Four Way Books), copyright © 2008 by Daniel Tobin. Reprinted by permission of the author.

Alison Townsend: "My Life as a Horse" from *The Blue Dress* by Alison Townsend (White Pine Press), copyright © 2003 by Alison Townsend. Reprinted by permission of the author.

Eric Trethewey: "Fools and Horses" from *Evening Knowledge* by Eric Trethewey (Cleveland State University Poetry Center), copyright © 1991 by Eric Trethewey, and originally published in *The Sewanee Review,* Vol. 99, No. 2, Spring 1991. Reprinted by permission of the author.

University of Akron Press: "My Father's Horses" from *Ohio Blue Tips* by Jeanne E. Clark, copyright © 1999 by Jeanne E. Clark. Reprinted by permission the University of Akron Press.

University of Iowa Press: "Mark Time," "Little girls and horses," and "Blue-eyed Horse" from *American Spikenard* by Sarah Vap, copyright © 2007 by Sarah Vap. Reprinted by permission of the University of Iowa Press.

University of Pittsburgh Press: "There Are Two Worlds" from *Winter Stars* by Larry Levis, copyright ©1985. Reprinted by permission of the University of Pittsburgh Press; "The Horse Fair" and "Phaeton" from *The Horse Fair: Poems* by Robin Becker, copyright © 2000. Reprinted by permission of the University of Pittsburgh Press; "Risk" and "The Ribbon" from *All-American Girl* by Robin Becker, copyright © 1996. Reprinted by permission of the University of Pittsburgh Press; "The Round Barn," "Riding Lesson," and "Floating Farm" from *Giacometti's Dog* by Robin Becker, copyright ©1990. Reprinted by permission of the University of Pittsburgh Press.

Miles Waggener: "Equuleus" from *Phoenix Suites* by Miles Waggener (The Word Works), copyright © 2003 by Miles Waggener also won the 2002 Word Works Washington Prize; "Horse," originally published in *Crazyhorse,* No. 70, Fall 2006. Reprinted by permission of the author.

Scott Ward: "Strike" from *Wayward Passages* by Scott Ward (Black Bay Books), copyright © 2006 by Scott Ward, originally published in *Washington Square.* Reprinted by permission of the author.

Ellen Waterston: "Sacking Out the Roan Filly" from *I Am Madagascar* by Ellen Waterston (Ice River Press), copyright © 2004 by Ellen Waterston. Reprinted by permission of the author.

Jonathan Weinert: "Manipura, Out of Tiphereth" from *In The Mode Of Disappearance* by Jonathan Weinert (forthcoming from Nightboat Books), copyright © 2008. Reprinted by permission of the author.

Don Welch: "Two Horses" from *Inkling* by Don Welch (Sandhill Press), copyright © 2001 by Don Welch. Reprinted by permission of the author.

Patricia Wellingham-Jones: "Contest," originally published in *Advocate,* August/September 2006; "Ghost Horses," originally published in *Advocate,* February/March 2005. Reprinted by permission of the author.

Wesleyan University Press: "Thoroughbreds" from *Luster* by Don Bogen, copyright © 2003 by Don Bogen. Reprinted by permission of Wesleyan University Press; "After Work," "Heat," "At Night," and "Tamara Stands in Straw" from *Of Gravity & Angels* by Jane Hirshfield, copyright © 1988 by Jane Hirshfield. Reprinted by permission of Wesleyan University Press.

Laurelyn Whitt: "The Eyes of a Dark Horse," originally published in *Hawaii Review,* Vol. 15, Issue 31, No. 1, Winter 1990. Reprinted by permission of the author.

Sam Witt: "Black Pony on a Bank of the James" and "Late Summer Fever," from *Sunflower Brother* by Sam Witt (Cleveland State University Press), copyright © 2007 by Sam Witt. Reprinted by permission of the author.

Deborah Woodard: "Plato's Bad Horse" from *Plato's Bad Horse* by Deborah Woodard (Bear Star Press), copyright © 2006 by Deborah Woodard. Reprinted by permission of the author.

Word Press: "Like Horses" from *Eden in the Rearview Mirror* by Susan Elbe, copyright © 2007 by Susan Elbe. Reprinted by permission of the author.

W. W. Norton & Company, Inc: "October Storm" from *Midwest Eclogue* by David Baker, copyright © 2005 by David Baker. Reprinted by permission of W. W. Norton & Company, Inc.; "The Agnostic Speaks to Her Horse's Hoof" and "Amanda is Shod" from *Selected Poems 1960-1990* by Maxine Kumin, copyright © 1996 by Maxine Kumin. Reprinted by permission of W. W. Norton & Company, Inc.; "In A Long Line Of Horses" from *Cornucopia: New and Selected Poems* by Molly Peacock, copyright © 2002 by Molly Peacock. Reprinted by permission of W. W. Norton & Company, Inc.; "Praise Be" and "Ars Poetica" from *Looking For Luck* by Maxine Kumin, copyright ©1992 by Maxine Kumin. Reprinted by permission of W. W. Norton, Inc.; "Jack" from *Jack And Other New Poems* by Maxine Kumin, copyright ©2005 by Maxine Kumin. Reprinted by permission of W. W. Norton & Company, Inc.

Su Zi: "12" from *The Tissue of Language* by Su Zi (Basilik Press), copyright © 2007 by Su Zi. Reprinted by permission of the author.